MONEY AND THE RULE OF LAW

Contemporary monetary institutions are flawed at a foundational level. The reigning paradigm in monetary policy holds up constrained discretion as the preferred operating framework for central banks. However, no matter how smart or well-intentioned are central bankers, discretionary policy contains information and incentive problems that make macroeconomic stability systematically unlikely. Furthermore, central bank discretion implicitly violates the basic jurisprudential norms of liberal democracy. Drawing on a wide body of scholarship, this volume presents a novel argument in favor of embedding monetary institutions into a rule-of-law framework. The authors argue for general, predictable rules to provide a sturdier foundation for economic growth and prosperity. A rule-of-law approach to monetary policy would remedy the flaws that resulted in misguided monetary responses to the 2007–2008 financial crisis and the COVID-19 pandemic. Understanding the case for true monetary rules is the first step toward creating more stable monetary institutions.

Peter J. Boettke is a University Professor of Economics and Philosophy at George Mason University, Director of the F. A. Hayek Program for Advanced Study in Philosophy, Politics, and Economics, and BB&T Professor for the Study of Capitalism at the Mercatus Center at George Mason University.

Alexander William Salter is an Associate Professor of Economics in the Rawls College of Business at Texas Tech University and the Comparative Economics Research Fellow at TTU's Free Market Institute.

Daniel J. Smith is an Associate Professor of Economics in the Jones College of Business at Middle Tennessee State University and the Director of the Political Economy Research Institute.

Money and the Rule of Law

Generality and Predictability in Monetary Institutions

PETER J. BOETTKE

George Mason University

ALEXANDER WILLIAM SALTER

Texas Tech University

DANIEL J. SMITH

Middle Tennessee State University

CAMBRIDGE
UNIVERSITY PRESS

CAMBRIDGE
UNIVERSITY PRESS

University Printing House, Cambridge CB2 8BS, United Kingdom

One Liberty Plaza, 20th Floor, New York, NY 10006, USA

477 Williamstown Road, Port Melbourne, VIC 3207, Australia

314–321, 3rd Floor, Plot 3, Splendor Forum, Jasola District Centre, New Delhi – 110025, India

79 Anson Road, #06–04/06, Singapore 079906

Cambridge University Press is part of the University of Cambridge.

It furthers the University's mission by disseminating knowledge in the pursuit of education, learning, and research at the highest international levels of excellence.

www.cambridge.org
Information on this title: www.cambridge.org/9781108479844
DOI: 10.1017/9781108806787

First published 2021

A catalogue record for this publication is available from the British Library.

Library of Congress Cataloging-in-Publication Data
Names: Boettke, Peter J., author. | Salter, Alexander William, author. | Smith, Daniel J., 1984– author.
Title: Money and the rule of law : generality and predictability in central banks and other monetary institutions / Peter J. Boettke, George Mason University, Virginia, Alexander William Salter, Texas Tech University, Daniel J. Smith, Middle Tennessee State University.
Description: Cambridge, United Kingdom ; New York, NY : Cambridge University Press, 2021. | Includes bibliographical references and index.
Identifiers: LCCN 2020042237 (print) | LCCN 2020042238 (ebook) | ISBN 9781108479844 (hardback) | ISBN 9781108790840 (paperback) | ISBN 9781108806787 (epub)
Subjects: LCSH: Monetary policy. | Banks and banking, Central.
Classification: LCC HG230.3 .B638 2021 (print) | LCC HG230.3 (ebook) | DDC 339.5/3–dc23
LC record available at https://lccn.loc.gov/2020042237
LC ebook record available at https://lccn.loc.gov/2020042238

ISBN 978-1-108-47984-4 Hardback
ISBN 978-1-108-79084-0 Paperback

This book is dedicated to the memory of Fredrich A. Hayek, Milton Friedman, and James M. Buchanan. May their work continue to inspire scholars for generations to come.

Contents

Preface

"Money Changes Everything" is the title of a popular song from the 1980s performed by Cyndi Lauper. But it is also the title of a sweeping economic history published in 2016. William Goetzmann's *Money Changes Everything* (2016) explores how money and finance provide the foundation for social order and civilization. The reason money changes everything, Goetzmann argues, is that, there is a wide divergence in prosperity and overall human flourishing between societies that maintain "good" money and those that do not. We strongly agree, which is why we wrote this book.

Money, of course, is one of several foundational social institutions. Others include private property, the rule of law, and the freedom to exchange. Each of these is necessary for economic prosperity (Acemoglu and Robinson 2012; Cooter and Schäfer 2012; Easterly 2001; Gwartney et al. 1999; North et al. 2009; Rodrik 2005; Smith 1776 [1982]). These institutions promote human prosperity by enabling peaceful social cooperation under the division of labor, including creative acts of innovation that give rise to sustained economic growth (Baumol 2002; Nordhaus 2004; Ridley 2020).

When money and finance function well, humans are able to "imagine and calculate the future" (Goetzmann 2016, p. 2). One of the underappreciated ways money does this is by permitting a quantification of the past. This enables us to gain a deeper understanding of our history and thereby improve our ability to plan for the future. Money and finance provide crucial "aids to the human mind"[1] that can foster the "sophisticated tools

---

[1] This phrase comes from Ludwig von Mises, *Theory of Money and Credit* (1912 [1981]) and is critical to his later work on the problem of economic calculation under socialism (see Mises 1920 [1990], 1922 [1988]). This insight is also highly relevant to his arguments in *Liberalism* (1927 [2005]) and *Human Action* (1949) about how monetary calculation is

for managing the economics of time and risk" (Goetzmann 2016, p. 2).[2] Prices provide an ex ante guide to economic planning and decision-making. Profits and losses provide an ex post assessment of economic planning, rewarding productive uses of resources and discouraging unproductive ones. The danger of monetary instability is not just that we lose this aid to planning and assessing, but that the aid will provide incorrect and unreliable assessments, causing plan miscoordination, malinvestment, and the overall misuse of scarce resources. The price system only works to its full potential when money, which underpins market prices, is responsibly governed (cf. Friedman 1992; Hayek 1931; Horwitz 2000). Thus, monetary mischief can impair our ability to engage in mutually beneficial exchanges, hampering economic prosperity and human well-being.

Throughout most of human history, of course, the economic well-being of societies across the globe was barely above subsistence. Some ancient civilizations did have complicated financial arrangements and, given the state of technological knowledge and other human and social capital constraints, quite sophisticated tools for managing risk. Yet, even the powerful and wealthy lived a precarious existence due to famine and disease, as well as intrigue and violence. Life was, to use the much-abused phrase of Thomas Hobbes (1651 [2017]), "nasty, brutish, and short."

Then something drastic happened: Humanity experienced what Deirdre McCloskey has called "The Great Enrichment," which resulted in an estimated improvement in the material conditions of humanity by a factor of 30 (McCloskey 2006, 2010, 2016, 2019).[3] This improvement is not only seen in caloric intake, clothing, and shelter, but also in better medicine, more education, and greater opportunities for leisure: in short, longer and better lives.

---

the critical component in the entrepreneurial theory of the market process. Our book explores the intricate relationship between the institutional framework of public and private ordering with monetary policy, as well as the consequences for rational economic calculation.

[2] Also see Yongseok Shin's (2018) review of Goetzmann in the *Journal of Economic Literature*.

[3] In *The Conservative Sensibility* (2019), George Will points out that too many public policymakers fail to see how small differences in growth rates, given enough time, can result in massive differences in living standards. It is vitally important to appreciate what McCloskey describes. We are talking about a *3,000 percent increase* in economic output from the eighteenth to the twenty-first century. This is an almost unfathomable growth in material prosperity. Understanding it is both a scientific and moral imperative – doubly so for policymakers, whose actions directly impinge on this process!

McCloskey attributes the material bounty we currently enjoy to *liberalism*: the philosophy of liberty and equality that freed ordinary people to "have a go" at bettering themselves. The result was thriving commercial societies. We find much of value in McCloskey's thesis, which is why the scholarly projects we have undertaken over the years seek better to understand the political economy of liberalism. Here, we focus on an area that has been relatively overlooked: what liberalism has to say about monetary institutions and policy. Money, finance, and their host of attendant institutions are not merely of interest in the "short run." How they work bears directly on the wealth and poverty of nations. Thus, understanding contemporary institutions for promulgating monetary policy, namely central banking, is essential for those working within the liberal project.

Monetary regimes operate within a network of institutions of private and public ordering. Disruptions along this path of increasing economic prosperity can be linked, in part, to monetary and financial breakdowns. Why did the Roman Empire collapse? How did the French Revolution veer off the rails? What precipitated Hitler's rise to power? What caused the 2007–2008 financial crisis? All these vexing questions of human history cannot be fully explained without recourse to failures of monetary and financial institutions.

Adam Smith, in *The Wealth of Nations* (1776, Book V, chapter 3, pp. 466–468), warned that governments, ancient as well as modern, continually demonstrated a penchant to engage in a pernicious juggling trick: spending in excess of revenue (deficit finance), accumulating these deficits into long-standing public debt, and paying off the debt through the debasement of their currency. "Deficits, Debt, Debasement" is the governmental version of Cyndi Lauper's tune. We could call it the "governmental habit" as it appears to be a natural proclivity of ruling powers once the state establishes its geographic monopoly of coercion. Political economy must take this governmental habit into account. It should also try to come up with ways to constrain this tendency so that institutions of money and finance enable civilizational progress rather than catalyze its decline.

The network of institutions in the public, private, and independent sectors that constitute liberal society is intricate and complex. We believe that monetary institutions are not peripheral, but central, to human betterment. Money matters in conjunction with institutions that protect persons and property, as well as expand trade and commerce. This is why the question of what monetary institutions we ought to adopt is really a part of the broader social discussion about liberalism. What we need is a conversation of *ideas*, but it must be remembered that such conversations are not mere academic playthings. Ideas have incalculable power. McCloskey puts particular stress on ideas, especially the spread of liberal sensibilities throughout the population. The bourgeois virtues, she argues, grant dignity to commerce and trade, and result in an ethos of social equality. We are all, regardless of our background, one another's free and dignified equals, recognized and protected in our personhood by the rule of law. In this story, money and finance matter because it is only through these institutions that we are able to secure the *anonymous cooperation* among free people required to maintain peace and prosperity. Empowered in part by money and finance, the bourgeois era unleashed people's entrepreneurial energy so they could come up with ideas, as well as harness the capital to bet on those ideas. In this process, scientific discoveries are transformed into commercially useful knowledge, and economic calculation filters out from the vast array of technologically feasible investment projects those that will be economically viable. It is this intricate matrix of ideas and legal, political, social, and financial institutions that produced the "The Creative Powers of a Free Civilization" that Hayek talks about in *The Constitution of Liberty* (1960).

Our book explores the relationship between monetary policy and the rule of law. The rule of law is an essential component to the story of liberalism. Political economists, however, have not seen much relevance of the rule of law to monetary institutions and policy. We believe it is, in fact, quite relevant. To start, there is always a tension between public monetary institutions and the rule of law because of Adam Smith's juggling trick, which we mentioned earlier. To preview one of our most important claims: *A monetary policy grounded in the rule of law would effectively tie the hands of the juggler.*

We want to make clear what we see as our contribution. We are not trying to help the juggler become more technically proficient at his trick. We are trying to stop the trick! The sort of economic thinking that we offer in this book is thus not intended as a guidebook for master jugglers. Our argument is much more radical than that. Yet at the same time, it is more modest. Our argument is that sound economics teaches us that the jugglers must be constrained, or else they will continue to pull their tricks. What this means for monetary institutions is that central bankers should be bound by *rules* rather than permitted *discretion*. Besides Adam Smith, in this book, you will encounter F. A. Hayek, Milton Friedman, and James M. Buchanan, the three great classically liberal Nobel laureates of the twentieth century, as well as a host of others who have consistently argued for rule-based governance, including monetary policy.

We are set to publish this book at a seemingly inauspicious time to argue for rules instead of discretion. The COVID-19 pandemic is sowing economic chaos throughout the world. In the United States, as was the case during the financial crisis of 2007–2008, the Federal Reserve has embarked on a series of extraordinary policies that, as a consequence, are precipitously shrinking the distance between monetary and fiscal authorities.[4] This poses unique challenges for those who care about the rule of law in monetary affairs. While we appreciate the severity of the public health crisis, and we empathize with the hardship suffered by millions of Americans, we worry that this scenario is too tempting for the juggler to resist. As much as we may wish to ease suffering by adopting a "no-holds-barred" approach to stabilizing markets, we must recognize that the abandonment of humility and restraint by monetary policymakers will eventually result in trouble. The governmental habit of deficits, debt, and debasement promises short-term relief only at the expense of long-run prosperity. The politics of panic and patronage is a recipe for economic stagnation. Economic decline will ultimately make us less capable of overcoming future challenges.

We should not expect dispassionate deliberation of the costs and benefits of alternative courses of action amid political emergencies. Emotional and *politicized* economics give rise to policy justifications to which sound and sober *economic* analysis would never lend credence (Hazlitt 1946). As Hayek told us: "'Emergencies' have always been the pretext on which the safeguards of individual liberty have been eroded – and once they are suspended it is not difficult for anyone who has assumed such emergency powers to see to it that the emergency will persist" (Hayek 1979, p. 124). We should add that Hayek does acknowledge the reality of true emergencies: situations in which the rules that constrain the coercive powers of government must be temporarily suspended in order to ensure the long-run preservation of a free society. Liberal civilization must be able to sustain itself against the threat of collapse due to catastrophic events, whether natural or human-made. But unless these suspensions are timely, targeted, and temporary, there is a very real risk that liberalism will be an unintended casualty. Perhaps in the realm of economic policy, what is most important is maintaining a commitment to ordinary economics even in the most extraordinary of times.

---

[4] Bassetto and Sargent (2020) describe the joint operation of monetary and fiscal policy during a crisis as a "shotgun wedding."

Money and the Rule of Law articulates a vision of monetary policy for a free society informed by the teachings of classical and modern political economy. The book contains both technical analyses of monetary policy and broader philosophical discussions of monetary institutions. We are working, for the most part, within the existing institutional structures of liberal democracy and the "best practice" model for a central bank. As we discuss in Chapter 5 on the evolving views of Hayek, Friedman, and Buchanan, it is frequently difficult to reconcile the theory of central banking with actual central bank behavior. This should impel us to reconsider whether actual policy can approximate ideal policy, given deviations from idealized incentives and information. Because of these imperfections, we should take seriously the promise of a rule-of-law approach to money.

To conclude, money does indeed change everything. And since it does, we had better get our monetary and financial institutions right. We argue that getting them right depends on making monetary policy consistent with the rule of law. Money needs to be treated as a right of citizens, not a privilege of central banks. Monetary policy not bound by the rule of law, but instead at the discretion of unaccountable experts, is a wrench in the gears of commerce and risks derailing the progress of civilization. We must not lose sight of what money is *for*. The function of money is to facilitate mutually beneficial exchange. Because money is one-half of all exchanges, monetary mischief causes havoc throughout the intricate web of commercial relationships that make up the economic and social order. Our goal in writing this book is to show how monetary institutions must work if they are to promote social cooperation, instead of social control.

In a self-governing society, the rule of law is a requirement to which all public institutions must adhere. What follows is our attempt to convince others to think seriously about how to extend this requirement to monetary institutions as well.

References

Acemoglu, Daron and James A. Robinson (2012). *Why Nations Fail*. Crown Business.

Baumol, William (2002). *Free Market Innovation Machine*. Princeton University Press.

Bassetto, Marco and Thomas Sargent (2020). Shotgun Wedding: Fiscal and Monetary Policy. NBER Working Paper No. 27004.

Cooter, Robert D. and Hans-Bernd Schäfer (2012). *Solomon's Knot: How Law Can End the Poverty of Nations*. Princeton University Press.

Easterly, William (2001). Can Institutions Resolve Ethnic Conflict? *Economic Development and Cultural Change*, 49(4), 687–706.

Friedman, Milton (1992). *Monetary Mischief*. Harcourt Brace & Company.

Goetzmann, William (2016). *Money Changes Everything*. Princeton University Press.

Gwartney, James, Robert Lawon, and Randall G. Holcombe (1999). Economic Freedom and the Environment for Economic Growth. *Journal of Institutional and Theoretical Economics*, 155(4), 643–663.

Hayek, Friedrich August von (1931). *Prices and Production*. Augustus M. Kelly.

(1960). *The Constitution of Liberty*. University of Chicago Press.

(1979). *Law Legislation and Liberty: The Political Order of a Free People*. University of Chicago Press.

Hazlitt, Henry (1946). *Economics in One Lesson*. Harper & Brothers Publishers.

Hobbes, Thomas (1651 [2017]). *Leviathan*. Penguin Classics.

Horwitz, Steven (2000) *Microfoundations and Macroeconomics: An Austrian Approach*. Routledge.

McCloskey, Deidre (2006). *The Bourgeois Virtues*. University of Chicago Press.

(2010). *Bourgeois Dignity*. University of Chicago Press.

(2016). *Bourgeois Equality*. University of Chicago Press.

(2019). *Why Liberalism Works*. Yale University Press.

Mises, Ludwig von (1912 [1981]). *Theory of Money and Credit*. Liberty Fund, Inc.

(1920 [1990]). *Economic Calculation in the Socialist Commonwealth*. Liberty Fund, Inc.

(1922 [1988]). *Socialism: An Economic and Sociological Analysis*. Liberty Fund, Inc.

(1927 [2005]). *Liberalism*. Liberty Fund, Inc.

(1949). *Human Action*. Yale University Press.

Nordhaus, William D. (2004). Schumpeterian Profits in the American Economy: Theory and Measurement. NBER Working Paper No. 10433.

North, Douglass C., John Joseph Wallis, and Barry R. Weingast (2009). *Violence and Social Orders*. Cambridge University Press.

Ridley, Matt (2020). *How Innovation Works: And Why It Flourishes in Freedom*. Harper.

Rodrik, Dani (2005). Growth Strategies. *Handbook of Economic Growth*, 1, 967–1014.

Shin, Yongseok (2018). Finance and Economic Development in the Very Long Run: A Review Essay. *Journal of Economic Literature*, 56(4), 1577–1586.

Smith, Adam (1776 [1982]). *An Inquiry into the Nature and Causes of the Wealth of Nations*. Liberty Fund, Inc.

Will, George (2019). *The Conservative Sensibility*. Hachette Book Group.

Acknowledgments

This book draws upon, synthesizes, and extends nearly a decade of independent and coauthored research projects between the authors. The following published book chapters and academic journal articles served as the foundation for this project:

Boettke, Peter J. and William J. Luther (2010). The Ordinary Economics of an Extraordinary Crisis. In Steven Kates (Ed.), *Macroeconomic Theory and Its Failings: Alternative Perspectives on the Global Financial Crisis*. Cheltenham, UK, and Northampton, MA: Edward Elgar, pp. 14–25.

Boettke, Peter J., Alexander W. Salter, and Daniel J. Smith (2018). Money as Meta-Rule: Buchanan's Constitutional Economics as a Foundation for Monetary Stability. *Public Choice*, 176(3–4), 529–555.

Boettke, Peter J. and Daniel J. Smith (2013). Federal Reserve Independence: A Centennial Review. *Journal of Prices and Markets*, 1(1), 31–48.

Boettke, Peter J. and Daniel J. Smith (2016). Evolving Views on Monetary Policy in the Thought of Hayek, Friedman, and Buchanan. *The Review of Austrian Economics*, 29(4), 351–370.

Furton, Glenn and Alexander Slater (2017). Money and the Rule of Law. *Review of Austrian Economics*, 30(4), 517–532.

Hogan, Thomas, Linh Le, and Alexander W. Salter (2015). Ben Bernanke and Bagehot's Rules. *Journal of Money, Credit and Banking*, 47(2–3), 333–348.

Hogan, Thomas L., Daniel J. Smith, and Robin P. K. Aguiar-Hicks (2018). Central Banking without Romance. *European Journal of Comparative Economics*, 15(2), 293–314.

Salter, Alexander W. (2014). Is There a Self-Enforcing Monetary Constitution? *Constitutional Political Economy*, 25(3), 280–300.

Salter, Alexander W. (2016). Robust Political Economy and the Lender of Last Resort. *Journal of Financial Services Research*, 50(1), 1–27.

Salter, Alexander W. and Daniel J. Smith (2017). What You Don't Know Can Hurt You: Knowledge Problems in Monetary Policy. *Contemporary Economic Policy*, 35(3), 505–517.

Salter, Alexander W. and Daniel J. Smith (2018). Political Economists or Political Economists? The Role of Political Environments in the Formation of Fed Policy under Burns, Greenspan, and Bernanke. *Quarterly Review of Economics and Finance*, 71(1), 1–13.

Smith, Daniel J. and Peter J. Boettke (2015). An Episodic History of Modern Fed Independence. *The Independent Review: A Journal of Political Economy*, 20(1), 99–120.

We owe a special thanks to our coauthors on these articles: Glenn Furton, Robin P. K. Aguiar-Hicks, Thomas L. Hogan, Linh Le, and William J. Luther. We also acknowledge the helpful research assistance of Justin Callais, Michael Makovi, and, especially, Louis Rouanet.

We owe a special debt of gratitude to the Mercatus Center and Malia Dalesandry, Stefanie Haeffele, Haley Larsen, Patrick Horan, and Giorgio Castiglia for hosting a manuscript conference on an earlier draft of this book. We thank the conference participants for their valuable feedback: David Beckworth, Rachael Behr, Rosolino Candela, Chris Coyne, Bryan Cutsinger, Peter Jacobsen, Jayme Lemke, William Luther, Louis Rouanet, Richard Wagner, and Lawrence White. We also thank Ed Weick for feedback on the manuscript.

Administrative staff at our respective institutions and centers played an important role in providing support for the completion of this project. Pete would like to thank Karla Segovia and Jessica Carges; Alex would like to thank Amanda Smith; and Dan would like to thank Henrietta Bailey, Gabriel Fancher, and Brian Delaney.

We thank Robert Dreesen and Karen Maloney at Cambridge University Press. Their support for this project was and is appreciated throughout this process.

Introduction

1.1 Rules vs. Discretion Redivivus

On November 8, 2002, Ben Bernanke, then a member of the Federal Reserve's Board of Governors, gave a speech at a conference honoring Milton Friedman. Along with Anna Schwartz, Friedman's scholarship on the monetary history of the United States (Friedman and Schwartz 1963) was crucial in drawing the economics profession's attention to how monetary mismanagement helped put the "Great" in "Great Depression." Bernanke (2002) ended his speech with an institutional mea culpa and an important promise: "Let me end my talk by abusing slightly my status as an official representative of the Federal Reserve. I would like to say to Milton and Anna: Regarding the Great Depression. You're right, we did it. We're very sorry. But thanks to you, we won't do it again."

But the Fed did do it again. Although there was no dramatic collapse in narrow money in the early days of the 2007–2008 crisis as there was in the Great Depression, monetary mismanagement did bear a significant share of the blame for the severity of the financial crisis's effects. Part of this was before Bernanke's tenure as Fed Chairman, which began in early 2006. The inflated asset markets that began to collapse in 2007 were the responsibility of the then-Chairman Alan Greenspan's Fed (Taylor 2009; White 2012). The secondary consequences of financial collapse, however, did happen under Bernanke's watch. In key ways, the event bears an uncanny resemblance to its counterpart during the Great Depression, which Bernanke had vowed would not repeat itself. This is not an indictment of Ben Bernanke or Alan Greenspan. Bernanke and Greenspan are first-rate economists and, from what we can know from their tenures as public servants, men of integrity. The mistakes made by the Fed during the financial crisis demonstrate that it is not enough to get smart and well-intentioned practitioners at the helm of central banks. The problem is *institutional*. Uncovering the institutional problems that plague contemporary central banking is our purpose in this book. Our thesis, in brief, is that *discretion* on the part of monetary policymakers is to blame. Discretion in monetary policy is the reason central banking fails to live up to its lofty promises of economic and financial stability.

Since the 2007–2008 financial crisis, scholars have increasingly paid attention to the relationship between monetary institutions and economic stability. While these discussions had some impact on internal operations, such as the Fed undertaking a systematic review of its strategy, tools, and communication practices (cf. Board of Governors of the Federal Reserve System 2018), the only proposals seriously considered are minor operational reforms. This is not to say monetary policy has not changed significantly. It has. The Fed's unprecedented monetary expansion and its transition from a corridor system to a floor system represent a radical break in monetary policy practice. What is curious is that this monumental shift has occurred with minimal reflection on central bank *governance*. Procedurally, little has changed.

In the academic literature, there has been an explosion of interest in topics related to unconventional monetary policy and expanded regulatory mandates for financial stability. Each of these discussions, while important, overlooks fundamental questions about central banking's institutional underpinnings. These institutional considerations are an essential part of any discussion of how central banks influence macroeconomic and financial conditions. If scholars of monetary policy want to make lasting progress, they must address these considerations head-on. We contend that existing monetary institutions have not delivered macroeconomic and financial stability because they are inherently incapable of achieving these ends. The dominant form of monetary institution in the world today is discretionary central banking. There are serious knowledge and incentive problems inherent in discretionary central banking that render it systematically unable to mitigate economic volatility, let alone stem a full-blown financial panic. In fact, we argue that discretionary central banking actually increases the likelihood that we will encounter financial instability in the first place. To put it more bluntly: The firefighters called upon to put out the fires are the very ones responsible for starting them.

Discretion on the part of monetary policymakers undermines the purposes for which we would want a central bank in the first place. We come down firmly on the side of rules in the ongoing (and seemingly interminable) debate between advocates of rules versus discretion in monetary policy. The consensus among central bankers that discretion was preferable to a fixed rule, due chiefly to the complexities of monetary policy and the uniqueness of particular macroeconomic circumstances, was challenged by studies that recognized the strategic interaction between policymakers and market actors (Barro and Gordon 1983; Calvo 1978; Kydland and Prescott 1977). Time inconsistency emerges because monetary authorities have the incentive to deviate from nonbinding rules.[1]

While macroeconomists and monetary economists came to appreciate the importance of rules, a full commitment to rules never became professional orthodoxy. Rather, the consensus that emerged was "constrained discretion" (Bernanke 2003; Bernanke and Mishkin 1997; Bianchi and Melosi 2018, p. 187; Friedman 2006). Under constrained discretion, "the central bank retains some flexibility in deemphasizing inflation stabilization so as to pursue alternative short-run objectives such as unemployment stabilization. However, such flexibility is constrained to the extent that the central bank should maintain a strong reputation for keeping inflation and inflation expectations firmly under control" (Bianchi and Melosi 2018, p. 187; see also Bernanke 2003).

Proponents of constrained discretion have a three-component solution to time inconsistency problems. First, appoint central bankers with the appropriate preexisting policy views (Herrendorf and Lockwood 1997; Lohmann 1992; Lossani et al. 1998; Persson 1993; Rogoff 1985; Romer and Romer 1997; Tillmann 2008; Waller and Walsh 1996; Walsh 1995). Second, grant appointed central bankers the necessary independence to exercise their discretion (Crowe and Meade 2007; Fischer 1995). Third, require central bank transparency (Blinder et al. 2001; Crowe and Meade 2007; Faust and Svensson 2001; Geraats 2002). Thus, constrained discretion offers the alluring promise of allowing monetary policymakers the best of both discretion and rules. It ensures the benefits of stable economic activity, especially price stability, while retaining the ability to veer from stability in the short run to combat financial turbulence. Ben Bernanke (2003), chairman of the Fed during the financial crisis, put it this way:

---

[1] Blinder (1998), a former governor of the Fed, argues that central bankers do not have time inconsistent incentives. Sargent (1999) provides a theoretical critique of Blinder (1998). Ireland (1999) and Berlemann (2005) empirically test for time inconsistency and find that the evidence suggests central bankers do behave in a time inconsistent fashion. McCallum (1995) argues that the government has a time inconsistency problem as well, and thus cannot be trusted to discipline the Fed.

Constrained discretion is an approach that allows monetary policymakers considerable leeway in responding to economic shocks, financial disturbances, and other unforeseen developments. Importantly, however, this discretion of policymakers is constrained by a strong commitment to keeping inflation low and stable. In practice ... this approach has allowed central banks to achieve better outcomes in terms of *both* inflation and unemployment, confounding the traditional view that policymakers must necessarily trade-off between the important social goals of price stability and high employment.

If constrained discretion can be reasonably expected to work better than either fixed rules or complete discretion, and if many of the world's most important central banks have already adopted this operating regime, then our argument is dead before it even begins. We concede the second point but vehemently deny the first. Constrained discretion does *not* offer a viable middle ground between fixed rules and complete discretion. This is because constrained discretion is really just discretion, with all the attendant information and incentive problems therein.

Each part of the three-step solution to time inconsistency problems fails due to the epistemic limitations and misaligned incentives of central bankers. Knowledge problems render discretionary central banking not just difficult, but impossible. Discretionary central banks, as monopoly suppliers of (base) money, eliminate the market mechanisms that adjust the supply of money to changes in the demand for money. Monetary authorities, even with hundreds of Ph.D. economists at their disposal, do not have the real-time knowledge or prescience to measure and forecast changes in the demand for money in a dynamic world of macroeconomic shocks, financial innovations, and regulatory changes. This causes persistent disequilibrium in the money market; because money is one-half of all market exchanges, the result is general economic discoordination.

The knowledge problems inherent in discretionary central banking give rise to the incentive problems. If the ends and means of monetary policy are uncertain, then it gives more leeway for discretionary central bankers to adjust monetary policy to achieve other objectives. Even if the appropriate economists are appointed as central bankers, they must operate within the bureaucratic environment of a central bank, which can impel them to change their views. Central bank independence often fails in practice under pressure from executive, legislative, and special interest groups precisely because there is genuine uncertainty about the "correct" course for monetary policy. Central bank transparency, such as required testimonies, reports, and audits, often only open another channel for policymakers to exert pressure on discretionary central bankers.

We realize that this is a bold claim. It will take the rest of the book to convince our readers. In fact, it took notable scholars of monetary economics and macroeconomics, such as F. A. Hayek and Milton Friedman, nearly a lifetime of wrestling with these ideas to come to this conclusion at the end of their scholarly careers. The role of monetary policy in promulgating and then failing to stem the 2007–2008 financial crisis, however, makes a compelling case for undertaking this task.

1.2 Central Banking and Monetary Mismanagement

Our claim about the systematic inefficacy of discretionary central banking may appear outlandish. After all, the monetary economics profession regards the theory and practice of central banking as having markedly improved since the early twentieth century, and that the resulting knowledge and competence are largely responsible for increased macroeconomic stability. This narrative, while widely believed, is questionable at best. At least in the US context, recent works have called into question the supposed improvements in economic performance brought about by central banking. Although the National Banking System, which preceded the Fed, was highly flawed, we can justifiably suspect that the Fed did not improve things (Hogan 2015; Hogan et al. 2018; Selgin et al. 2012; White 2015). Economic outcomes under the classical gold standard, which prevailed internationally from 1879 to 1914, may very well have been "superior in some respects and no worse in others" (Cutsinger 2020, p. 1).

What about the Great Moderation? A case can be made that the reduction in economic volatility beginning in the mid-1980s and prevailing until the 2007–2008 crisis was due to central banking. But it is highly suspect to attribute it to *discretionary* central banking. This is because Fed policy during this era was at its most rule-like. Alan Meltzer (2014, p. 162) contends that the Great Moderation was due to the Fed's "reliance on the Taylor rule to guide policy."[2] Elsewhere Meltzer (2012, p. 630) claims that "Abandoning the rule in 2003 contributed to the housing and finance crisis that followed." John Taylor, after whom the Taylor rule is named, concurs. Beginning in 2003, Fed policy deviated from Taylor rule-like behavior and as a result "macroeconomic policy became more interventionist, less rules

---

[2] There are studies suggesting that the Great Moderation was also caused by other factors, such as fewer destabilizing shocks (Clark 2009; Summers 2005). It is worth noting that the reduction in volatility during the Great Moderation was also accompanied by an increase in substantial economic contractions (Jenson et al. 2020; Jordà et al. 2017).

based, and less predictable" (Taylor 2010b, p. 1, emphasis removed; see also Taylor 2012, 2013). This was one of the many contributors to the 2007–2008 crisis.

Any account of this crisis must include misguided central bank policies. Those policies, in turn, resulted from central banks embracing constrained discretion. Adding the discretionary element does not improve monetary policy outcomes. Instead, it invites the kinds of mistakes that were made before, during, and after the crisis. In what follows, we briefly go over the mistakes made before the crisis, the mistakes made during and after the crisis, and what these mistakes tell us about the feasibility of central banking under constrained discretion.

1.2.1 Before the Crisis: First Too Loose

Prior to the 2007–2008 crisis, theories linking artificially low interest rates (induced by monetary policy) to the business cycle were held in low regard by the economics profession. They were endorsed by adherents of the "Austrian" school of economics (Hayek 1933 [2008], 1935 [2008]; Mises 1949, 1953), but few others.[3] This has changed since the crisis. There is a growing body of literature that finds merit in the Mises–Hayek theory of the business cycle (e.g., Borio and Disyatat 2011; Caballero 2010; Calvo 2013; Diamond and Rajan 2012; Gjerstad and Smith 2014, ch. 6; Leijonhufvud 2009; Schwartz 2009; Taylor 2007, 2009, 2014; see Cachanosky and Salter 2017 for a summary and analysis). While sometimes disagreeing with specific components of the theory, belief in a link between artificially low interest rates and unsustainable economic activity is no longer untenable.

The Fed, under Alan Greenspan's chairmanship, set the stage for the 2007–2008 financial crisis. It did so through excessively expansionary monetary policy in the years following the dot-com crash.[4] At the start of 2001, the federal funds rate was 6.25 percent; by the end of the year, it had fallen to 1.75 percent. In 2003, the rate fell further to 1 percent. These rates were so low that *real* interest rates were negative. Furthermore, this was a significant deviation from previous rule-like behavior. This can be

---

[3] The standard New Keynesian framework contains a link between low interest rates and a welfare-reducing expansion, but this is not a boom–bust cycle with investment errors driven by credit, as in the Austrian theory.

[4] For a dissenting view, see Henderson and Hummel (2008). Horwitz and Luther (2011) offer a critique of that dissenting view. Also, see Taylor (2009, pp. 6–7) for an argument that a global "savings glut" cannot explain the low interest rates that preceded the crisis.

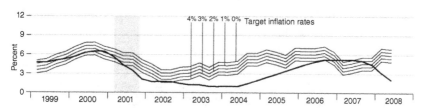

Figure 1.1. Federal funds rate and inflation targets.
Source: Federal Reserve Bank of St. Louis, *Monetary Trends* (October 2008), p. 10. Available online: https://s3.amazonaws.com/files.research.stlouisfed.org/datatrends/pdfs/mt/20081001/mtpub.pdf

considered in the context of the Taylor rule. Figure 1.1, taken from the Federal Reserve Bank of St. Louis's *Monetary Trends* (October 2008), shows the actual federal funds rate compared to the path it ought to have followed, had the Fed been targeting the indicated inflation rate.

As Figure 1.1 shows, before 2001, the Fed kept the federal funds rate at a level consistent with approximately 2 percent inflation. After 2001, however, deviations arose between the rate consistent with 2 percent inflation and the actual market rate. The deviations were especially pronounced from 2003 through 2005.[5] Excessively loose monetary policy contributed to excessively easy credit, which eventually found its way into the housing sector. To be clear, monetary policy alone cannot explain why unsustainable economic activity occurred in the housing market specifically. Other public policies for which the central bank was not responsible, such as various federal policies aimed at increasing homeownership, are viable candidates (Gjerstad and Smith 2014, ch. 6; Koppl 2014; Mueller 2019). But, excessively loose money can and does explain why there was a credit bubble in the first place.

1.2.2 During and After the Crisis: Now Too Tight

The Fed, now under Bernanke's chairmanship, made the opposite mistake once turmoil developed in financial markets and began spilling over into

---

[5] Bernanke (2010, 2015), Kohn (2007), Mehra and Sawhney (2010), and Orphanides and Wieland (2008) argue that a modified Taylor rule, which adjusts for inflation using the forecasted PCE rather than the CPI, does justify the Fed's course of monetary policy during this period. Nikolsko-Rzhevskyy and Papell (2013) examine modified Taylor rules and conclude that, while varying the measure of inflation and the output gap can produce a Taylor rule consistent with monetary policy from 2003 to 2005, these assumptions are not consistent with historical experience. Taylor (2010a, 2012) argues that forecasted inflation is an inappropriate measure.

the real economy. When the housing bubble burst, the Fed began drastically expanding its balance sheet in an attempt to stabilize markets. The Fed's portfolio, which totaled $900 billion in mid-2008, grew to nearly $3 trillion by early 2012, and then grew again to $4.5 trillion by mid-2016. This was accompanied by a significant change in the composition of the assets held by the Fed. The Fed no longer restricted its asset purchases to short-term government debt. It instead began to purchase longer-term government debt and in a "creative interpretation of the Fed's power" (Bernanke et al. 2019, p. 50), the now infamous mortgage-backed securities.

Normally, a monetary expansion as aggressive as this would significantly increase aggregate demand, putting upward pressure on employment, prices, and output. That did not occur. This can be attributed to the Fed policy, adopted in October 2008, of paying interest on excess reserves (additional reserves above the reserve requirement) held by financial institutions in their accounts at the Fed. This was done because Fed officials were worried that the expansion of the Fed's balance sheet would result in significant growth in broader monetary aggregates, which then would result in higher-than-desirable inflation (Selgin 2019). In April 2008, core inflation was above the Fed's implicit 2 percent target, and headline inflation was even higher. But, when the Fed began paying interest on excess reserves, it essentially sterilized its monetary expansion during the early days of the crisis, arguably when the economy most urgently needed the effects of such an expansion. As a result of its interest on excess reserves policy, financial institutions did not lend out or otherwise channel the monetary injections by the Fed into the broader economy. Rather, the money sat in banks' accounts at the Fed.

The result was a precipitous decline in aggregate demand. As Figure 1.2 shows, this decline in nominal gross domestic product (aggregate demand) began with a slowdown in growth in early 2008; by late 2008 total nominal spending started to contract. The Fed failed to act decisively at the necessary time to stabilize the nominal economy because it was unduly worried about inflation. Although the Fed eventually recognized the turmoil in financial markets, beginning the first round of its quantitative easing programs in November 2008, it maintained its policy of paying interest on excess reserves, which limited the efficacy of these programs' countercyclical effects. The unemployment rate stood at 6.8 percent in November 2008; it would climb as high as 10 percent in October 2009 before declining.

Bernanke's Fed failed to live up to the promise made at the conference honoring Milton Friedman. The errors of the Great Depression–era Fed stemmed from a desire to protect external reserve drains and worries over

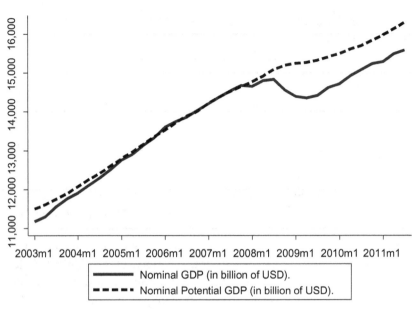

Figure 1.2. NGDP vs. potential.
Source: FRED, Federal Reserve Bank of St. Louis

excessive speculation in financial markets. In contrast, the errors of the Great Recession–era Fed stemmed from an excessive concern for inflationary trends during the early days of the crisis, followed by policies that ensured a breakdown between the Fed's monetary injections and overall economic stabilization. Although the circumstances were different, the result was the same. Once again, the Fed bears significant responsibility for the economic turmoil that developed on its watch.

1.2.3 What It All Means

The previous discussion is a very brief distillation of an incredibly complex event in recent economic history. We do not intend to "prove" that the Fed caused the initial credit bubble and the subsequent economic downturn. Instead, we use the 2007–2008 financial crisis as an illustration of the argument we make in this book: The Fed's modus operandi of constrained discretion prevents it from achieving macroeconomic and financial stability. This is essentially a means–ends argument: Constrained discretion is an inappropriate operating framework for securing broadly held goals about what we want central banks to do. Constrained discretion fails because it places insurmountable information and incentive burdens on those whom we ask to run central banks and implement monetary policy. In terms of information, it is incredibly difficult in real time to maintain allocatively neutral demand stabilization at the macroeconomic level, which entails obtaining monetary equilibrium at the microeconomic level. It is equally difficult to ascertain the degree to which monetary factors spill over into financial markets, causing either asset bubbles or systemic illiquidity. Note that Bernanke, himself an expert on how credit and financial markets affect the macroeconomy, along with many other monetary and financial policymakers, failed to recognize the nascent economic turmoil as it developed.

In terms of incentives, we must remember that central banking is a bureaucracy. Even well-intentioned people can fall prey to problems stemming from poor incentives in nonmarket hierarchies (Niskanen 1968; Tullock 2005). Furthermore, money and finance is a highly political field and has been so throughout the entire history of the United States (Calomiris and Haber 2014). Despite the appearance of formal independence from politicians, there are many ways political pressure can be and is brought to bear on monetary policy decision-makers. These sources of incentive problems undermine central banks' ability to act in the public interest.

1.3 Real Monetary Rules: Still the Only Game in Town

Selgin (2016, p. 282) usefully distinguishes between pseudo- and real monetary rules. A pseudo-monetary rule "is one that is either not well enforced or not expected to last." Monetary rules that allow discretion, but do not specify conditions for when deviations are permitted, are "mere guidelines for monetary policy too vague to be operational" (Sevensson 2003, p. 3). A real monetary rule, in contrast, is both specified and enforced.[6] There is some institutional technology that binds the hands of monetary policymakers in such a way that they cannot deviate from the rule. In addition, a true monetary rule is also "robust," meaning that "it must be chosen so that its strict enforcement is not likely to be a cause of such regret as might lead to its frequent revision or abandonment" (Selgin 2016, p. 287). Selgin's analysis of what kinds of arrangements constitute real monetary rules considers several information and incentive frictions, which focus scholars'

---

[6] See Drazen and Masson (1994), Florez-Jimenez and Parra-Polania (2016), and Obstfeld (1997) for the literature on formalizing escape clauses to specify when and how discretion is permitted.

attention on how actually existing discretion compares to actually existing rules. This is precisely the kind of institutional analysis we intend to conduct in our study, and it is something we believe should be much more common in contemporary monetary economics and macroeconomics.

In light of Selgin's analysis, when revisiting Bernanke's (2003) speech, we see that constrained discretion is not categorically distinct from discretion itself. Bernanke contends that, under constrained discretion,

the central bank is free to do its best to stabilize output and employment in the face of short-run disturbances, with the appropriate caution born of our imperfect knowledge of the economy and of the effects of policy. However, a critical proviso is that, in conducting stabilization policy, the central bank must also maintain a strong commitment to keeping inflation – and, hence, public *expectations* of inflation – firmly under control.

Here, Bernanke discusses inflation targeting (or price-level targeting) as an application of rule-like behavior. Ultimately, the choice of a nominal anchor is of secondary importance. What matters most is whether rule-like behavior is similar enough to true rules for rule-like behavior to enjoy the benefits of rules while avoiding the costs. The crucial issue, as Bernanke recognizes, is that of public expectations. Can monetary policymakers credibly commit to rule-like behavior, such that the public can form its plans as if monetary policy unfolds according to a rule? Recent monetary and financial history suggests a cautious optimism. In ordinary times, when the financial system is operating well enough, monetary policymakers can concern themselves exclusively with aggregate demand management. However, the troubling possibility of institutionalized moral hazard in the financial system throws the above into serious doubt. The Fed's history of bailouts – the Franklin National Bank in 1974, the First Pennsylvania Bank and Trust Company in 1980, the Continental Illinois in 1984, the Long-Term Capital Management in 1999, and several organizations during the most recent crisis – suggests credible commitment *in the other direction*: Because the Fed has a history of not allowing "important" financial institutions that became insolvent to fail, the public has a reasonable expectation that the Fed will not constrain itself to limited and predictable responses in the event of potential systemic events (e.g., Goodfriend and Lacker 1999; Hetzel 2012; Meltzer 2009, pp. 881, 1055n55; Miller et al. 2002; Salter 2016; White 2012).[7]

---

[7] Many of these bailouts violate Bagehot's famous last-resort lending rules (Bernanke et al. 2019, p. 119; Hogan et al. 2015; Meltzer 2009, pp. 881, 1053n55, 1173–1174, 1248–1150). We explore this in greater detail in Chapter 4.

But wait. Have we moved the goalposts? After all, Bernanke was clearly discussing constrained discretion in the context of nominal stabilization policy. Financial crises are something else entirely. In fact, it is precisely the possibility of a financial crisis that makes the "discretion" part of constrained discretion valuable.[8] Rule-like behavior during ordinary times, and discretion in the service of firefighting during turbulent times, is the best response. But this counterargument fails. It is the "discretionary" part of constrained discretion that increases the likelihood that we will find ourselves in turbulent times in the first place, as well as making those turbulent times more severe and prolonged. That is what the institutionalization of moral hazard ("too big to fail") means.[9]

More broadly, we cannot neatly separate monetary policy from financial stability, because financial panics involve a crucial transition from systemic *illiquidity* to systemic *insolvency*, and the central bank has the monopoly on the economy's most liquid asset: the supply of narrow money. To be clear, we also contend that there are serious information and incentive problems with discretionary monetary policy even during ordinary times. Detailing those problems and their consequences will be a large part of our argument. But when push comes to shove, the ultimate breakdown point for constrained discretion is that it does not allow monetary policymakers to commit themselves, effectively and robustly, to responses to financial turbulence such that market actors are disincentivized from engaging in reckless behavior in the first place. Part of the problem is that there is no enforcement mechanism for making central bankers adhere to the kinds of responses that can achieve stability. Another part is that the implicit self-adopted framework is not robust: it breaks down when stressed. Our larger argument is a plea for monetary economists and macroeconomists to take these problems seriously and to reallocate their substantial intellectual capital toward discovering effective alternatives. These alternatives must include meaningful enforcement mechanisms and exhibit robustness in the face of challenges.

---

[8] One of the primary alternative monetary institutions to discretionary central banking, the gold standard, is often rejected because it cannot be used to mitigate short- and medium-run fluctuations (Bernanke 2013; Hogan et al. 2018; Kydland and Wynne 2002). However, the gold standard has a better record of generating long-term price stability.

[9] As Meltzer (2009, p. 1250) explains, "Banks and financial firms should not have incentives to become so large that they cannot fail. 'Too big to fail' encourages excessive risk taking and imposes costs on the taxpayers."

1.4 Rediscovered Country: The Classically Liberal Perspective

There is another reason that constrained discretion is objectionable as a central bank operating framework, one that most monetary economists and macroeconomists do not consider. Constrained discretion is problematic not just on positive, but normative, grounds. In brief, discretion on the part of monetary policymakers is inconsistent with basic jurisprudential tenets of post-Enlightenment political thought. It is worth quoting at length Robert Hetzel (1997, pp. 45–46), a monetary economist who has seriously grappled with the political economy issues inherent in central banking:

Constitutional democracy protects individual liberty. It does so by placing restraints on the arbitrary exercise of power by government. A primary restraint is the constitutional protection of property rights. The monetary arrangements of a country either promote or undermine that protection.

Money is unique in that its value in exchange far exceeds the cost of producing an additional unit. On the one hand, governments have an incentive to print additional money to gain "free" resources, or seigniorage revenues. On the other hand, the central bank must limit the quantity of money in circulation to control prices.

Through its influence on seigniorage, money creation affects how government raises revenue. It can also affect who within government decides how that revenue is spent. Through its influence on fluctuations in the price level, money creation influences the extent of arbitrary redistributions of wealth among individuals. The institutional arrangements that govern the creation of money then bear on two aspects of the protection of property rights: the taking and disposition of wealth from the public and the distribution of wealth by government between individuals.

A legislative mandate from Congress requiring the Federal Reserve (the Fed) to stabilize the price level and to hold only government securities in its portfolio would complement the rules in a constitutional democracy that protect property rights.

Hetzel makes a simple but profound point: In a constitutional democracy, the *rule of law* is the standard to which self-governing citizens demand that a public institution conform itself. This includes central banks such as the Fed. These institutions are ultimately created and justified by the consent of citizens and are chartered to serve their interests. They also must be accountable to the citizenry. Central banking by discretion, constrained or otherwise, violates these basic norms of modern politics.

Our concerns differ somewhat from Hetzel's. We will not pay much attention to the temptation to generate seigniorage, and we are not as convinced of the desirability of a price-level target as he. We are much more concerned with instances where politics impinged on Fed operations, especially the de facto politicization of money and credit that has followed from the Fed's expansive new powers acquired during the darkest days of the financial crisis (Meltzer 2011). But our basic perspective on the desirability of true rules for monetary policy is the same as his.

One of our objectives in this study is to (re-)introduce classically liberal political economy to monetary economics and macroeconomics scholarship. Classically liberal political economy refers to the "mainline" of economic thought proceeding in an unbroken line since Adam Smith (Boettke 2012). As the mainstream of contemporary economics, this kind of political economy recognizes that how economies work and how they ought to work are different questions. But it also insists that the second question is just as much a concern for scholarly inquiry as the first. The hallmark of classically liberal political economy is using the core tools of the economic way of thinking, namely price-theoretic reasoning, to conduct comparative institutional analyses for ascertaining what kinds of rules best contribute to human flourishing. James Buchanan, the 1986 Nobel laureate in economics, offers the best summary of this approach:

> Political economists stress the technical economic principles that one must understand in order to assess alternative arrangements for promoting peaceful cooperation and productive specialization among free men. Yet political economists go further and frankly try to bring out into the open the philosophical issues that necessarily underlie all discussions of the appropriate functions of government and all proposed policy measures. They examine philosophical values for consistency among themselves and with the ideal of human freedom. (Buchanan 1958, p. 5)

Currently, the mainstream of the profession in monetary economics and macroeconomics only tangentially engages the mainline. This is unfortunate. It is the scholarly equivalent to $20 bills laying on the sidewalk. However, this by necessity implies an opportunity for intellectual arbitrage – one we are happy to exploit! Informed by classically liberal political economy, our argument will contain both positive and normative components. The positive component will resemble the kind of economics practiced by Ronald Coase, Douglass North, and Elinor Ostrom: comparative institutional analysis grounded in the rationality postulate, to demonstrate that constrained discretion is means–ends inconsistent as a central bank operating framework. It will also draw on the three great classically liberal political economists of the twentieth century, Friedrich von Hayek, Milton Friedman, and James M. Buchanan, each of whom devoted significant scholarly attention to monetary institutions and policy. Our normative component is grounded in the fact that money and its attendant operating system are institutions of public importance, implying that the same justificatory standards that apply to other institutions of public importance apply to the monetary system as well.

1.5 The Map and the Territory

Readers familiar with mainstream monetary economics and macroeconomics may find our methods and arguments unusual. We will not construct any mathematical models nor test econometrically any hypotheses. Instead, we will explicate, using simple verbal logic grounded in the economic way of thinking, why we believe constrained discretion cannot be adopted by central banks if their goal is economic stability, as well as why discretion is incompatible with the justificatory tenets of constitutional democracy. Furthermore, we will support our arguments by drawing on the history of the Fed. We firmly reject the standard rejoinder that our approach is "unscientific" or "unrigorous." The questions we address are the foundational ones about what monetary policy is, what we want it to achieve, what institutions we construct to help us achieve it, and whether those institutions are morally commensurate with self-governance. The methods we adopt are those we believe are best suited to answer the questions, as with any scientific study. Our goal is to persuade monetary economists and macroeconomists as well as those conducting scholarship on the relationship between institutions and human flourishing in political science, philosophy, and other subfields of economics.

We close this introductory chapter by offering a brief outline of the remainder of the book. Chapter 2 argues that there is an insuperable knowledge problem with discretionary monetary policy. It is not merely difficult for central bankers to maintain aggregate nominal stability (which implies monetary equilibrium at the micro-level) by discretionary means. It is impossible. Our arguments mirror many of those made by Mises, Hayek, and others on the impossibility of rational economic calculation under socialism. Discretionary monetary policy thus is systematically unlikely to achieve economic stability.

Chapter 3 focuses on incentive problems with discretionary monetary policy. Central bankers are bureaucrats, and thus confront the standard range of peculiar nonmarket incentives that result in phenomena such as status quo bias and "mission creep." Furthermore, central banks are susceptible to political interference. The widespread perception that the Fed is politically independent is unjustified. Taken collectively, these incentive problems prevent us from uncritically assuming that central banks can advance the public interest so long as they retain discretion.

Chapter 4 focuses on financial crises. Fighting such crises and preventing them from toppling the financial system is one of the strongest arguments for a degree of discretion in monetary policy. We will show this "challenge of the extraordinary" does not weaken the case for true rules. Drawing on the literature on last-resort lending, we will argue that true rules can deal not just with nominal instability as is typically assumed, but financial insolvency as well. The first four chapters establish the problems with discretion, including constrained discretion. The remainder of the book considers potential solutions.

Chapter 5 explores the monetary economics of Friedrich von Hayek, Milton Friedman, and James M. Buchanan. Each of these Nobel laureates devoted significant attention to the problem of how we can establish monetary institutions that are both effective and accountable. They came to different solutions, but reasoned in similar ways. We will argue it is not their specific recommendations, but their way of thinking, that monetary economists and macroeconomists must recover if they hope to make progress.

Chapter 6 is normatively focused. We introduce the ideal of the rule of law, detail its pedigree in classically liberal political economy, and show why monetary economists and macroeconomists should pay attention to it. We argue that this tenet underlies the justification for all institutions of public importance in constitutional democracies and that central banks cannot meet this standard so long as it retains discretion in its operations. If we want lawful monetary institutions, we must embrace true rules.

Chapter 7, the concluding chapter, explores the relationship between monetary institutions and the liberal project of creating a society of free and equal persons. This project has important implications for the structure of public institutions, including monetary institutions. We also discuss a global crisis that unfolded just as we finished this manuscript: the COVID-19 pandemic and the economic fallout it created. We survey the Fed's response to the pandemic, focusing on how monetary institutions can help us respond to crises without undermining self-governance. Our takeaway message is that if monetary economists and macroeconomists want to make lasting contributions to the quest for economic stability in a self-governing society, they must think "constitutionally." Calibrating formal models and studying policy effects econometrically, while valuable, are of secondary importance. Fundamental institutional considerations come first.

References

Barro, Robert and David Gordon (1983). Rules, Discretion, and Reputation in a Model of Monetary Policy. *Journal of Monetary Economics*, 12(1), 101–121.

Berlemann, Michael (2005). Time Inconsistency of Monetary Policy: Empirical Evidence from Polls. *Public Choice*, 125(1–2), 1–15.

Bernanke, Ben (2002). Remarks by Governor Ben S. Bernanke. Given at the Conference to Honor Milton Friedman at the University of Chicago. Available online (accessed May 14, 2020), www.federalreserve.gov/BOARDDOCS/SPEECHES/2002/20021108/

(2003). "Constrained Discretion" and Monetary Policy. Remarks before the Monetary Marketers of New York University. Available online (accessed May 14, 2020), www.federalreserve.gov/boarddocs/speeches/2003/20030203/default.htm

(2010). Monetary Policy and the Housing Bubble. Speech at the Annual Meeting of the American Economic Association. Atlanta, GA. January 3. Available online (accessed June 20, 2019), www.federalreserve.gov/newsevents/speech/bernanke20100103a.htm

(2015). The Taylor Rule: A Benchmark for Monetary Policy? Brookings. Available online (accessed June 20, 2019), www.brookings.edu/blog/ben-bernanke/2015/04/28/the-taylor-rule-a-benchmark-for-monetary-policy/

Bernanke, Ben and Frederic Mishkin (1997). Inflation Targeting: A New Framework for Monetary Policy? *Journal of Economic Perspectives*, 11(2), 97–116.

Bernanke, Ben S. (2013). A Century of US Central Banking: Goals, Frameworks, Accountability. *Journal of Economic Perspectives*, 27(4), 3–16.

Bernanke, Ben S., Timothy F. Geithner, and Henry M. Paulson, Jr. (2019). *Firefighting: The Financial Crisis and Its Lessons*. Penguin Books.

Bianchi, Francesco and Leonardo Melosi (2018). Constrained Discretion and Central Bank Transparency. *Review of Economics and Statistics*, 100(1), 187–202.

Blinder, Alan (1998). *Central Banking in Theory and Practice*. The MIT Press.

Blinder, Alan, Charles Goodhard, Philipp Hildebrand, David Lipton, and Charles Wyplosz (2001). *How Do Central Banks Talk?* International Center for Monetary and Banking Studies and Centre for Economic Policy Research.

Board of Governors of the Federal Reserve System (2018). Review of Monetary Policy Strategy, Tools, and Communications. Available online (accessed June 19, 2019), www.federalreserve.gov/monetarypolicy/review-of-monetary-policy-strategy-tools-and-communications.htm

Boettke, Peter J. (2012). *Living Economics: Yesterday, Today, and Tomorrow*. Independent Institute.

Borio, Claudio and Piti Disyatat (2011). Global Imbalances and the Financial Crisis: Link or No Link? BIS Working Paper No. 346.

Buchanan, James (1958). The Thomas Jefferson Center for Studies in Political Economy. *University of Virginia Newsletter*, 35(2), 5–8.

Caballero, Ricardo (2010). Macroeconomics after the Crisis: Time to Deal with the Pretense-of-Knowledge Syndrome. *Journal of Economic Perspectives*, 24(4), 85–102.

Cachanosky, Nicolas and Alexander William Salter (2017). The View from Vienna: An Analysis of the Renewed Interest in the Mises-Hayek Theory of the Business Cycle. *The Review of Austrian Economics*, 30(2), 169–192.

Calomiris, Charles and Stephen Haber (2014). *Fragile by Design: The Political Origins of Banking Crises and Scarce Credit*. Princeton University Press.

Calvo, Guillermo A. (1978). On the Time Consistency of Optimal Policy in a Monetary Economy. *Econometrica: Journal of the Econometric Society*, 46(6), 1411–1428.

(2013). Puzzling over the Anatomy of Crises: Liquidity and the Veil of Finance. Bank of Japan Monetary and Economic Studies (November), Working Paper, 39–63.

Clark, Todd E. (2009). Is the Great Moderation Over? An Empirical Analysis. Federal Reserve Bank of Kansas City. *Economic Review* (Fourth Quarter 2009), 5–42.

Crowe, Christopher and Ellen Meade (2007). The Evolution of Central Bank Governance around the World. *Journal of Economic Perspectives*, 21(4), 69–90.

Cutsinger, Bryan (2020). On the Feasibility of Returning to the Gold Standard. *Quarterly Review of Economics and Finance*, 78, 88–97.

Diamond, Douglas and Raghuram Rajan (2012). Illiquid Banks, Financial Stability, and Interest Rate Policy. *Journal of Political Economy*, 120(3), 552–591.

Drazen, Allan and Paul Masson (1994). Credibility of Policies versus Credibility of Policymakers. *The Quarterly Journal of Economics*, 109(3), 735–754.

Faust, Jon and Lars Svensson (2001). Transparency and Credibility: Monetary Policy with Unobservable Goals. *International Economic Review*, 42)(2), 369–397.

Fischer, Stanley (1995). Central-Bank Independence Revisited. *The American Economic Review*, 85(2), 201–206.

Florez-Jimenez, Maria Lucia and Julian Parra-Polania (2016). Forward Guidance with an Escape Clause: When Half a Promise Is Better Than a Full One. *Applied Economics*, 48(15), 1372–1381.

Friedman, Benjamin (2006). The Greenspan Era: Discretion, Rather Than Rules. *American Economic Review*, 96(2), 174–177.

Friedman, Milton and Anna Schwartz (1963). *A Monetary History of the United States, 1863–1960*. Princeton University Press.

Geraats, Petra (2002). Central Bank Transparency. *The Economic Journal*, 112(483), F532–F565.

Gjerstad, Steven and Vernon Smith (2014). *Rethinking Housing Bubbles*. Cambridge University Press.

Goodfriend, Marvin and Jeffrey Lacker (1999). Limited Commitment and Central Bank Lending. *Economic Quarterly-Federal Reserve Bank of Richmond*, 85(4), 1–27.

Hayek, Friedrich August (1933 [2008]). *Monetary Theory and the Trade Cycle*. Ludwig von Mises Institute.

(1935 [2008]). *Prices and Production*. Ludwig von Mises Institute.

Henderson, David and Jeffrey Rogers Hummel (2008). Greenspan's Monetary Policy in Retrospect: Discretion or Rules? Cato Institute Briefing Papers, No. 109. Available online (accessed June 17, 2019), https://object.cato.org/sites/cato.org/files/pubs/pdf/bp109.pdf

Herrendorf, Berthold and Ben Lockwood (1997). Rogoff's "Conservative" Central Banker Restored. *Journal of Money, Credit, and Banking*, 29(4), 476–495.

Hetzel, Robert (1997). The Case for a Monetary Rule in a Constitutional Democracy. *Federal Reserve Bank of Richmond Economic Quarterly*, 83(2), 45–65.

(2012). *The Great Recession: Market Failure or Policy Failure?* Cambridge University Press.

Hogan, Thomas (2015). Has the Fed Improved U.S. Economic Performance? *Journal of Macroeconomics*, 43, 257–266.

Hogan, Thomas, Linh Le, and Alexander William Salter (2015). Ben Bernanke and Bagehot's Rules. *Journal of Money, Credit and Banking*, 47(2–3), 333–348.

Hogan, Thomas, Daniel Smith, and Robin Aguiar-Hicks (2018). Central Banking without Romance. *The European Journal of Comparative Economics*, 15(2), 293–314.

Horwitz, Steven and William Luther (2011). The Great Recession and Its Aftermath from a Monetary Equilibrium Theory Perspective. In Steven Kates (Ed.), *The Global Financial Crisis: What Have We Learnt?* Edward Elgar Publishing, pp. 75–92.

Ireland, Peter (1999). Does the Time-consistency Problem Explain the Behavior of Inflation in the United States? *Journal of Monetary Economics*, 44(2), 279–291.

Jenson, Henrik, Evan Petrella, Søren Hove Ravn, and Emiliano Santoro (2020). Leverage and Deepening Business-Cycle Skewness. *American Economic Journal: Macroeconomics*, 12(1), 245–281.

Jordà, Òscar, Moritz Schularick, and Alan M. Taylor (2017). Macrofinancial History and the New Business Cycle Facts. In Martin Eichenbaum and Jonathan A. Parker (Eds.), *NBER Macroeconomics Annual*, volume 31, pp. 213–263.

Kohn, Donald (2007). John Taylor Rules. Speech at the Conference on John Taylor's Contributions to Monetary Theory and Policy. Federal Reserve Bank of Dallas, Dallas, TX. October 12. Available online (accessed June 20, 2019), www.federalreserve.gov/newsevents/speech/kohn20071012a.htm.

Koppl, Roger (2014). *From Crisis to Confidence: Macroeconomics after the Crash.* The Institute for Economic Affairs.

Kydland, Finn E. and Edward Prescott (1977). Rules Rather Than Discretion: The Inconsistency of Optimal Plans. *Journal of Political Economy*, 85(3), 473–491.

Kydland, Finn E. and Mark A. Wynne (2002). Alternative Monetary Constitutions and the Quest for Price Stability. *Federal Reserve Bank of Dallas, Economic & Financial Policy Review*, 1(1), 1–19.

Leijonhufvud, Axel (2009). Out of the Corridor: Keynes and the Crisis. *Cambridge Journal of Economics*, 33(4), 741–757.

Lohmann, Susanne (1992). Optimal Commitment in Monetary Policy: Credibility versus Flexibility. *The American Economic Review*, 82(1), 273–286.

Lossani, Marco, Piergiovanna Natale, and Patrizio Tirelli (1998). Incomplete Information in Monetary Policy Games: Rules Rather Than a Conservative Central Banker. *Scottish Journal of Political Economy*, 45(1), 33–47.

McCallum, Bennett (1995). Two Fallacies Concerning Central-Bank Independence. *American Economic Review*, 85(2), 207–211.

Mehra, Yash and Bansi Sawhney (2010). Inflation Measure, Taylor Rules, and the Greenspan-Bernanke Years. *Economic Quarterly*, 96(2), 123–151.

Meltzer, Alan (2009). *A History of the Federal Reserve*, volume II, Book Two, 1970–1986. University of Chicago Press.

(2011). Politics and the Fed. *Journal of Monetary Economics*, 58(1), 39–48.

(2012). The Federal Reserve at (Almost) 100. *Journal of Macroeconomics*, 34(3), 626–630.

(2014). Federal Reserve Independence. *Journal of Macroeconomic Dynamics and Control*, 49, 160–163.

Miller, Marcus, Paul Weller, and Lei Zhang (2002). Moral Hazard and the US Stock Market: Analyzing the "Greenspan Put." *The Economic Journal*, 112(478), C171–C186.

Mises, Ludwig von (1949). *Human Action: A Treatise on Economics*. Yale University Press.

(1953). *The Theory of Money and Credit*. Yale University Press.

Mueller, Paul (2019). *Ten Years Later: Why the Conventional Wisdom about the 2008 Financial Crisis Is Still Wrong*. Cambridge Scholars Publishing.

Nikolsko-Rzhevskyy, Alex and David Papell (2013). Taylor's Rule versus Taylor Rules. *International Finance*, 16(1), 71–93.

Niskanen, William (1968). The Peculiar Economics of Bureaucracy. *American Economic Review*, 58(2), 293–305.

Obstfeld, Maurice (1997). Destabilizing Effects of Exchange-Rate Escape Clauses. *Journal of International Economics*, 43(1–2), 61–77.

Orphanides, Athanasios and Volker Wieland (2008). Economic Projections and Rules of Thumb for Monetary Policy. *Federal Reserve Bank of St. Louis Review*, 90(4), 304–324.

Persson, Torsten (1993). Designing Institutions for Monetary Stability. *Carnegie-Rochester Conference Series on Public Policy*, 39, 53–84.

Rogoff, Kenneth (1985). The Optimal Degree of Commitment to an Intermediate Monetary Target. *Quarterly Journal of Economics*, 100(4), 1169–1189.

Romer, Christina and David Romer (1997). Institutions for Monetary Stability. In Christina Romer and David Romer (Eds.), *Reducing Inflation: Motivation and Strategy*. Chicago University Press, pp. 307–334.

Salter, Alexander William (2016). Robust Political Economy and the Lender of Last Resort. *Journal of Financial Services Research*, 50(1), 1–27.

Sargent, Thomas (1999). Central Banking in Theory and Practice: Lionel Robbins Lectures. *Journal of Political Economy*, 107(2), 419–425.

Schwartz, Anna (2009). Origins of the Financial Market Crisis of 2008. *Cato Journal*, 29 (1), 19–23.

Selgin, George (2016). Real and Pseudo Monetary Rules. *Cato Journal*, 36(2), 279–296.

(2019). The Fed's New Operating Framework: How We Got Here and Why We Shouldn't Stay. *Cato Journal*, 39(2), 317–326.

Selgin, George, William Lastrapes, and White, Lawrence (2012). Has the Fed Been a Failure? *Journal of Macroeconomics*, 34(3), 569–596.

Sevensson, Lars (2003). What Is Wrong with Taylor Rules? Using Judgement in Monetary Policy through Targeting Rules. *Journal of Economic Literature*, 41(2), 426–477.

Summers, Peter (2005). What Caused the Great Moderation? Some Cross-Country Evidence. *Federal Reserve Bank of Kansas City Economic Review*, (Third Quarter 2005), 5–32.

Taylor, John (2007). Housing and Monetary Policy. Proceedings – Economic Policy Symposium – Jackson Hole, Federal Reserve Bank of Kansas City, pp. 463–476.

(2009). *Getting Off Track*. Hoover Institute Press.

(2010a). The Fed and the Crisis: A Reply to Ben Bernanke. *The Wall Street Journal. Sunday*, January 10.

(2010b). Macroeconomic Lessons from the Great Deviation. *NBER Macroeconomics Annual*, 25, 387–395.

(2012). Monetary Policy Rules Work and Discretion Doesn't: A Tale of Two Eras. *Journal of Money, Credit and Banking*, 44(6), 1017–1032.

(2013). International Monetary Coordination and the Great Deviation. *Journal of Policy Modeling*, 35(3), 463–472.

(2014). The Role of Policy in the Great Recession and the Weak Recovery. *American Economic Review*, 104(5), 61–66.

Tillmann, Peter (2008). The Conservative Central Banker Revisited: Too Conservative Is More Costly Than too Liberal. *European Journal of Political Economy*, 24(4), 737–741.

Tullock, Gordon. (2005). *Bureaucracy*. Liberty Fund.

Waller, Christopher and Carl Walsh (1996). Central-Bank Independence, Economic Behavior, and Optimal Term Lengths. *The American Economic Review*, 86(5), 1139–1153.

Walsh, Carl (1995). Optimal Contracts for Central Bankers. *The American Economic Review*, 85(1), 150–167.

White, Lawrence (2012). Monetary Policy and the Financial Crisis. In Davide Beckworth (Ed.), *Boom and Bust Banking: The Causes and Cures of the Great Recession*. Independent Institute, pp. 13–26.

(2015). The Merits and Feasibility of Returning to a Commodity Standard. *Journal of Financial Stability*, 17, 59–64.

Knowledge Problems with Discretionary Monetary Policy

2.1 Introduction

When questioned by US Representative Alexandria Ocasio-Cortez about the Federal Reserve's inaccurate forecasts of long-run unemployment, Chairman Powell replied, "We have learned that – you can't identify – this is something you can't identify directly. I think we have learned its [the natural rate of unemployment] lower than we thought – it's substantially lower than we thought" (C-Span 2019). This was a surprisingly candid admission of the limits of expert knowledge by the head of one of the most important central banks in the world.[1]

The reason this matters is because the natural rate of unemployment (along with the natural rate of interest) is an important metric guiding both ordinary and extraordinary monetary policies. Chairman Powell acknowledged that we cannot directly observe or predict these natural rates in a changing economy. In more detailed remarks, Powell (2019a), referring to the tendency of economists to label these metrics as u* (natural rate of unemployment) and r* (natural rate of interest), explains, "Unlike celestial stars, these stars move unpredictably and cannot be directly observed. We must judge their locations as best we can based on incoming data and then add an element of risk management to be able to use them as guides." While both u* and r* were once thought to be roughly stable, recent changes in the economy have made it clear that they are far more

---

[1] Chairman Powell's frankness earned him both criticism and praise. For example, Williamson (2019) writes in response, "There's a lot Powell doesn't know, and it shows." Cochrane (2019b), responding to Williamson, writes, "I would much rather have Powell's healthily acknowledged uncertainty than a PhD economist who thinks he or she 'knows' how the Phillips curve really works."

unpredictable than economists previously thought (Abraham and Haltiwanger 2019; Powell 2018; Sablik 2018).[2]

Instead of an exact science, central banking is a process of educated guesses and trial and error (Hetzel 2016, p. 7). Things become even messier when central bankers act with a significant degree of discretion. This is further complicated by the fact that other government policies, such as tax policy and transfer programs, can affect the natural rates, and must also be taken into consideration (Barro and Gordon 1983; Daly et al. 2011; Drazen 2000, p. 120).

Furthermore, this is only one of several *technical* problems that discretionary central bankers face. Technical problems, at least in theory, are solvable. But central bankers also face unsurmountable *knowledge* problems (Salter and Smith 2017). Unlike technical problems, knowledge problems do not have solutions. The best we can do is ascertain which institutions best cope with knowledge problems so that they are not left to the fragile decisions of a single mind or group of minds (cf. Hayek 1948 [1980]). Collectively, economists working on monetary theory and policy have made substantial advancements in our technical modeling and data collection techniques. Yet, despite these refinements and the intellectual firepower at the disposal of central banks, uncertainty and guesswork still characterize decision-making at the Fed (Axilrod 2011; Bernanke 2003; Bernanke et al. 2019, pp. 7–8; Bernanke and Mishkin 1997, p. 106; Goodhart 1989, p. 150; Greenspan 1997; Meltzer 2009, p. 1234; Pollock 2018; Posen 2011; Romer 1989).[3]

This uncertainty does not just emerge during extraordinary times. It is present during ordinary times as well. Writing about monetary policy over a period that includes the Great Moderation, so called due to its uncharacteristic stability, Alan Greenspan (2004, pp. 36–37) contends,

The Federal Reserve's experiences over the past two decades make it clear that uncertainty is not just a pervasive feature of the monetary policy landscape; it is the defining characteristic of that landscape. The term "uncertainty" is meant here to encompass both "Knightian uncertainty," in which the probability distribution of outcomes is unknown, and "risk," in which uncertainty of outcomes is delimited by a known probability distribution. In practice, one is never quite sure what type

---

[2] Some research even questions whether u* is an acceptable guidepost for monetary policy (e.g., Borio et al. 2019).

[3] Central banks tend to be some of the largest employers of PhD economists. For instance, White (2005) notes that the Fed employs over 400 staff economists. This does not include the hundreds of additional economists affiliated with the Fed as consultants, visiting scholars, or conference participants.

of uncertainty one is dealing with in real time, and it may be best to think of a continuum ranging from well-defined risks to the truly unknown.

That uncertainty, of course, is strongly amplified during extraordinary times, such as economic crises. These extraordinary times are precisely the circumstances that central bankers are commissioned in to use their judgment to stabilize markets (Bernanke 2012; Husted et al. 2020; Kuttner and Posen 2004; Pollock 2018; Ramey and Zubairy 2018).[4]

In this chapter, we argue that the inherent uncertainty in central bank decision-making makes rules more desirable than discretion. This fact is not sufficiently appreciated in the literature. Many critiques of rule-based monetary policy in favor of discretionary central banking detail the extreme epistemic difficulties involved in setting an appropriate rule ahead of time based on historical relationships that are unlikely to continue in the future (Bernanke 2015c; Orphanides 2003; Svensson 2002). The alleged advantage of discretion over rules is that discretionary policymakers can use the most recent models and data, and can act in a way that fits the particulars of the situation. But given the demonstrated unreliability and contradictions of real-time data, the argument for discretionary central banking ultimately boils down to trusting and empowering the judgment calls of monetary authorities. Given that the data on which central bankers have to draw is inherently noisy, this is a dubious proposition at best. In the words of Chairman Powell (2019b), "Good decisions require good data, but the data in hand are seldom as good as we would like. Sound decision-making, therefore, requires the application of good judgment and a healthy dose of risk management." But we are justified in questioning the efficacy of "good judgment" and "risk management" when they can rarely be guided by adequate knowledge of the relevant facts.

Trusting the judgment of monetary policymakers has not worked well in practice. While Bernanke et al. (2019, pp. 11–12) describe the 2007–2008 financial crisis as having some similarities to past crises, they state it had "modern twists that made the panic even more difficult to anticipate and contain." The 2007–2008 financial crisis and the lack of consensus for addressing future recessions in its wake (Bernanke 2013; Cochrane 2019a; Sumner 2019; Svensson 2019; Taylor 2009) suggest that discretionary central bankers are, and will continue, operating in an uncertain

---

[4] Uncertainty arises for reasons other than narrowly economic phenomena. For instance, Bernanke (2015a, p. 73) notes that following the US invasion of Iraq, the Fed released a statement essentially admitting that "uncertainty was so high we couldn't usefully characterize the near-term course of the economy or monetary policy."

environment. More fundamentally, the persistence of monetary and macroeconomic volatility under the Fed, even in comparison to the imperfect institutions in place prior to its establishment (e.g., Hogan 2015; Pollock 2018; Selgin et al. 2012), suggests that we have not reached the "end of history" in central banking.

We contend that discretionary central banking, as judged by its own objectives, falls prey not just to technical problems but also to true knowledge problems. Even hundreds of PhD economists do not have the collective knowledge required to steward the macroeconomy. Central banks do not have, and will never have, the knowledge of the public's demand for money required to manage the money supply. This means the central bank cannot fulfill its most basic task, as a supplier and controller of the monetary base. This failure undermines the functioning of the price system, which plays a crucial epistemic and motivational role in a market economy (Hayek 1945).[5]

Simply put, discretionary central banking is not only difficult; it is impossible. The impossibility stems from the knowledge problem inherent in centralized monetary policy (Selgin 1988). Macroeconomic stewardship via central bank discretion fails in the same way that classical liberal scholars have demonstrated that hierarchical planning of an economy fails because such planning inadvertently destroys crucial information mechanisms (Hayek 1948 [1980]; Lavoie 1985; Mises 1936 [1981]; see also Kiesling 2015).

Here, we detail the specific technical and knowledge problems that plague discretionary central banking. We first discuss the technical difficulties that central bankers face before moving on to our discussion of the knowledge problems proper. The technical problems can possibly be ameliorated with (much) further advancement in data collection and model refinement. Although these are not true knowledge problems, and hence are solvable *in principle*, they merit discussion due to the inherent difficulty of the task. True monetary knowledge problems, however, are impossible to overcome within a central banking regime that maintains centralized control over the monetary base, so long as central banks are run by discretionary monetary policymakers.[6]

---

[5] See also O'Driscoll (1977), Caldwell (2005), and Kiesling (2015) for an elaboration of the coordination problem that the price system solves in a complex modern economy.

[6] Importantly, if a central bank also has regulatory roles, as the Fed does, this introduces additional technical difficulties and knowledge problems, especially in forecasting their interaction affects, beyond those considered here.

2.2 The Technical Problems of Monetary Policy

The technical problems with monetary policy can be split into four categories: problems with (1) objectives, (2) targets, (3) instruments, and (4) model calibration. In this section, we detail and provide examples of each of these kinds of problems.

2.2.1 Problems with Objectives

The first technical difficulty in discretionary central banking is in determining the concrete objectives of monetary policy. That we identify this as a technical difficulty may be puzzling since there is broad agreement among monetary economists and central bankers that the objective of monetary policy is the maximization of short-term employment subject to the constraint of maintaining long-run price stability (Bean et al. 2010, p. 269; Greenspan 1993; Powell 2019a, 2019b; Yellen 2017). Since 2012, the Fed has set its objectives as an inflation target of 2 percent and maximum employment (Federal Reserve 2012a).[7,8]

The consensus on the objectives of inflation and unemployment is central to the very design of modern central banking institutions and is an underlying assumption in orthodox monetary models. Yet the short- and medium-term objectives of monetary policy are open to interpretation, especially given the trade-off between short- and medium-term employment and long-term price stability (Goodhart 1989, ch. 12; Rangarajan 1997–1998, 2001).[9]

How do central bankers navigate the trade-offs associated with pursuing these goals? A famous monetary rule modeling this trade-off, the Taylor Rule, defaults to an equal priority on each goal (Taylor 1993). While Taylor

---

[7] In an updated statement, the Fed (2016) reaffirms its 2012 statement, with this same target, defined in terms of the personal consumption expenditure price index, but clarifies that it is a long-term goal, jointly with maximum employment.

[8] These are the current prevailing objectives, but the Fed operating framework has changed repeatedly through the Fed's history and is certainly subject to change going forward (Fuhrer et al. 2018). The objective to "promote effectively the goals of maximum employment, stable prices, and moderate long-term interest rates" has officially been the stance of the Fed since 1977 (Steelman 2011, p. 1).

[9] This is admittedly a short-run trade-off. In the long run, the economy's potential, in terms of output and unemployment, is independent of the stance of monetary policy. Even in the short to medium run, if the central bank provides a nominal anchor, the economy can adjust its plans to this anchor and reach its potential. This, of course, requires the central bank's stated policy to be credible – which, we note in passing, would certainly be promoted by a true monetary rule!

(1999, p. 14) argues that the rule was simply a guideline to be used in tandem with other policy rules, former Chairman Bernanke (2015b) and Chairwoman Yellen (2012a) have both explicitly confirmed that the Fed prioritizes these objectives equally.

Yet, there appears to be disagreement over whether these objectives should always be pursued equally, even among the same central bankers. Bernanke (2015c), for instance, writes separately that the relative priorities depend on whether "policymakers are willing to accept greater variability in inflation in exchange for greater stability in output" and that "there is no agreement on what the Taylor rule weights on inflation and the output gap should be, except with respect to their signs." Yellen (2012b, p. 15) separately says, "I think it is essential that policy rules incorporate a sufficiently strong response to resource slack, typically either the output gap or the unemployment gap, to help bring the economy back toward full employment expeditiously." In this statement, "sufficiently strong" suggests that the weights can change based on the circumstances.

In practice, the Fed has deviated from equally prioritizing these objectives.[10] For instance, Narayana Kocherlakota, the President of the Federal Reserve Bank of Minneapolis, in the March 2014 conference call of the Federal Open Market Committee (FOMC) said, "Markets are likely to turn back to those pre-crisis historical relationships, like the Taylor (1993) rule or the Taylor (1999) rule, to provide their guide to future FOMC behavior. The problem is that, as the Summary of Economic Projections indicates, monetary policy is likely to be more accommodative than either of these rules for years to come" (Federal Reserve 2014b, pp. 7–8). A 2012 Fed memo shows that the Fed was actively exploring the potential use of alternative rules (Del Negro et al. 2012a).

---

[10] Decision-making at the Fed has also been characterized by changes in the weights (Danis 2017; Dolado et al. 2005; Judd and Rudebusch 1998; Khoury 1990; Lakdawala 2016; McNees 1992). For instance, a Fed (2018b, p. 6) memo states,

> In response to this asymmetric risk, the Committee might choose to follow some simple rule once the economic recovery was firmly entrenched, but nonetheless remain more accommodative than suggested by the rule for some time while the recovery gains strength, thereby reducing the risk of a return to poor economic performance and the effective lower bound soon after the initial firming. Specifically, it is desirable to follow a more accommodative policy stance than implied by a simple "Taylor-style" linear rule if economic conditions suggest considerable risk that the economy may become constrained by the effective lower bound the medium term.

Central bankers may, in fact, prefer to keep their exact prioritization unspecified to provide more flexibility in setting policy as circumstances develop. As Federal Reserve Bank of Philadelphia President Charles Plosser said during the October 29–30, 2013, meeting, there is a "fundamental tension between having a clearly articulated reaction function and the Committee's desire for discretion – that is, the desire to keep open the possibility of doing whatever seems right at any particular moment in time" (Federal Reserve 2013b, p. 90). Federal Reserve Bank of Atlanta President Dennis Lockhart said in the January 28–29, 2014 FOMC meeting that "I would prefer to keep our explanation of the Committee's reaction ... more qualitative than quantitative, if that can be done" (Federal Reserve 2014a, p. 118).

Leaving the priority on these objectives unspecified necessarily creates room for strong disagreements over the proper course of monetary policy. As Federal Reserve Bank of Richmond President Jeffery Lacker noted in the October 23–24, 2012 FOMC meeting, "Disagreement is clearly less about the economic forecast than it is about the reaction function" (Federal Reserve 2012b, p. 14). That is a strong admission given the inherent uncertainty in forecasting (more on this later).

But the priority of these objectives is not the only technical objective problem in conducting monetary policy. Given the wide-ranging effects of monetary policy, it is difficult for central bankers to stay narrowly focused on just these objectives. The Fed has introduced several "unofficial" objectives, further complicating the setting and maintenance of a consensus objective. As former Fed governor Sherman Maisel (1973, p. 303) writes, "The fact that monetary policy has indirect impacts on jobs, output, and prices through its effects on the level of spending means that all of these semicompetitive goals, and not any single one, must be taken into account."

Some of the unofficial objectives adopted at the Fed include federal fund rate smoothing (Clarida et al. 1998; Goodfriend 1998; Jackson et al. 2018), financial stability (Bernanke 2011; Caballero and Simsek 2019; Haltom and Lacker 2013; Kashyap and Siegert 2019; Puzzanghera and Lee 2015), exchange rate stabilization (Dorn and Niskanen 1989; Rangarajan 2001), and expanding the availability and affordability of housing (Fieldhouse and Mertens 2017, pp. 131–136). On adding objectives to pursue, President Plosser of the Federal Reserve Bank of St. Louis said,

There's a lot of discussion about getting to 6½ percent [unemployment], and not being happy about the participation rate or the employment-to-population ratio or U-6 or temporary workers or something. I think we're just moving the goalposts on ourselves. We can't keep adding real gaps to our reaction function ad infinitum. If we were worried about the participation rate or the employment-to-population ratio, we don't have very good models of either one of those. And for us to try to set policy based on some gap between a model – we have a hard enough time defining output gaps and unemployment gaps without defining participation rate gaps and employment-to-population rate gaps – is just a dead-end strategy leading to both confusion and lack of clarity. (Federal Reserve 2013a, p. 135)

During the March 4, 2014 FOMC conference call, there was a discussion about possibly changing the reaction function variable of unemployment to employment; switching to an alternative variable, such as output growth; or simply just putting more emphasis on the inflation variable (moving toward stricter inflation-targeting) (Federal Reserve 2014b). In that same call, the FOMC clearly struggled with the role that financial stability should have as a separate argument in their reaction function. Senior Vice President of the Federal Reserve Bank of Kansas City, John A. Weinberg (Federal Reserve 2014b, p. 31), for instance, said,

Finally, we're against including a reference to financial-stability concerns or financial market developments. Aside from a concern for financial stability, it's not clear on what basis one would want to single out for special consideration the implication of financial market developments for our goals, compared with the full array of factors taken into consideration. Further, the notion of highlighting concerns about financial stability in a monetary policy context creates some difficulties. Would people conclude that the Committee would compromise on employment and inflation objectives for the sake of financial stability? Or would they conclude that large asset price increases would induce tighter monetary policy, or that large asset price declines would induce easier policy? Might they conclude that the Committee would ease policy in response to distress at one or more large financial institutions? Without a shared understanding of how financial market developments ought to enter into the monetary policy reaction function, communicating to the public about the role of financial-stability considerations could create more problems than it solves. (Federal Reserve 2014b, p. 31)

Each unofficial objective that enters into the analysis of discretionary central bankers surely has trade-offs against long-run price stability or other unofficial and official objectives (El Herradi and Leroy 2019; Ferguson 2003; Issing 2003; Jordà et al. 2015; Saiki and Frost 2014; Shukayev and Ueberfeldt 2018; Smets 2013).

2.2.2 Problems with Targets

After objectives are defined, the next technical problem discretionary central bankers face is the selection of the appropriate targets to achieve those objectives. Even with a given set of objectives, the range of potential target variables gives monetary authorities wide discretion in practice (Axilrod 1970, pp. 5, 15). Potential intermediate targets for long-run price stability include the federal funds rate and the term structure of interest rates; more direct targets would be inflation or nominal gross domestic product (NGDP).[11] Recounting a 1983 FOMC discussion on which monetary metric to use as their target, Meltzer (2009, p. 1145) writes, "The consensus was not complete, and agreement was surrounded by ambiguity, reflecting the uncertainty the members felt." Paul Volcker and Christine Harper (2018, p. 105) recount the FOMC transitioning from trying to control interest rates to trying to control the money supply. Even if there is a very well-specified objective, such as 2 percent inflation, there is leeway for central banks to determine what specific measure of inflation to target as well as the acceptable range for hitting that target. For instance, during the July 30–31, 2019 FOMC meeting, the minutes state the following:

> A few participants suggested that an alternative means of delivering average inflation equal to the Committee's longer-run objective might involve aiming for inflation somewhat in excess of 2 percent when the policy rate was away from the ELB [effective lower bound], recognizing that inflation would tend to move lower when the policy rate was constrained by the ELB. Another possibility might be for the Committee to express the inflation goal as a range centered on 2 percent and aim to achieve inflation outcomes in the upper end of the range in periods when resource utilization was high. (Federal Reserve 2019a, p. 4)

And, even when a target range is specified, there is leeway for discretionary central bankers to run outside of that range. For example, the minutes of the October 29–30, 2019, FOMC meeting summarize it as follows:

> Some participants indicated that, in such an environment, they would have some tolerance for allowing the federal funds rate to vary from day to day and to move occasionally outside its target range, especially in those instances associated with easily identifiable technical events; a couple of participants expressed discomfort with such misses. (Federal Reserve 2019b, p. 6)

The Fed's primary target has in recent history been the Effective Federal Funds Rate (EFFR). The EFFR is the rate that emerges in the overnight lending market between banks. Banks are required by the Fed to have a certain percentage of their liabilities as reserves at the end of the business

---

[11] The federal funds rate is frequently referred to as an instrument in the monetary policy literature. Technically, this is incorrect; to qualify as an instrument, it must be something that the Fed directly controls, such as the monetary base.

day. Banks with excess reserves lend at the emergent EFFR to banks with a shortage of reserves.

But the EFFR can always be replaced by a different target. In the November 7–8, 2018 FOMC meeting, the minutes state the following:

Participants cited several potential benefits of targeting the OBFR [overnight bank funding rate] rather than the EFFR: The larger volume of transactions and greater variety of lenders underlying the OBFR could make that rate a broader and more robust indicator of banks' overnight funding costs, the OBFR could become an even better indicator after the potential incorporation of data on onshore wholesale deposits, and the similarity of the OBFR and the EFFR suggested that transitioning to the OBFR would not require significant changes in the way the Committee conducted and communicated monetary policy. Some participants saw it as desirable to explore the possibility of targeting a secured interest rate. Some also expressed interest in studying, over the longer term, approaches in which the Committee would target a mixture of secured and unsecured rates. (Federal Reserve 2018a, p. 4)

This is related to the transition of the Fed from a corridor operating system to a floor system with the 2008 implementation of interest on excess reserves (IOER), which dried up the market that generated the EFFR (Selgin 2018). Essentially, the Fed switched from EFFR to IOER as its main target. Importantly, the FOMC, which determines the target EFFR, delegates the IOER rate to the Federal Reserve Board of Governors (a subgroup of the FOMC). The introduction of overnight reverse repurchase agreements introduced yet another target for the Fed (Selgin 2018; Williamson 2016), the implicit interest rate from the terms of the repo contract.

2.2.3 Problems with Instruments

Once objectives and targets are agreed upon, the monetary authority then faces the technical problem of selecting and properly using the instruments at its disposal. The first step of this process is selecting the appropriate policy tool or mix of policy tools. Given the wide variety of tools, ends, and durations, the selection problem is extremely complicated (Butos 1986; Federal Reserve 2009; Johnson 1988, p. 253; Lombra and Moran 1980; Meltzer 2009, p. 1134). As Jordan (2017, p. 362) writes, inflation and unemployment "may be appropriate intermediate or longer-term object-ives for policymakers consider, but translating them into a policy that can be implemented requires some identifiable linkages between what can be controlled – the size and composition of the central bank balance sheet, and administered interest rates charged to borrowing banks or paid on reserve balances – and financial indicators of the stance of policy."

The traditional tools at the disposal of monetary authorities to tighten or loosen monetary policy are buying and selling treasury securities (open market operations), the required reserve ratio, and the penalty rate for banks requesting a loan from the Fed (the discount rate). When faced with a crisis, however, central banks have shown a willingness to explore unconventional policies even before those policies are well understood (Bernanke et al. 2004; Hamada 2004). For instance, as is well known concerning the 2007–2008 financial crisis, "the Fed and other central banks were forced to resort to unconventional and at that time untested monetary policy tools" (Kashyap and Siegert 2019, p. 232; see also Bernanke et al. 2019, p. 2 and Del Negro et al. 2012b). Monetary scholars are still exploring the implications and nuances of the Fed's policies, such as interest on excess reserves, direct lending to nonbank financial institutions, large-scale asset purchases (quantitative easing), and maturity extensions. Several postcrisis debates, such as whether the Fed should return to a corridor operating system or continue to remain on the floor system, reflect the inherent difficulty of not only specifying the appropriate policy tools but the operating system itself (Cochrane 2019a; Selgin 2018, 2020).

Once an instrument is selected, monetary authorities must decide upon the appropriate magnitude and timing for using that instrument. Discussing the difficulties of policy interventions during the 2007–2008 financial crisis, Bernanke et al. (2019, p. 8) write:

As hard as it is to predict crises in advance, it's also hard to know early in a crisis whether it's just a brush fire or the start of a five-alarm conflagration . . . . Responding too quickly can encourage risk-takers to believe they'll never face consequences for their bad bets, creating "moral hazard" than can promote even more irresponsible speculation and set the state for future crises. But once it's clear that a crisis is truly systemic, underreacting is much more dangerous than overreacting, too late creates more problems than too early, and half measures can just pour gasoline on the flames.

These technical problems include the task of deciding, concomitantly with other policymakers and other appointed officials, where to interject the policy tool. For instance, monetary policy can work by injecting bank reserves to lower interest rates, or (much more worryingly) it can be used to finance deficit spending, enabling policymakers to potentially direct it toward specific industries or groups (Horwitz 2000, p. 117).[12] Measures such as this often skirt the line between fiscal and monetary policy.

---

[12] The Bank of Japan, which has extensive experience with discretionary policy in low interest rate environments, attempted monetary injections via the purchase of exchange-

2.2.4 Problems with Calibrating Models

Forecasting models are necessary to gauge the appropriateness and extent of proposed monetary interventions, as well as to assess their effectiveness. Calibrating these models represents the final technical problem that discretionary central bankers face.

The possible barometers for measuring the state of the economy range from the conventional, such as interest rates, the labor market, and the housing market, to the unconventional, such as dry cleaning and men's underwear sales (Pashman 2007) or the price of gold (Lastrapes and Selgin 1996). Once an economic indicator (or a weighted group of economic indicators) can be identified from the endless list of potential barometers, monetary authorities then face the technical problem of identifying the specific measurement of that indicator that would be most appropriate.

These technical problems emerge, in part, because it is often difficult to define these indicators, let alone agree on an indicator. The very definition of money, for instance, is open to interpretation. As Kay and King (2020, p. 96) write, "But central banks report many different quantitative measures of 'the money supply' and the expression M in a mathematical model is as imprecise as the confused references to 'money supply' in much popular writing. And what is meant by 'money' is temporally and geographically specific."

Once an indicator can be agreed upon, then discretionary central bankers must wrestle with the problems associated with measuring that indicator. GDP, a primary indicator of the economy, for instance, has well-known measurement problems (Coyle 2015).[13] The New York Fed and the Federal Reserve Bank of Atlanta even publish methodologically distinct indices of US GDP growth (Burne et al. 2016). Another primary indicator of the economy, inflation, also has well-known measurement and

---

traded funds and real estate investment funds (Hamada 2004). Informed in part by Japan's experience, monetary economists have considered so-called helicopter drops, which inject money directly into households, to their repertoire to fight the next recession (Ball 2008; Bernanke 2003; Caballero and Farhi 2018). When considering the level, timing, and injection point, monetary authorities must anticipate possible interaction and amplification affects, including with any recent or expected regulatory or fiscal policy measures. It goes without saying that the judgment burdens this places on discretionary central bankers are extraordinary.

[13] Kay and King (2020, p. 95, footnote omitted) write, "GDP is a very different kind of measure form, say, temperature or velocity, which are empirical facts which can be observed with the aid of suitable instruments, and in respect of which any competent observer will come up with the same answer. There is no such thing as aggregate output."

weighting biases and noise problems (Cecchetti 1997; Kay and King 2020, p. 95; Shapiro and Wilcox 1996; Stock and Watson 2019). In yet another example, ascertaining labor productivity and employment data is fraught with measurement issues (Houseman 2018).

Given the amount of noise in any single variable, such as unemployment, focus on just one barometer is often deemed inappropriate (Davig and Mustre-del-Rio 2013; Summers 1981). For instance, measurements of the labor market can include unemployment, the labor force participation rate, job openings, and hiring rates.

Importantly, as the vignette at the beginning of the chapter demonstrates, substantial technical difficulties emerge in interpreting these variables in comparison to other measures of that same barometer and, in particular, to their baseline "natural rates" (Blanchard and Katz 1997; Beyer and Wieland 2019; Orphanides 2003; Tasci and Verbrugge 2014; Taylor and Wieland 2016; Weidner and Williams 2011).[14] As Ashley et al. (2018, p. 4) explain that,

estimates of u_t^* are inherently problematic in that they are estimated very imprecisely, are subject to large revisions, and typically hinge on untested (and perhaps untestable) auxiliary assumptions about the natural-rate data-generating process (such as an explicit formulation of its persistence). Any or all of these may well be substantially incorrect. As might be expected, then, the u_t^* estimates vary widely across concepts and methods.

The technical problems become more severe as central bankers move on to the task of modeling and forecasting the state of the economy using these barometers, necessarily based on contingent historical relationships, while also accounting for measurement lags in the data. The real-time data available to central bankers operating in the short term is often unreliable (Cassou et al. 2018; Croushore 2011; Goodhart 1989, pp. 150–151).

Central bankers, of course, must go a step further and forecast these barometers due to the "long and variable" lags required to implement any given course of monetary policy (Friedman 1961). Experience and advancements in modeling have not solved the complex problem posed by forecasting errors (Meltzer 2009, pp. 1197, 1235). As the "Forecast Uncertainty" portion of the FOMC's meeting minutes state that, "Considerable uncertainty attends these projections, however. The economic and statistical models and relationships used to help produce

---

[14] For a recent attempt to draw the conflicting methodological approaches to estimating the natural rate of unemployment into consensus, see Crump et al. (2019).

economic forecasts are necessarily imperfect descriptions of the real world, and the future path of the economy can be affected by myriad unforeseen developments and events." Forecasting models, due to the necessities of tractability, can leave important segments of the economy outside the purview of these models. These segments can sometimes be brought into the model, but this is often only done after a problem has already emerged. For instance, Kay and King (2020, p. 348), reflecting on the financial crisis, write,

It will come as a surprise to many that forecasting models used by most central banks had no ability to explain borrowing or lending as the models had no place for banks, ignored most financial assets, and assumed that all people were identical. In short, these models assumed an economy shorn of a financial system, and an economic crisis originating in the financial system was therefore impossible.

In addition to accurately forecasting economic variables, monetary authorities must also account for the impact of recent and expected changes in regulatory or fiscal policy in their forecasts. For instance, even looking back historically, economists come up with a wide range of estimates for how government spending, the fiscal multiplier, will affect the economy (Carroll 2014; Ramey 2011). Unemployment programs can also affect the natural rate of employment (Daly et al. 2011). During a recession the economy is often hit with a confluence of fiscal, regulatory, and monetary initiatives often influenced by the particulars of the recession and political environment, making this a particularly difficult, and probably even impossible, task for monetary authorities.

Even more difficult is predicting how the prevailing psychology and expectations of market participants affect a given course of monetary policy (Axilrod 2011, p. 205; Greenspan 1997; Holland 1985; Keynes 1936; Maisel 1973, pp. 262–263; Tobias 1982; Volcker and Harper 2018, p. 36). This is especially true in the presence of uncertainty over the underlying policy regime, which can occur when governments consider or impose drastic changes in their efforts to combat a crisis (Higgs 1997).[15] In discussing their difficulty in deciding the appropriate level of intervention during the financial crisis, Bernanke et al. (2019, p. 60), write, "our show of force did not have the effect we intended. Markets didn't breathe a sigh of relief, they concluded that if the government was worried enough to take such extraordinary measures, the situation must be even worse than it

---

[15] This is further complicated by regime uncertainty: policy-induced confusion as to how new rules will be interpreted and enforced.

looked. Uncertainty drives fear, and nobody felt certain . . .. We weren't certain either."

Recognizing the difficulty of incorporating psychology into theoretical models, Janet Yellen, the then-President of Federal Reserve Bank of San Francisco, said during a January 15, 2009, FOMC conference call, "I think that the inflationary psychology that exists right now is especially delicate and doesn't correspond well to our theoretical models" (Federal Reserve 2009, p. 21). To be fair, this point is well captured in the strategic scenario between central bankers and market actors from the rules versus discretion literature (e.g., Taylor 2017; Van Lear 2000). Although these insights are several decades old, however, they have only been halfheartedly engaged by advocates of monetary policy discretion.

Perhaps the greatest difficulty with forecasting the economy and crafting a monetary response stems from the "Lucas critique" (Lucas 1976) and "Goodhart's law" (Goodhart 1975). The takeaway from these works is that basing government policy on historical data necessarily means using relationships involving *past* expectations and beliefs to make *current* policy. Since these expectations and beliefs can and do change, sometimes drastically, out-of-sample generalizations of policy effects are unreliable. This becomes even more difficult when the policy in question causes changes in expectations. The Fed monitors the market as part of formulating its course of action but at the same time the market monitors the Fed to ascertain how it should respond. This potentially creates a "circularity problem" where market data may fail to register risks or concerns because they expect the Fed to respond (Bernanke and Woodford 1997). Attempts to anchor expectations, for example, by announcing the future path of a policy (e.g., Woodford 2003) attempt to circumvent this problem but have not yielded lasting success in terms of stability.

One final point before we move on to true knowledge problems: While the difficulties associated with selecting the appropriate policy tools, levers, and injection points are hard enough during normal economic times, they become positively nightmarish for discretionary central bankers during abnormal times. We have in mind financial crises, both developing and full-blown. In such scenarios, the existing monetary policy playbook is of little to no help. As Jean-Claude Trichet (2010), then-president of the European Central Bank during the financial crisis, writes, "As a policymaker during the crisis, I found the available models of limited help. In fact, I would go further: in the face of the crisis, we felt abandoned by the conventional tools." We have (and will continue to make) references to crisis management where it impinges on the technical problems and knowledge problems associated with monetary policy but postpone an extended and focused discussion of financial crises until Chapter 4.

2.3 Monetary Knowledge Problems

While technical problems may be lessened with better models and data, true monetary knowledge problems represent an insurmountable burden for discretionary central banking. To achieve and maintain monetary equilibrium, central bankers must be able to continuously, and presciently, discern and meet the public's demand for money. Yet, without the aid of a feedback mechanism that provides monetary policymakers with the relevant knowledge, they are systematically unlikely to achieve or maintain monetary equilibrium. Thus, discretionary central banking inescapably generates monetary disequilibrium. Given that money serves as one-half of all exchanges, playing a crucial role in economic coordination, accounting, and planning, monetary disruption can severely affect the overall efficiency of the market (Hayek 2008; Horwitz 2000; Yeager 1986, 1988). The monetary knowledge problem is the same kind of problem Mises (1936 [1981]) and Hayek (1948 [1980]) identified for centrally planned economies (see also Boettke 2000, 2001; Kiesling 2015; Kirzner 2018; and Lavoie 1985).

Central planning fails because it abolishes the mechanism by which consumers and producers coordinate their activities. Without private property, market prices, and profit-and-loss calculations, the informational feedback loop that facilitates economy-wide coordination is destroyed. Setting aside incentive problems, the impossibility of central planning is ultimately due to knowledge problems that arise from a lack of any sort of a feedback mechanism that can do the same work as the market price system.

Likewise, monetary policymakers lack a feedback mechanism that generates the requisite knowledge to maintain, or even tend toward, monetary equilibrium. There is nothing to provide them contextual knowledge for the stance of policy ex ante, nor anything for them to check their policies against ex post. Without something to shoulder this knowledge burden, the only recourse monetary policymakers have is to various statistical aggregates (Rothbard 1960). But while these statistics can be used to devise policy, there is no reason to believe they can steer monetary policymakers toward monetary equilibrium. Discretionary central banking is thus the same *type* of problem as central planning, although on a smaller scale.

Predicting these shifts in demand are complicated by the fact that supply shocks and changes in productivity create an "information extraction problem" that makes it difficult to discern between changes in monetary velocity and these other factors (Selgin 1997, p. 10). We first address the knowledge problems embedded in adjusting monetary policy to changes in the velocity of money and then, separately, discuss supply shocks and changes in productivity.

2.3.1 Changes in the Velocity of Money

Changes in monetary velocity, the rate at which money "turns over" in the course of economic activity, are driven by changes in the demand for money. The demand for money, in turn, is affected by numerous factors, including the demand for consumer goods, demographics, economic uncertainty, income, inequality, inflation, interest rates, international trade, investment, political uncertainty, regulation, seasonal changes, unemployment, and taxation. These variables can be further split into subfactors based on short- and long-term or current and expected components.

Each of these identified factors has associated technical problems of measuring, interpreting, and modeling them (Laidler 1993, ch. 8). As Goodhart (1989, p. 84) writes, "some of the variables influencing the demand for money balances can only be measured with difficulty, if at all." Cooley and LeRoy (1981) write of their attempt to use macroaggregates to determine a long-run money demand function, "we are unpersuaded by existing attempts to estimate a money demand equation, but we are unable to supply an attractive alternative." More recently, Knell and Stix (2006) find a wide degree of variance in their analysis of nearly 1,000 estimates of money demand. Wang (2011, p. 62) writes that "the evidence in favor of an existing stable long-run money demand is, at most, weak."[16]

Certainly, there have been modern attempts to estimate a reliable money demand function (Anderson et al. 2017; Ball 2012; Benati et al. 2016). Nevertheless, even if advances in the literature allow us to identify a reasonably predictive long-run money demand function, the case for

---

[16] We believe that evidence is lacking for a stable money demand function because such stability *requires a clear commitment to rules* by the monetary authority. If there is no firm rule behind the money creation process, there will be no stable demand to hold money. This important point is at the heart of Buchanan and Brennan's (1980) argument for a monetary constitution. We discuss "constitutional" money at greater length in Chapters 5 and 6.

discretionary central banking is premised on the ability of monetary authorities to exercise that discretion not in the long-run but during abnormal times of short- and medium-run volatility. It is precisely during episodes of short- and medium-run volatility that long-run estimates of money demand break down (Heller 1965, p. 292; Horwitz 1990; Maisel 1973, p. 261). While attempting to advance our understanding of money demand, Brunner and Meltzer (1963, p. 319) concede that

there is no accepted theoretical explanation of the short-run behavior of velocity, which is to say that there is no theory of the demand function for money that is sufficiently in accord with the observed short-run behavior of velocity to be useful for prediction and that explains relatively constant long-run velocity.

There are two primary reasons that estimating a short- or medium-run money demand function is not just technically difficult, but impossible. First, the demand for money can manifest itself in various, and often unpredictable, forms (Maisel 1973, p. 57). The variety of forms money can take makes it difficult for economists to even form a consensus as to which assets count as money (Goodhart 1989, pp. 25, 155; Laidler 1993, pp. 93–98; Lombra and Moran 1980; Mason 1976). The demand for money can manifest itself in demand for cash balances, checking accounts, money market funds, certificates of deposits, bonds, stocks, durable consumer goods, and in new financial products (Alvarez and Lippi 2009; Butos 1986, pp. 93–98; Laidler 1993). While we may be able to trace what forms of wealth economic actors prefer ex post (Dutkowsky and Cynamon 2003; Teles and Zhou 2005), we cannot forecast what new financial products will be introduced and, once introduced, which ones will succeed. As Paul Volcker and Christine Harper (2018, p. 32) write that "in the short run, institutional changes made it difficult to precisely define what we meant by 'money'."[17]

The innovation of new financial products makes it impossible to predict and accurately gauge changes in the demand for money, especially during an economic recession or crisis when economic actors are prone to changing their behavior. For instance, in the 1990s, existing estimates of the relationship between money demand and interest rates became inoperative due to the introduction of sweep technology (Berentsen et al. 2015). Greenspan (1997) notes, regarding this period, that "As an indicator, M2 served us well for a number of years. But by the early 1990s, its usefulness was undercut by the increased attractiveness and availability of alternative

---

[17] See also Goodhart (1989, p. 25).

outlets for saving, such as bond and stock mutual funds, and by mounting financial difficulties for depositories and depositors that led to a restructuring of business and household balance sheets." Even over a decade after they were introduced, economists still cannot agree on whether digital currencies, such as Bitcoin, represent money or how, if they will (or should), affect monetary policy (Dyhrberg et al. 2018; Fernández-Villaverde and Sanches 2019; Pagano and Sedunov 2018; Yermack 2015).

Given the accelerated pace of financial innovation (Finnerty and Emery 2002; Frame and White 2004), we can expect financial innovation to remain a constant, insurmountable barrier to predicting the public's demand for money. For instance, Mishkin's (2013, p. 493) popular undergraduate textbook, *The Economics of Money, Banking, and Financial Markets* (10th edition), states that

the rapid pace of financial innovation, which changed the items that could be used for money, led to substantial instability in estimated money demand functions. The instability of the money demand function calls into question whether our theories and empirical analyses are adequate.

The second reason that estimating short- or medium-run demand for money is impossible is because of the unpredictable nature of financial regulation, which often follows financial innovation and crises. As Goodhart (1989, p. 25) writes,

the form of econometric relationships between certain monetary assets and economic developments may depend on the institutional and structural arrangements in the country, and also on the policy regime adopted by the authorities. If these change, previous apparently stable relationships may crumble.

For instance, in January 1976, the Fed found that money growth fell 6.25 percent below forecasts and attributed it to a shift in the demand for money (Meltzer 2009, p. 983). In hindsight, however, it appeared that the causal factors were a change in the regulatory rules that made "savings accounts closer substitutes for demand deposits ..." and financial innovation in payment systems spurred by higher interest rates (Meltzer 2009, p. 984). In 1980, President Carter's anti-inflation program, which included both budget cuts and controls on credit as well as a campaign to convince consumers to pay off their credit cards and cut them up, led to an unanticipated "sharp drop in bank deposits and the money supply" (Volcker and Harper 2018, p. 111). More recently, the financial crisis of 2007–2008 provides another example of this problem in practice. Anderson et al. (2017, fn. 3) write, "After the Great Recession, new bank regulations (e.g., new liquidity and higher capital requirements, plus bank 'stress tests'), low opportunity costs, and unattractive loan applicants likely discouraged lending and related deposit expansion."

Haphazard financial regulation is most likely to emerge in a financial crisis, often with an overemphasis on combating the perceived causes of the crisis, which are impossible to predict before the crisis takes place (Hoshi 2011; Levine 2012). While it is possible, of course, that the introduction of financial regulation, especially during crises, could be halted, it is not politically feasible.

The need to adjust the money supply in accordance to changes in money demand represents a substantial, and insurmountable, knowledge problem for monetary authorities. The demand for money, especially in the short- and medium-run is not stable. The foresight required to adjust the money supply correspondingly, especially in a predictive fashion, given the presence of long and variable lags (Friedman 1961), and the unpredictable nature of both financial innovation and regulation, is unobtainable. The real-time fluctuations in the demand for money, which would be necessary to execute discretionary central banking without generating monetary disturbances, are both unpredictable and unobservable.

Long-run patterns of money demand are insufficient for the task of discretionary central banking if it hopes to prevent short- and medium-term fluctuations. The research finding historical series of stable money demand is based on macroeconomic aggregates with no direct causal effects on each other. Yet, changes in the demand for money reflect continuous, individual-level decisions, frequently driven by uncertainty about the future. Thus, macroaggregates, the best tool available to monetary authorities, are unreliable (Lucas 1976; Goodhart 1989, chs. 2–3). As Paul Volcker and Christine Harper (2018, p. 113) write, "the Federal Reserve's seeming inability to assure, week by week, confidence-building control of the money supply, something that we learned is technically impossible to do."

The inability of monetary authorities to gauge and predict money demand means that discretionary central banking will generate monetary disequilibrium whenever there are discrepancies between the amount of money demanded, no matter the form that the demand for money takes, and the amount of money supplied at the going price level (Horwitz 2000; Yeager 1986). This is because monetary equilibrium requires that the supply of money be adjusted in accordance with changes in the demand for money. Without a grasp of what drives short- and medium-run changes in money demand, central bankers can deliver monetary equilibrium only by chance. Given that money is one-half of all exchanges, the resultant monetary disequilibrium will disrupt the economy. An oversupply (undersupply) of currency, relative to the money demand, results in economic actors transitioning away (toward) from cash toward (away) nonmonetary assets. This will necessarily affect relative prices, resulting in changes in output, labor, and capital. Thus, monetary disruption can seriously undermine economic calculation and coordination (Yeager 1988, p. 267). As Greenspan (1997) said, "Inflation impairs economic efficiency in part because people have difficulty separating movements in relative prices from movements in the general price level."

Given these difficulties with measuring the demand for money, some models simply leave it out of the analysis. For instance, a Federal Reserve Bank of New York forecasting model states that "Since money balances enter separably [sic], and we do not use money balances as an observable in estimating the model, the 'demand for money' is irrelevant for the dynamics of the model, and we will subsequently ignore it" (Federal Reserve 2011, p. 26). Though it may improve model tractability, this approaches a de facto renunciation of the very economic problem monetary authorities are supposed to manage. Ultimately, it is further evidence of the inability of central bankers to forecast money demand and engage the correct tools at the appropriate time and to the right degree. This was one of the reasons that economists such as Milton Friedman proposed constant money growth rules (Friedman 1968, p. 17).

Fundamentally, advocates for money growth rules concede that the inherent knowledge problems in discretionary central banking are too complex. However, even a money growth rule will necessarily generate monetary disequilibrium in the short- and medium-term as the public's demand for money fluctuates. Other rules, such as the Taylor Rule, also assume that monetary authorities have real-time access to both real and potential GDP, which is a heroic assumption (Beckworth 2019, p. 21; Beckworth and Hendrickson 2019; Orphanides 2001, 2002a, 2002b, 2002c, 2003). Again, the primary argument for central banking is that monetary authorities can use central banking tools to adjust the economy to avoid short- and medium-run fluctuations in a fashion superior to other institutional alternatives, such as the gold standard (Hogan et al. 2018). This argument fails.

One key assumption driving theoretical central bank reaction functions is the assumption that money demand can be inferred by proxy from its direct and predictable relationship with interest rates (Laidler 1993, p. 19; Mishkin 2013, pp. 492–493). But focusing on interest rates as the relevant link or descriptive statistic offers no way around the knowledge barrier. Similar to long-run money demand functions, descriptive studies help determine casual factors after the fact, but economists cannot reliably use them to predict short- and medium-run fluctuations (Holston et al. 2017; Laubach and Williams 2016). As Mallaby (2016, p. 461) writes, "the mechanism linking the Fed's interest-rate lever to the real economy was a prime example of a phenomenon that could *not* be modeled. It changed character so fast that a statistical study of its past told you little about its future." Factors such as individuals' discount rates, projected consumption patterns, expected income and economic growth, and investment opportunities all contribute to the formation of the natural interest rate.

The connections between market interest rates and money demand become indiscernible during times of economic uncertainty, such as liquidity traps, periods of low interest rates, or in a low interest rate environment (Caballero and Farhi 2018; Laidler 1993, pp. 19–23; Mishkin 2013, pp. 492–493). As Wieland (2018, p. 58) writes, "these estimates [of the natural rate of interest] are highly imprecise and unstable. They do not indicate an empirically significant decline [in the natural interest rate] and may suffer from omitted variable bias. Thus they are not that helpful for monetary policy practice." Ohanian (2018, p. 79), in accepting the drastic knowledge problems associated with central bankers attempting to forecast the natural rate of interest, writes, "Taken together, these data suggest that monetary policy makers should consider placing less emphasis on short-run demand management through monetary policy. As an alternative, monetary policy makers could work on developing policies that promote long-run growth and investment."

2.3.2 Supply Shocks

Supply shocks, such as the unexpected change in the availability of a widely used input, can generate monetary disequilibrium when prices are costly to change (Yeager 1988). In the presence of sticky prices, supply shocks thus pose another challenge to monetary authorities (Hall 1986; Schmitt-Grohe and Uribe 2004). While flexible prices reduce the effect of money supply changes on real income and employment, sticky prices can amplify money supply changes (Laidler 1993, p. 8). To fully understand and predict the extent that a course of monetary policy will have on the economy, therefore, requires a comprehensive understanding of not only the extent of sticky prices or information across the economy but also the factors that influence price flexibility and the costs of disseminating and acquiring information. This is because price adjustment, in response to inflation or deflation, is not an instantaneous or mechanical process, rather the adjustment is sequential and staggered, meaning that nominal changes can have real effects (Horwitz 2000). The literature on sticky prices and sticky information suggests that we have not achieved a rigorous understanding of this process (Beckman and Czudaj 2018; Blinder 1994; Kiley 2016; Mankiw and Reis 2002). Economists have found it difficult even to find data on this, but even if they could, sticky prices are likely to vary drastically across firms, industries, economies, and time (Anderson et al. 2015).

The origin of a supply shock, its magnitude, the state of the economy when it hits, and what markets it affects will all influence the degree of monetary disequilibrium. Furthermore, supply shocks may become more difficult to interpret and forecast in a low interest rate environment (Garín et al. 2016). Whether a supply shock is predicted or not, and by whom, will also influence how a specific supply shock affects the economy. Further complications emerge due to the fact that a supply shock can interact with money demand. In discussing this possible interaction, Laidler (1993, p. 36) notes that "The only general conclusion we can draw from the above discussion is that the interaction is likely to differ from time to time and from place to place."

Consider a specific kind of supply shock: changes in productivity. Productivity shocks generate unpredictable changes to an economy, especially in factor markets. The economic effects of a productivity shock depend on where the productivity shock occurs and the overall state of the economy.[18]

Monetary authorities must take forecasts of productivity into account in setting monetary policy (Muto 2013). When productivity increases in a specific industry, it often reduces the prices of the goods or services in that industry, and thereby the overall price level. An increase in the money supply in response to this decline in the overall price level would distort market prices (Horwitz 2000, p. 77; Selgin 1997).

In the presence of regular changes in productivity, monetary authorities are thus faced with the knowledge problem of distinguishing between real changes in money demand and the effects of those productivity changes on the economy, as well as how those productivity changes will affect the course of monetary policy. In a dynamic, open economy with a wide range of industries experiencing periodic changes in productivity, this is an incredible knowledge problem for discretionary central bankers. At a

---

[18] For example, monetary disequilibrium can result from a positive productivity shock in an industry where demand for the good is greater than unit-elastic and from a negative productivity shock in an industry where demand for the good is less than unit-elastic.

speech at Stanford University, Greenspan (1997) acknowledged the inherent difficulties of this task: "But we have found that very often historical regularities have been disrupted by unanticipated change, especially in technologies." Greenspan goes on to say that "Such changes mean that we can never construct a completely general model of the economy, invariant through time, on which to base our policy." Or, as Svensson (2002, p. 3, in parentheses) writes, "Estimating potential output is a non-trivial matter, though, and a major challenge in practical monetary policy."

2.4 No Escape from the Knowledge Problem

Macroeconomic stewardship requires maintaining monetary equilibrium at the micro-level. So long as central banks operate discretionarily, it will be impossible for them to achieve this in a systematic way. Monetary authorities simply do not have the real-time knowledge to measure and predict changes in the demand for money. Nor can this knowledge ever be approximated, even with hundreds of economists collecting data and refining models. Given the impossibility of measuring and predicting the demand for money, discretionary central banking will generate monetary disequilibrium *as a regular matter of course*, as the money supplied by the central bank periodically falls short or exceeds the money demanded by the public. With no real-time feedback mechanism, central banks cannot adjust to constant changes in money demand. This monetary disequilibrium undermines the accuracy and reliability of the price system, undermining economic coordination among consumers and producers. This is hugely significant. Coordination of consumption and production plans is the ultimate economic justification for market economies. That discretionary central banking necessarily impairs this process is a significant strike against it.

References

Abraham, Katharine and John Haltiwanger (2019). How Tight Is the Labor Market? Working Paper presented at the Conference on Monetary Policy Strategy, Tools, and Communication Practices. Federal Reserve Bank of Chicago, Chicago, IL. June 4. Available online (accessed June 20, 2019), www.federalreserve.gov/confer ences/conference-monetary-policy-strategy-tools-communications-20190605.htm

Alvarez, Fernando and Francesco Lippi (2009). Financial Innovation and the Transactions Demand for Cash. *Econometrica*, 77(2), 363–402.

Anderson, Eric, Nir Jaimovich, and Duncan Simester (2015). Price Stickiness: Empirical Evidence of the Menu Cost Channel. *Review of Economics & Statistics*, 97(4), 813–826.

Anderson, Richard, Michael Bordo, and John Duca (2017). Money and Velocity during Financial Crises: From the Great Depression to the Great Recession. *Journal of Economic Dynamics and Control*, 81 (August), 32–49.

Ashley, Richard, Kwok Ping Tsang, and Randal Verbrugge (2018). All Fluctuations Are Not Created Equal: The Differential Roles of Transitory versus Persistent Changes in Driving Historical Monetary Policy. Federal Reserve Bank of Cleveland Working Paper 18-14. Available online (accessed March 24, 2020), www.clevelandfed.org/en/newsroom-and-events/publications/working-papers/2019-working-papers/wp-1814r-a-new-look-at-historical-monetary-policy-and-the-great-inflation.aspx

Axilrod, Stephen (2011). *Inside the Fed: Monetary Policy and Its Management, Martin through Greenspan to Bernanke*. The MIT Press.

Axilrod, Stephen H. (1970). The FOMC Directive as Structured in the Late 1960s: Theory and Appraisal. Available online (accessed December 8, 2020), https://fraser.stlouisfed.org/title/fomc-directive-structured-late-1960s-1185

Ball, Laurence (2008). Helicopter Drops and Japan's Liquidity Trap. *Monetary and Economic Studies*, 26 (December), 87–106.

——— (2012). Short-Run Money Demand. *Journal of Monetary Economics*, 59(7), 622–633.

Barro, Robert and David Gordon (1983). A Positive Theory of Monetary Policy in a Natural Rate Model. *Journal of Political Economy*, 91(4), 589–610.

Bean, Charles, Matthias Paustian, Adrian Penalver, and Tim Taylor (2010). Monetary Policy after the Fall, Macroeconomic Challenges: The Decade Ahead. Available online (accessed May 28, 2020), www.kansascityfed.org/publicat/sympos/2010/Bean_final.pdf

Beckman, Joscha and Robert Czudaj (2018). Monetary Policy Shocks, Expectations, and Information Rigidities. *Economic Inquiry*, 56(4), 2158–2176.

Beckworth, David (2019). *Facts, Fears, and Functionality of NGDP Level Targeting: A Guide to a Popular Framework for Monetary Policy*. Special Study. Mercatus Center at George Mason University.

Beckworth, David and Joshua Hendrickson (2019). Nominal GDP Targeting and the Taylor Rule on an Even Playing Field. *Journal of Money, Credit and Banking*, 52 (1), 269–286.

Benati, Luca, Robert Lucas, Juan Pablo Nicolini, and Warren Weber (2016). International Evidence on Long Run Money Demand. NBER Working Paper No. 22475.

Berentsen, Aleksander, Samuel Huber, and Alessandro Marchesiani. (2015). Financial Innovations, Money Demand, and the Welfare Costs of Inflation. *Journal of Money, Credit and Banking*, 47(S2), 223–261.

Bernanke, Ben (2003). "Constrained Discretion" and Monetary Policy. Remarks before the Money Marketeers of New York University, New York. February 3. Available online (accessed May 31, 2019), www.federalreserve.gov/boarddocs/speeches/2003/20030203/default.htm#fn4

——— (2011). Implementing a Macroprudential Approach to Supervision and Regulation. Speech at the 47th Annual Conference on Bank Structure and Competition, Chicago, IL. Available online (accessed May 31, 2019), www.federalreserve.gov/newsevents/speech/bernanke20110505a.htm

——— (2012). *The Federal Reserve and the Financial Crisis*. Princeton University Press.

(2015a). *The Courage to Act: A Memoir of a Crisis and Its Aftermath.* W. W. Norton & Company.

(2015b). Remarks at the Brookings Institution on the FORM Act. Video. Brookings Institution. March 2. Available online (accessed March 19, 2020), www.youtube .com/embed/KJmA5JDNpKg?start=42&end=60&version=3

(2015c). The Taylor Rule: A Benchmark for Monetary Policy? Brookings Institute blogpost. April 28. Available online (accessed March 20, 2020), www.brookings .edu/blog/ben-bernanke/2015/04/28/the-taylor-rule-a-benchmark-for-monetary-policy/

Bernanke, Ben, Timothy Geithner, and Henry Paulson (2019). *Firefighting: The Financial Crisis and Its Lessons.* Penguin Books.

Bernanke, Ben and Frederic Mishkin (1997). Inflation Targeting: A New Framework for Monetary Policy? *Journal of Economic Perspectives,* 11(1), 97–116.

Bernanke, Ben, Vincent Reinhart, and Brian Sack (2004). Monetary Policy Alternatives at the Zero Lower Bound: An Empirical Assessment. *Brookings Papers on Economic Activity,* 2, 1–100.

Bernanke, Ben and Michael Woodford (1997). Inflation Forecasts and Monetary Policy. *Journal of Money, Credit and Banking,* 29(4), 653–684.

Bernanke, Ben S. (2013). *The Federal Reserve and the Financial Crisis.* Princeton University Press.

Beyer, Robert and Volker Wieland (2019). Instability, Imprecision and Inconsistent Use of Equilibrium Real Interest Rate Estimates. *Journal of International Money and Finance,* 94 (June), 1–14.

Blanchard, Olivier and Lawrence Katz (1997). What We Know and Do Not Know about the Natural Rate of Unemployment. *Journal of Economic Perspectives,* 11(1), 51–72.

Blinder, Alan (1994). On Sticky Prices: Academic Theories Meet the Real World. In N. Gregory Mankiw (Ed.), *Monetary Policy.* University of Chicago Press, pp. 117–154.

Boettke, Peter J. (2000). *Socialism and the Market: The Socialist Calculation Debate Revisited.* Routledge.

(2001). *Calculation and Coordination: Essays on Socialism and Transitional Political Economy.* Routledge.

Borio, Claudio, Piti Disyatat, and Phurichai Rungcharoenkitkul (2019). What Anchors for the Natural Rate of Interest? BIS Working Papers No. 777. Available online (accessed March 13, 2020),www.bis.org/publ/work777.htm

Brunner, Karl and Allan Meltzer (1963). Predicting Velocity: Implications for Theory and Policy. *The Journal of Finance,* 18(2), 319–354.

Buchanan, James and Geoffrey Brennan (1980). *The Power to Tax: Analytic Foundations of a Fiscal Constitution.* Cambridge University Press.

Burne, Katy, Ben Eisen, and Paul Vigna (2016). Fed Banks Spar Over GDP Data. *The Wall Street Journal,* April 12. Available online (accessed June 6, 2019), www.wsj .com/articles/the-fed-fights-itself-over-gdp-data-1460503606

Butos, William (1986). The Knowledge Problem under Alternative Monetary Regimes. *Cato Journal,* 5(3), 849–876.

C-Span (2019). Clip of Federal Reserve Chair Jerome Powell Testifies on the State of the Economy. July 10. Available online (accessed March 24, 2020), www.c-span.org/ video/?c4806495/user-clip-aoc-asks-phillips-curve-fairy-tale&start=7501

Carroll, Daniel R. (2014). Why Do Economists Still Disagree over Government Spending Multipliers? Federal Reserve Bank of Cleveland Economic Commentary, No. 2014-09. Available online (accessed December 8, 2020), www .clevelandfed.org/newsroom-and-events/publications/economic-commentary/ 2014-economic-commentaries/ec-201409-why-do-economists-still-disagree-over- government-spending-multipliers

Caballero, Ricardo and Emmanuel Farhi (2018). The Safety Trap. *Review of Economic Studies*, 85(1), 223–274.

Caballero, Ricardo and Alp Simsek (2019). Prudential Monetary Policy. NBER Working Paper No. 25977. Available online (accessed June 25, 2019), www.nber .org/papers/w25977#fromrss

Caldwell, Bruce (2005). The Road to Serfdom Symposium: Comments on Papers by Rosser and by Levy, Peart, and Farrant. *European Journal of Political Economy*, 21 (4), 1054–1059.

Cassou, Steve, Patrick Scott, and Jesús Vázquez (2018). Optimal Monetary Policy Revisited: Does Considering US Real-Time Data Change Things? *Applied Economics*, 50(57), 6203–6219.

Cecchetti, Stephen (1997). Measuring Short-Run Inflation for Central Bankers. *Review of the Federal Reserve Bank of Saint Louis*, 79(3), 143–155.

Clarida, Richard, Jordi Gali, and Mark Gertler (1998). Monetary Policy Rules in Practice: Some International Evidence. *European Economic Review*, 42(6), 1033–1067.

Cochrane, John (2019a). Operating Procedures. *The Grumpy Economist*. May 29. Available online (accessed June 6, 2019), https://johnhcochrane.blogspot.com/ 2019/03/operating-procedures.html

    (2019b). Whither the Fed? *The Grumpy Economist*. August 12. Available online (accessed May 28, 2020), https://johnhcochrane.blogspot.com/2019/08/whither- fed.html

Cooley, Thomas and Stephen LeRoy (1981). Identification and Estimation of Money Demand. *American Economic Review*, 71(5), 825–844.

Coyle, Diane (2015). *GDP: A Brief but Affectionate History*. Princeton University Press.

Croushore, Dean (2011). Frontiers of Real-Time Data Analysis. *Journal of Economic Literature*, 49(1), 72–100.

Crump, Richard, Stefano Eusepi, Marc Giannoni, and Ayşegül Şahin (2019). A Unified Approach to Measuring u*. NBER Working Paper No. 25930.

Daly, Mary, Bart Hobign, and Rob Valletta (2011). The Recent Evolution of the Natural Rate of Unemployment. Federal Reserve Bank of San Francisco Working Paper Series. Available online (accessed March 23, 2020), www.federalreserve.gov/mon etarypolicy/files/FOMC20110117memo01.pdf

Danis, Hakan (2017). Nonlinearity and Asymmetry in the Monetary Policy Reaction Function: A Partially Generalized Ordered Probit Approach. *Eurasian Economic Review*, 7, 161–178.

Davig, Troy and Jose Mustre-del-Rio (2013). The Shadow Labor Supply and Its Implications for the Unemployment Rate. *Federal Reserve Bank of Kansas City Economic Review*, 5–29. Available online (accessed June 11, 2019), www .kansascityfed.org/publicat/econrev/pdf/13q3Davig-Mustre.pdf

Del Negro, Marco, Michael Dotsey, Marc Giannoni, and Argia Sbordone (2012a). DSGE Policy Scenarios Project. Memo. December 3, 2012. Available online (accessed March 20, 2020), www.federalreserve.gov/monetarypolicy/files/ FOMC20121203memo01.pdf

Del Negro, Marco, Marc Giannoni, and Christina Patterson (2012b). The Forward Guidance Puzzle. Staff Reports 574, Federal Reserve Bank of New York, revised December 1, 2015. Available online (accessed June 25, 2019), www.newyorkfed .org/medialibrary/media/research/staff_reports/sr574.pdf

Dolado, Juan, María-Dolores Ramón, and Manuel Naveira (2005). Are Monetary-Policy Reaction Functions Asymmetric?: The Role of Nonlinearity in the Phillips Curve. *European Economic Review*, 49(2), 485–503.

Dorn, James and William Niskanen, eds. (1989). *Dollars Deficits & Trade*. Kluwer Academic Publishers.

Drazen, Allan (2000). *Political Economy in Macroeconomics*. Princeton University Press.

Dutkowsky, Donald and Barry Cynamon (2003). Sweep Programs: The Fall of M1 and Rebirth of the Medium of Exchange. *Journal of Money, Credit and Banking*, 35(2), 263–279.

Dyhrberg, Anne, Sean Foley, and Jiri Svec (2018). How Investible Is Bitcoin? Analyzing the Liquidity and Transaction Costs of Bitcoin Markets. *Economics Letters*, 171 (October), 140–143.

El Herradi, Mehdi and Aurélien Leroy (2019). Monetary Policy and the Top One Percent: Evidence from a Century of Modern Economic History. De Nederlandsche Bank Working Paper No. 632. Available online (accessed June 5, 2019), www.dnb.nl/en/binaries/Working%20paper%20No.%20632_tcm47-383633.pdf

Federal Reserve (2009). Conference Call of the Federal Open Market Committee. January 16. Available online (accessed March 23, 2020), www.federalreserve.gov/ monetarypolicy/files/FOMC20090116confcall.pdf

(2011). FRBNY DSGE Model: Research Directors Draft. June. Available online (accessed March 25, 2020), www.federalreserve.gov/monetarypolicy/files/ FOMC20110609memo03.pdf

(2012a). Federal Reserve Issues FOMC Statement of Longer-Run Goals and Policy Strategy. Press Release. January 25. Available online (accessed March 18, 2020), www.federalreserve.gov/newsevents/pressreleases/monetary20120125c.htm

(2012b). Meeting of the Federal Open Market Committee on October 23–24, 2012. Available online (accessed March 20, 2020), www.federalreserve.gov/monetarypo licy/files/FOMC20121024meeting.pdf

(2013a). Meeting of the Federal Open Market Committee on July 30–31, 2013. Available online (accessed March 20, 2020), www.federalreserve.gov/monetarypo licy/files/FOMC20130731meeting.pdf

(2013b). Meeting of the Federal Open Market Committee on October 29–30, 2013. Available online (accessed March 20, 2020), www.federalreserve.gov/monetarypo licy/files/FOMC20131030meeting.pdf

(2014a). Meeting of the Federal Open Market Committee on January 28–29, 2014. Available online (accessed March 20, 2020), www.federalreserve.gov/monetarypo licy/files/FOMC20140129meeting.pdf

(2014b). Conference Call of the Federal Open Market Committee on March 4. Available online (accessed March 20, 2020), www.federalreserve.gov/monetarypo licy/files/FOMC20140304confcall.pdf

(2016). Statement on Longer-Run Goals and Monetary Policy Strategy Adopted effective January 24, 2012; as amended effective January 26, 2016. Press Release. January 26. Available online (accessed March 18, 2020), www.federalreserve.gov/ monetarypolicy/files/FOMC_LongerRunGoals_20160126.pdf

(2018a). Minutes of the Federal Open Market Committee. November 7–8. Available online (accessed March 23, 2020), www.federalreserve.gov/monetarypolicy/ fomcminutes20181108.htm

(2018b). Further Analysis of Simple Policy Rules in the Current Environment. Federal Reserve Memo. Available online (accessed July 20, 2020), www .federalreserve.gov/monetarypolicy/files/FOMC20120718memo03.pdf

(2019a). Minutes of the Federal Open Market Committee. July 30–31. Available online (accessed March 23, 2020), www.federalreserve.gov/monetarypolicy/files/ fomcminutes20190731.pdf

(2019b). Minutes of the Federal Open Market Committee. October 29–30. Available online (accessed May 27, 2020), www.federalreserve.gov/monetarypolicy/files/ fomcminutes20191030.pdf

Ferguson, Roger (2003). Should Financial Stability Be an Explicit Central Bank Objective? BIS Papers No. 18: Monetary Stability, Financial Stability and the Business Cycle: Five Views, pp. 7–15. Available online (accessed May 31, 2019), www.bis.org/publ/bppdf/bispap18.pdf

Fernández-Villaverde, Jesús and Daniel Sanches (2019). Can Currency Competition Work? *Journal of Monetary Economics*, 106, 1–15.

Fieldhouse, Andrew and Karel Mertens (2017). A Narrative Analysis of Mortgage Asset Purchases by Federal Agencies. NBER Working Paper No. 23165. Available online (accessed June 5, 2019), www.nber.org/papers/w23165

Finnerty, John and Douglas Emery (2002). Corporate Securities Innovation: An Update. *Journal of Applied Finance*, 12(1), 21–47.

Frame, Scott and Lawrence. White (2014). Empirical Studies of Financial Innovation: Lots of Talk, Little Action? *Journal of Economic Literature*, 42(1), 116–144.

Friedman, Milton (1961). The Lag in Effect of Monetary Policy. *Journal of Political Economy*, 69(5), 447–466.

(1968). The Role of Monetary Policy. *American Economic Review*, 58(1), 1–17.

Fuhrer, Jeff, Giovanni Olivei, Eric Rosengren, and Geoffrey Tootell (2018). Should the Federal Reserve Regularly Evaluate Its Monetary Policy Framework? *Brookings Papers on Economic Activity*, Fall, 443–517.

Garín, Julio, Robert Lester, and Eric Sims (2016). Are Supply Shocks Contractionary at the ZLB? Evidence from Utilization-Adjusted TFP Data. *The Review of Economics and Statistics*, 101(1), 160–175.

Goodfriend, Marvin (1998). Using the Term Structure of Interest Rates for Monetary Policy. *Federal Reserve Bank of Richmond Economic Quarterly*, 84(3), 13–30.

Goodhart, Charles (1975). Problems of Monetary Management: The U.K. Experience. Papers in Monetary Economics, 1. Reserve Bank of Australia.

(1989). *Money, Information and Uncertainty* (2nd Edition). Macmillan Press.

Greenspan, Alan (1993). The Fed Aims for Price Stability. *Challenge*, September–October, 36, 4–10.

(1997). Rules vs. Discretionary Monetary Policy. Speech at the 15th Anniversary Conference of the Center for Economic Policy Research at Stanford University. Stanford, CA. September 5. Available online (accessed May 28, 2020), www .federalreserve.gov/boarddocs/speeches/1997/19970905.htm

(2004). Risk and Uncertainty in Monetary Policy. *American Economic Review*, 94(2), 33–40.

Hall, Robert (1986). Optimal Monetary Institutions and Policy. In Colin D. Campbell and William R. Dougan (Eds.), *Alternative Monetary Regimes*. Johns Hopkins University Press, pp. 224–239.

Haltom, Renee and Jeffrey Lacker (2013). Does the Fed Have a Financial Stability Mandate? *Economic Brief,* 17-06, Federal Reserve Bank of Richmond. Available online (accessed May 31, 2019), www.richmondfed.org/-/media/richmondfedorg/ publications/research/economic_brief/2017/pdf/eb_17-06.pdf

Hamada, Koichi (2004). Policy Making in Deflationary Japan. *The Japanese Economic Review*, 55(3), 221–239.

Hayek, Friedrich August (1945). The Use of Knowledge in Society. *The American Economic Review*, 35(4), 519–530.

(1948 [1980]). *Individualism and Economic Order*. University of Chicago Press.

(2008). *Prices & Production and Other Works*. Joseph Salerno (Ed.). Ludwig von Mises Institute.

Heller, Robert (1965). The Demand for Money: The Evidence from the Short-Run Data. *Quarterly Journal of Economics*, 79(2), 291–303.

Hetzel, Robert (2016). A Proposal to Clarify the Objectives and Strategy of Monetary Policy. *Journal of Macroeconomics*, 54, 72–89.

Higgs, Robert (1997). Regime Uncertainty: Why the Great Depression Lasted So Long and Why Prosperity Resumed after the War. *The Independent Review*, 1(4), 561–590.

Hogan, Thomas (2015). Has the Fed Improved U.S. Economic Performance? *Journal of Macroeconomics*, 43, 257–266.

Hogan, Thomas, Daniel Smith, and Robin Aguiar-Hicks (2018). Central Banking without Romance. *European Journal of Comparative Economics*, 15(2), 293–314.

Holland, Steven (1985). Rational Expectations and the Effects of Monetary Policy: A Guide for the Uninitiated. *Federal Reserve Bank of St. Louis Review*, May, 67, 5–11.

Holston, Kathryn, Thomas Laubach, and John Williams (2017). Measuring the Natural Rate of Interest: International Trends and Determinants. *Journal of International Economics*, 108 (May), S59–S75.

Horwitz, Steven (1990). A Subjectivist Approach to the Demand for Money. *Journal des Economistes et des Etudes Humaines*, 1(4), 459–471.

(2000). *Microfoundations and Macroeconomics: An Austrian Perspective*. Routledge.

Hoshi, Takeo (2011). Financial Regulation: Lessons from the Recent Financial Crises. *Journal of Economic Literature*, 49(1), 120–128.

Houseman, Susan N. (2018). Understanding the Decline of U.S. Manufacturing Employment, Upjohn Institute Working Paper No. 18-287. Available online (accessed May 28, 2020), https://research.upjohn.org/cgi/viewcontent.cgi?article=1305&context=up_workingpapers

Husted, Lucas, John Rogers, and Bo Sun (2020). Monetary Policy Uncertainty. *Journal of Monetary Economics*, 115, 20–36.

Issing, Otmar (2003). Monetary and Financial Stability: Is There a Trade-off? BIS Papers No. 18: Monetary Stability, Financial Stability and the Business Cycle: Five Views, pp. 16–23. Available online (accessed May 31, 2019), www.bis.org/publ/bppdf/bispap18.pdf

Jackson, Laura, Michael Owyang, and Daniel Soques (2018). Nonlinearities, Smoothing and Countercyclical Monetary Policy. *Journal of Economic Dynamics and Control*, 95, 136–154.

Johnson, Manuel (1988). Current Perspectives on Monetary Policy. *Cato Journal*, 8(2), 253–260.

Jordà, Òscar, Moritz Schularick, and Alan Taylor (2015). Betting the House. *Journal of International Economics*, 96(1), S2–S18.

Jordan, Jerry L. 2017. Rethinking the Monetary Transmission Mechanism. *Cato Journal*, 37(2), 361–384.

Judd, John and Glenn Rudebusch (1998). Taylor's Rule and the Fed: 1970–1997. *Federal Reserve Bank of San Francisco Economic Review*, 3, 3–16.

Kashyap, Anil and Caspar Siegert (2019). Financial Stability Considerations and Monetary Policy. *International Journal of Central Banking*, 16(1), 231–266.

Kay, John and Mervyn King (2020). *Radical Uncertainty*. W. W. Norton & Company.

Keynes, John Maynard (1936). *The General Theory of Employment, Interest, and Money*. Harcourt, Brace & World.

Khoury, Salwa (1990). The Federal Reserve Reaction Function: A Specification Search. In Thomas Mayer (Ed.), *The Political Economy of American Monetary Policy*. Cambridge University Press, pp. 27–41.

Kiesling, Lynne (2015). The Knowledge Problem. In Peter J. Boettke and Christopher J. Coyne (Eds.), *The Oxford Handbook of Austrian Economics*. Oxford University Press, pp. 45–64.

Kiley, Michael (2016). Policy Paradoxes in the New Keynesian Model. *Review of Economic Dynamics*, 21 (July), 1–15.

Kirzner, Israel (2018). *Competition, Economic Planning, and the Knowledge Problem*. Peter Boettke and Frédéric Sautet (Eds.). Liberty Fund, Inc.

Knell, Markus and Helmut Stix (2006). Three Decades of Money Demand Studies. Some Differences and Remarkable Similarities. *Applied Economics*, 38(7), 805–818.

Kuttner, Kenneth and Adam Posen (2004). The Difficulty of Discerning What's Too Tight: Taylor Rules and Japanese Monetary Policy. *The North American Journal of Economics and Finance*, 15(1), 53–74.

Laidler, David E. W. (1993). *The Demand for Money* (4th Edition). HarperCollins College Publishers.

Lakdawala, Aeimit (2016). Changes in Federal Reserve preferences. *Journal of Economic Dynamics and Control*, 70 (September), 124–143.

Lastrapes, William and George Selgin (1996). The Price of Gold and Monetary Policy. Working Paper. Available online (accessed June 14, 2019), https://pdfs.semanticscholar.org/c5d5/77dd46e898781bfeff704436a483b6ac72db.pdf

Laubach, Thomas and John Williams (2016). Measuring the Natural Rate of Interest Redux. Board of Governors of the Federal Reserve System Finance and Economics Discussion Series 2016-011. Available online (accessed June 12, 2019), www .federalreserve.gov/econresdata/feds/2016/files/2016011pap.pdf

Lavoie, Donald (1985). *Rivalry and Central Planning: The Socialist Debate Reconsidered.* Cambridge University Press.

Levine, Ross (2012). The Governance of Financial Regulation: Reform Lessons from the Recent Crisis. *International Review of Finance,* 12(1), 39–56.

Lombra, Raymond and Michael Moran (1980). Policy Advice and Policymaking at the Federal Reserve. *Carnegie-Rochester Conference Series on Public Policy,* 13, 9–68.

Lucas, Robert (1976). Econometric Policy Evaluation: A Critique. *Carnegie-Rochester Conference Series on Public Policy,* 1(1), 19–46.

Maisel, Sherman (1973). *Managing the Dollar.* W. W. Norton & Company.

Mallaby, Sebastian (2016). *The Man Who Knew: The Life and Times of Alan Greenspan.* Penguin Press.

Mankiw, Gregory and Ricardo Reis (2002). Sticky Information versus Sticky Prices: A Proposal to Replace the New Keynesian Phillips Curve. *Quarterly Journal of Economics,* 117(4), 1295–1328.

Mason, Will (1976). The Empirical Definition of Money: A Critique. *Economic Inquiry,* 14(4), 525–538.

McNees, Stephen (1992). A Forward-Looking Monetary Policy Reaction Function: Continuity and Change. *New England Economic Review* (November/December), 3–13.

Meltzer, Allan (2009). *A History of the Federal Reserve, Volume II, Book Two, 1970–1986.* University of Chicago Press.

Mises, Ludwig von (1936 [1981]). *Socialism: An Economic and Sociological Analysis.* Liberty Fund, Inc.

Mishkin, Frederic (2013). *The Economics of Money, Banking, and Financial Markets* (10th Edition). Pearson.

Muto, Ichiro (2013). Productivity Growth, Transparency, and Monetary Policy. *Journal of Economic Dynamics and Control,* 37(1), 329–344.

O'Driscoll, Gerald (1977). *Economics as a Coordination Problem.* Sheed, Andrews, and McMeel.

Ohanian, Lee (2018). Should Policy Makers Worry about R-Star? In Michael Bordo and John Cochrane (Eds.), *The Structural Foundations of Monetary Policy.* Hoover Institution Press, pp. 62–80.

Orphanides, Athanasios (2001). Monetary Policy Rules Based on Real-Time Data. *American Economic Review,* 91(4), 964–985.

(2002a). Activist Stabilization Policy and Inflation: The Taylor Rule in the 1970s. Center for Financial Studies Working Paper No. 2002/15.

(2002b). Monetary Policy Rules and the Great Inflation. Finance and Economics Discussion Series 2002-8. Board of Governors of the Federal Reserve System.

(2002c). The Unreliability of Output-Gap Estimates in Real Time. *The Review of Economics and Statistics,* 84(4), 569–583.

(2003). Historical Monetary Policy Analysis and the Taylor Rule. *Journal of Monetary Economics,* 50(5), 983–1022.

Pagano, Michael and John Sedunov (2018). Bitcoin and the Demand for Money: Is Bitcoin More Than Just a Speculative Asset? SSRN Working Paper. Available online (accessed May 28, 2020), https://papers.ssrn.com/sol3/papers.cfm?abstract_id=3293998

Pashman, Dan (2007). Krulwich Exposes Greenspan's Underwear Secret, Bryant Park Project, NPR. Available online (accessed June 25, 2019), www.npr.org/sections/bryantpark/2007/09/robert_krulwich_exposes_greens_1.html

Pollock, Alex (2018). *Finance and Philosophy: Why We're Always Surprised.* Paul Dry Books.

Posen, Adam (2011). Monetary Policy, Bubbles, and the Knowledge Problem. *Cato Journal,* 31(3), 461–471.

Powell, Jerome (2018). Monetary Policy and Risk Management at a Time of Low Inflation and Low Unemployment. Speech at the Revolution or Evolution? Reexamining Economic Paradigms. 60th Annual Meeting of the National Association for Business Economics, Boston, MA. Available online (accessed March 13, 2020), www.federalreserve.gov/newsevents/speech/powell20181002a.htm

(2019a). Challenges for Monetary Policy. Speech at the Challenges for Monetary Policy Symposium sponsored by the Federal Reserve Bank of Kansas City, Jackson Hole, WY. August 23. Available online (accessed March 13, 2019), www.federalreserve.gov/newsevents/speech/powell20190823a.htm

(2019b). Data-Dependent Monetary Policy in an Evolving Economy. Speech at Trucks and Terabytes: Integrating the "Old" and "New" Economies, the 61st Annual Meeting of the National Association for Business Economics, Denver, CO. October 8. Available online (accessed March 13, 2020), www.federalreserve.gov/newsevents/speech/powell20191008a.htm.

Puzzanghera, Jim and Don Lee (2015). Financial Stability May be X Factor in Fed's Interest Rate Decisions. *Los Angeles Times.* September 16. Available online (accessed May 21, 2020), www.latimes.com/business/la-fi-fed-rate-mandate-20150916-story.html

Ramey, Valerie (2011). Can Government Purchases Stimulate the Economy? *Journal of Economic Literature,* 49(3), 673–685.

Ramey, Valerie and Sarah Zubairy (2018). Government Spending Multipliers in Good Times and in Bad: Evidence from U.S. Historical Data. *Journal of Political Economy,* 126(2), 850–901.

Rangarajan, Chakravarthi (1997–1998). Role of Monetary Policy. *Economic and Political Weekly,* 32(52), 3325–3328.

(2001). Some Critical Issues in Monetary Policy. *Economic and Political Weekly,* 36 (24), 2139–2146.

Romer, David (1989). Comments and Discussion on Institutional Change and the Efficacy of Monetary Policy by Barry Bosworth. *Brookings Papers on Economic Activity,* 1, 77–124.

Rothbard, Murray (1960). The Politics of Political Economists: Comment. *The Quarterly Journal of Economics,* 74(4), 659–665.

Sablik, Tim (2018). The Fault in R-Star, *Econ Focus,* Federal Reserve Bank of Richmond. Fourth Quarter. Available online (accessed March 13, 2020), www

.richmondfed.org/-/media/richmondfedorg/publications/research/econ_focus/2018/q4/federal_reserve.pdf.

Saiki, Ayako and Jon Frost (2014). Does Unconventional Monetary Policy Affect Inequality? Evidence from Japan. *Applied Economics*, 46(36), 4445–4454.

Salter, Alexander and Daniel Smith (2017). What You Don't Know Can Hurt You: Knowledge Problems in Monetary Policy. *Contemporary Economic Policy*, 35(3), 505–517.

Schmitt-Grohe, Stephanie and Martin Uribe (2004). Optimal Fiscal and Monetary Policy under Sticky Prices. *Journal of Economic Theory*, 114, 198–230.

Selgin, George (1988). *The Theory of Free Banking*. Rowman & Littlefield.

(1997). *Less than Zero: The Case for a Falling Price Level in a Growing Economy*. Institute for Economic Affairs.

(2018). *Floored!: How a Misguided Fed Experiment Deepened and Prolonged the Great Recession*. Cato Institute.

(2020). *The Menace of Fiscal QE*. Cato Institute.

Selgin, George, William Lastrapes, and Lawrence White (2012). Has the Fed Been a Failure? *Journal of Macroeconomics*, 34(3), 569–596.

Shapiro, Matthew and David Wilcox (1996). Mismeasurement in the Consumer Price Index: An Evaluation. In Ben Bernanke and Julio Rotemberg (Eds.), *NBER Macroeconomics Annual 11*. The MIT Press, pp. 93–154.

Shukayev, Malik and Alexander Ueberfeldt (2018). Monetary Policy Tradeoffs between Financial Stability and Price Stability. *Canadian Journal of Economics*, 51(3), 901–945.

Smets, Frank (2013). Financial Stability and Monetary Policy: How Closely Interlinked? *Economic Review, Sveriges Riksbank*, 3, 121–159.

Steelman, Aaron (2011). The Federal Reserve's "Dual Mandate": The Evolution of an Idea. *Federal Reserve Bank of Richmond Economic Brief*, December (11–12), 1–6.

Stock, James and Mark Watson (2019). Slack and Cyclically Sensitive Inflation. NBER Working Paper No. 25987.

Summers, Lawrence (1981). Measuring Unemployment. *Brookings Papers on Economic Activity*, 2, 609–620.

Sumner, Scott (2019). Don't Target Interest Rates. *TheMoneyIllusion*. Available online (accessed June 25, 2019), www.themoneyillusion.com/dont-target-interest-rates/

Svensson, Lars (2002). What Is Wrong with Taylor Rules? Using Judgement in Monetary Policy through Targeting Rules. *Journal of Economic Literature*, 41(2), 426–477.

(2019). Monetary Policy Strategies for the Federal Reserve. Paper presentation on the Conference on Monetary Policy Strategy, Tools, and Communication Practices (A Fed Listens Event). Federal Reserve Bank of Chicago, Chicago. Available online (accessed June 25, 2019), www.federalreserve.gov/conferences/conference-monet ary-policy-strategy-tools-communications-20190605.htm

Tasci, Murat and Randal Verbrugge (2014). How Much Slack Is in the Labor Market? That Depends on What You Mean by Slack. *Federal Reserve Bank of Cleveland Economic Commentary*, 2014-12 (October). Available online (accessed December 8, 2020), www.clevelandfed.org/en/newsroom-and-events/publications/economic-commentary/2014-economic-commentaries/ec-201421-how-much-slack-is-in-the-labor-market.aspx

Taylor, John (1993). Discretion versus Policy Rules in Practice. *Carnegie-Rochester Conference Series on Public Policy*, 39 (December), 195–214.

(1999). Introduction. In John Taylor (Ed.), *Monetary Policy Rules*. University of Chicago Press, pp. 1–14.

(2017). Rules versus Discretion: Assessing the Debate over the Conduct of Monetary Policy. NBER Working Paper No. 24149.

(2009). The Financial Crisis and the Policy Responses: An Empirical Analysis of What Went Wrong. *Critical Review: A Journal of Politics and Society*, 21(2–3), 341–364.

Taylor, John and Volker Wieland (2016). Finding the Equilibrium Real Interest Rate in a Fog of Policy Deviations. *Business Economics*, 51(3), 147–154.

Teles, Pedro and Ruilin Zhou (2005). A Stable Money Demand: Looking for the Right Monetary Aggregate. *Journal of Payment Systems Law*, 3(May), 281–298.

Tobias, Andrew (1982). A Talk with Paul Volcker, *The New York Times*, September 19. Available online (accessed June 10, 2019), www.nytimes.com/1982/09/19/maga zine/a-talk-with-paul-volcker.html

Trichet, Jean-Claude (2010). Reflections on the Nature of Monetary Policy Non-standard Measures and Finance Theory. Opening address at the ECB Central Banking Conference, Frankfurt, Germany. November 18. Available online (accessed March 19, 2020), www.ecb.europa.eu/press/key/date/2010/html/ sp101118.en.html

Van Lear, William (2000). A Review of the Rules versus Discretion Debate in Monetary Policy. *Eastern Economic Journal*, 26(1), 29–39.

Volcker, Paul and Christine Harper (2018). *Keeping at It: The Quest for Sound Money and Good Government*. Public Affairs.

Wang, Yiming (2011). The Stability of Long-Run Money Demand in the United States: A New Approach. *Economic Letters*, 111(1), 60–63.

Weidner, Justin and John Williams (2011). What Is the New Normal Unemployment Rate? *Federal Reserve Bank of San Francisco Economic Letter*, 2011-05 (February 14). Available online (accessed June 11, 2019), www.frbsf.org/economic-research/ publications/economic-letter/2011/february/new-normal-unemployment-rate/

White, Lawrence (2005). The Federal Reserve System's Influence on Research in Monetary Economics. *Econ Journal Watch*, 2(2), 325–354.

Wieland, Volker (2018). R-Star: The Natural Rate and Its Role in Monetary Policy. In Michael Bordo and John Cochrane (Eds.), *The Structural Foundations of Monetary Policy*. Hoover Institution Press, pp. 45–61.

Williamson, Stephen (2016). Interest Rate Control Is More Complicated Than You Thought, Federal Reserve Bank of St. Louis. *Regional Economist*. April. Available online (accessed March 23, 2020), www.stlouisfed.org/publications/regional-econo mist/april-2016/interest-rate-control-is-more-complicated-than-you-thought

(2019). Is the Fed Doing Anything Right? New Monetarist Economics. Available online (accessed March 24, 2020), http://newmonetarism.blogspot.com/2019/08/ is-fed-doing-anything-right.html

Woodford, Michael. (2003). *Interest and Prices: Foundations of a Theory of Monetary Policy*. Princeton University Press.

Yeager, Leland (1986). The Significance of Monetary Disequilibrium. *Cato Journal*, 6 (2), 369–420.

(1988). Domestic Stability versus Exchange Rate Stability. *Cato Journal*, 8(2), 261–284.

Yellen, Janet (2012a). Revolution and Evolution in Central Bank Communications. Speech at the Haas School of Business, University of California, Berkeley, Berkeley, CA. November 13. Available online (accessed March 19, 2020), www .federalreserve.gov/newsevents/speech/yellen20121113a.htm

(2012b). The Economic Outlook and Monetary Policy. Speech at the Money Marketeers of New York University, New York. Available online (accessed March 20, 2020), www.federalreserve.gov/newsevents/speech/yellen20120411a .htm

(2017). The Goals of Monetary Policy and How We Pursue Them. Speech at the Commonwealth Club, San Francisco. January 18. Available online (accessed May 21, 2020), www.federalreserve.gov/newsevents/speech/yellen20170118a.htm

Yermack, David (2015). Is Bitcoin a Real Currency? An Economic Appraisal. In David Leed (Ed.), *The Handbook of Digital Currency*. Elsevier, pp. 31–44.

Incentive Problems with Discretionary Central Banking

3.1 Introduction

"The Fed Interest rate way too high, added to ridiculous quantitative tightening! They don't have a clue!" President Trump tweeted out, publicly upbraiding the Federal Reserve in a series of attempts to push the Board of Governors toward monetary easement (Blinder 2019; Condon 2019; Smialek 2019; also see Ballhaus et al. 2019 and Timiraos 2019).[1] President Trump's public targeting of the Fed on social media, interviews, and speeches was followed up with phone calls and other administrative pressures, including openly exploring the possibility of removing Governor Jerome Powell as Chairman and nominating unqualified, partisan appointees to the Board of Governors (Blinder 2019; Luther 2019). These actions were of such grave concern to the independent operation of the Fed that former Chairs Paul Volcker, Alan Greenspan, Ben Bernanke, and Janet Yellen (2019) co-authored an article in *The Wall Street Journal* writing that,

When the current chair's four-year term ends, the president will have the opportunity to reappoint him or choose someone new. We hope that when that decision is made, the choice will be based on the prospective nominee's competence and integrity, not on political allegiance or activism. It is critical to preserve the Federal Reserve's ability to make decisions based on the best interests of the nation, not the interests of a small group of politicians.

Bill Dudley (2019), the former President of the Federal Reserve Bank of New York, even went so far as to suggest that the Fed should actively "consider how their decisions will affect the political outcome in 2020"

---

[1] Available online (accessed July 9, 2019), https://twitter.com/realdonaldtrump/status/1138427450927529984

given that "Trump's reelection arguably presents a threat to the U.S. and global economy, to the Fed's independence and its ability to achieve its employment and inflation objectives."

While President Trump's public threats against the Fed are certainly more visible in the age of social media, they are not idiosyncratic to his administration.[2] In fact, the history of the Fed is replete with examples of political and bureaucratic pressures shaping both its institutional structure and policy. These pressures have compromised its operational independence and undermined its ability to achieve long-run price stability (Boettke and Smith 2013; Smith and Boettke 2015).

In this chapter, we explore the Fed's record of compromised independence. Despite being founded ostensibly as an independent monetary authority (Barron 1914; Bernanke 2010a), and acquiring additional protections from politics over time (Bordo and Prescott 2019; Hetzel and Leach 2001), we argue that true operational independence is lacking. In fact, we can make a stronger claim: bona fide independence *can never be* achieved under discretionary central banking institutions. We explain theoretically why incentive problems are unavoidable obstacles to discretionary central banking and detail the Fed's record of compromised independence. So long as central banks retain discretion – including "constrained discretion," which is discretion by another name – we have reasons to be concerned about political interference with central banking, and as Dudley's remarks demonstrate, central bank interference with politics.

3.2 Central Bank Incentive Problems

Institutions, by creating the "rules of the game," set the incentives that actors face and thereby influence their behavior (North 1991; Ostrom 2005). The same actors, under alternative institutional incentives, will behave differently (Boettke and Coyne 2009; Buchanan 2008; Nozick 1974, pp. 18–22). Institutions thus encourage certain behaviors and discourage others. In this way, institutions act as a filter that not only influences human behavior but drives changes in human behavior (Alchian 1950; Becker 2007; Gode and Sunder 1993).

---

[2] In contrast, William Dudley's remarks, where a central banker actively and openly seeks to influence a political election, appear to be unprecedented. Less obviously, there is evidence that the Fed's estimates of inflation systematically err, depending on the party of the sitting president (Gandrud and Grafström 2012), suggesting partisan bias.

That different institutions lead to different outcomes is a long-recognized insight in economics. Adam Smith (1776 [1976], pp. 758–761), for instance, observed that university professors in Scotland were more engaging teachers than university professors in England. The difference in outcomes was not because professors in Scotland were more talented or harder working than professors in England, rather the difference in classroom outcomes was driven by institutional differences in teaching. In Scotland, university professors were primarily compensated by fees paid directly by the student to the professor. This provided a strong incentive for Scottish professors to prepare engaging lectures. In England, university professors were primarily compensated by a salary paid regardless of student attendance in their course. This provided English professors with little incentive to prepare engaging lectures. Thus, differences in educational institutions explained variance in educational outputs. If English universities adopted the student fee model of compensation, it would have provided a different set of incentives that would have encouraged their boring professors to become more effective teachers. Similarly, a professor moving from an English to a Scottish university would have been incentivized by the institutional change to alter their behavior.

Despite appreciating that institutions matter in many aspects of their theoretical and applied work, economists tend to ignore this basic insight when studying monetary theory and policy. As Charles Plosser (2018, p. 2) writes (in describing Karl Brunner's views), "policy makers are not the romantic 'Ramsey planners' that we economists often assume in our models but actors responding to incentives and subject to institutional constraints, both of which shape policy choices and outcomes." When it comes to central banking, academic economists tend to forget that if you put the same players in a different game, you will get different results. Central banking institutions do affect the incentives of monetary authorities.

Thus, to achieve both analytical rigor and policy relevance, political economy can and must play a prominent role in our monetary models and policy prescriptions. More fundamentally, these considerations should be incorporated into the design of our monetary institutions to make them robust against policymakers deviating, sometimes widely so, from idealized public interest.

The failure to incorporate institutional incentives in our monetary models and policy prescriptions is likely due to the fact that, when it comes to central banking (and higher education, as in Adam Smith's example), economists themselves are often players in the game! The temptation for actors to rationalize their own behaviors, and thus overlook the institutional influences on their behavior, underlies the principle of *nemo judex in causa sua*, that no man should be his own judge. This is a troubling oversight.

Central banks, as institutions, create incentives for monetary authorities, including economists in research and policy roles, and can thus influence their behavior. As economists move from academia to central banks, they can be impelled to alter their views or actions due to these institutional influences. They are susceptible to influence primarily because of the latitude provided by discretionary central banking. The epistemic problems inherent in conducting discretionary monetary policy, as discussed in Chapter 2, generate uncertainty. This uncertainty opens the door for both internal and external pressure to be exerted on monetary authorities, allowing considerations beyond long-run price stability to influence monetary policy. In other words, when a decision-maker is uncertain as to what the optimal policy is, as is common in central banking, they are more likely to be swayed by pressures, however subtle, which stem from their institutional environment.

Perhaps the best way to analyze the influence of incentives is to compare the preexisting views of economists with their views after they become chairmen of the Fed (Salter and Smith 2019). In doing so, we often can see drastic changes in the views of economists transiting into policy roles, suggesting that the institutional incentives of the Fed impelled them to alter their preexisting views. For instance, when Arthur Burns was appointed chairman of the Fed in 1970, his former student Milton Friedman (1970a) praised his appointment. It did not take long, however, for Friedman to see Arthur Burns pursue a course of monetary policy inconsistent with his previous beliefs and then to reject responsibility for it. Friedman (1970b) wrote, in the same year in which he praised Burns' appointment that:

Central banks (like the rest of us) have a tendency to try to shift responsibility and blame to others for economic troubles. The favorite tactic of the Fed in earlier days was "moral suasion" in the field of credit – appeals to banks not to make "speculative" or inflationary loans. Today central bankers worldwide blame fiscal policy, on the one hand, and propose the exercise of "moral suasion" on business and labor, on the other. It is disheartening to observe so tough-minded, so independent, and so knowledgeable a person as Arthur Burns conform to this pattern so soon after becoming chairman of the Fed.

Alan Greenspan similarly changed his views as he transitioned to becoming a monetary policymaker. Prior to his political experience,

Greenspan famously questioned the need for the Fed, advocating instead for returning to commodity money, because he held that inflation was overwhelmingly driven by debt accommodation by the Fed, and staunchly opposed federal bailouts before his policy roles (Burck 1959, p. 201; Mallaby 2016, p. 4; Tuccille 2002, pp. 79–80, 114, 127). Following his appointment as chairman, however, he undertook actions inconsistent with these earlier views. For instance, he became known for the famous "Greenspan put," a promise by the Fed to provide liquidity to the market during downturns. Testifying before the Committee on Banking, Housing & Urban Affairs, Greenspan's justification was that "History teaches us that central banks have a crucial role to play in responding to episodes of acute financial distress" (Greenspan 1988, p. 2).[3] Throughout his tenure at the Fed, Greenspan supported using a mix of traditional and nontraditional monetary policy tools, including bailouts, to soften the blow to private financiers (Salter and Smith 2019).

Most recently, Ben Bernanke, once appointed as chairman, undertook policy actions drastically inconsistent with his previous research and teaching (Ball 2016; Caplan 2009; Hogan et al. 2015; Salter and Luther 2019). For instance, Bernanke's early views (Bernanke 2002; Bernanke and Mishkin 1997) tended to be critical of discretionary actions on the part of the Fed, which is why Bernanke was an advocate of central banks explicitly committing to inflation targeting (Bernanke 2003; Bernanke et al. 2001; Bernanke and Mishkin 1997; Mallaby 2016, p. 611). Bernanke's actions in the wake of the financial crisis, however, embraced and expanded upon the discretionary role of the Fed. Despite commissioning a committee to explore adopting an inflation target, Bernanke never implemented it as a formal policy (Harris 2008, ch. 8).[4] A former graduate student of

---

[3] While Mallaby (2016, pp. 386–387) initially attributes the put to Vice Chairman Manuel H. Johnson, Greenspan embraced it as official policy throughout his tenure at the Fed.

[4] In 2012, toward the end of Bernanke's tenure as chairman, the Fed publicly announced an inflation target of 2 percent. But inflation "fell short of the Fed's 2% target for much of the past decade" (Wessel 2018, p. 10). In the absence of an enforcement mechanism, it is more accurate to characterize this as a guideline. Even if this guideline were made more formal, lack of enforcement would prevent it from being a true rule. It is worth noting that the Fed's policy falls short of the kind of mandate for price stability that applies to, for example, the European Central Bank (ECB). The ECB system's constitution (European Central Bank 2011) explicitly says price stability is its "primary objective." However, even the ECB departed from its mandate by aggressively combating a nascent sovereign debt crisis in 2012 (yields on Spanish and Italian bonds rose sharply during that summer), which pushed inflation persistently above 2 percent. This calls to mind the distinction between real and pseudo rules (Selgin 2016) from Chapter 1.

Bernanke, Bryan Caplan (2012) wrote that "His [Bernanke's] behavior as Fed chairman seemed utterly disconnected from his lectures and writing."

The cases of Burns, Greenspan, and Bernanke show we cannot rely on beneficence to achieve good outcomes in central banking. It is time to pay much closer attention to the political realities and peculiar incentives confronting central bankers as a matter of course.

3.3 Pressures on the Federal Reserve

An obvious threat to the conduct of responsible central banking is the possibility of political interference. While economists sometimes acknowledge this has been a problem with the Fed in the past, they typically understate the problem historically and, more concerningly, fail to realize the prospect of political meddling still looming large.

However, before we get to external pressures on the Fed, we must discuss internal pressures: those stemming from within the Fed, due to its nature as a bureaucracy. These kinds of pressures, if anything, are even less well known and discussed than their more visible, and overtly concerning, external counterparts.

3.3.1 Internal Pressures

Internal pressures on monetary authorities emerge from the bureaucratic nature of central banks. As a bureaucracy, central banks are prone to the same tendencies of any other bureaucracy, including budget maximization, self-preservation, inertia, and groupthink (Auerbach 1991).

Most government bureaucracies, however, do not enjoy the advantage of having a self-financing budget. This benefit has enabled the Fed to generate discretionary profits (Toma 1982), which sometimes creates perverse bureaucratic incentives. For instance, Shughart II and Tollison (1983) find that the Fed has expanded the money supply to support its bureaucratic growth.[5] The Fed's self-financing budget has also been used by the Board of Governors to exert control over the Federal Reserve Banks and their research (Toma and Toma 1985a).[6] However, it is important to point out that this budgetary autonomy is still subject to the control of Congress. The 2015 FAST Act and the 2018 Economic Growth Act, both of which

---

[5] Also see Boyes et al. (1988).
[6] Rolnick (1985) provides a critical comment on this result. Toma and Toma (1985b) respond.

reduced the Fed's allowable Surplus Account, resulted in the Fed being forced to remit billions to the US Treasury (Selgin 2020, ch. 5).

As a bureaucracy, the Fed is subject to inertia (or status quo bias). As Milton Friedman (1982, p. 102) writes, "With perhaps a few minor exceptions, the system has relatedly been unable or unwilling to change its methods of operation in order to benefit from its own experience." Perhaps this is best exemplified by the fact that it took over 70 years after the Great Depression for the Fed to admit that its mismanagement of the money supply contributed to it (Bernanke 2002).[7] Mankiw (2006), arguing that economists at central banks have stubbornly clung to outdated models, shows how strong this inertia tends to be. Specifically speaking about Laurence Meyer's (2004) *A Term at the Fed*, Mankiw (2006, p. 40) writes, "The book leaves the reader with one clear impression: recent developments in business cycle theory, promulgated by both new classicals and new Keynesians, have had close to zero impact on practical policy-making." Mankiw holds that Meyer's views, as a central bank, are neither idiosyncratic nor atypical; they are representative of the top economists in central banks. In fact, Stephen Williamson (2019) argues that even the Fed's focus on the federal funds rate, a core component of the Fed's monetary policy until recently, may be the result of bureaucratic inertia. The Fed's decision, even following the recovery, to stick with the floor system, which was "triggered" by monetary authorities raising interest on excess reserve above the short-term market rates (Beckworth 2018b), also reflects bureaucratic inertia (Selgin 2018). The Fed's reluctance to seriously consider alternative monetary policy strategies (Selgin 2019), even in the midst of a review that was publicly touted to be doing so in 2018 (Federal Reserve 2020), further reflects its inflexible mindset.

This inertia may relate to the Fed's influence over the economics profession. Central banks, and in particular the Fed, are a major employer and research sponsor of monetary economists (White 2005). This leads to the Fed having substantial influence over the profession (Auerbach 2008, p. 141; Grim 2009; White 2005). As Milton Friedman (as quoted by Robert Auerbach 2008, p. 142) writes,

having something like 500 economists [employed by the Federal Reserve] is extremely unhealthy. As you say, it is not conducive to independent, objective

---

[7] It may be more appropriate to use the year Milton Friedman and Anna Schwartz (1963) published *A Monetary History of the United States*, which painstakingly detailed the Fed's responsibility for the Great Depression. That would mean that it still took the Fed nearly forty years to admit its mistakes.

research. You and I know there has been censorship of the material published. Equally important, the location of the economists in the Fed has a significant influence on the kind of research they do, biasing that research toward noncontroversial technical papers on method as opposed to substantive papers on policy and results.

This influence on the profession tends to generate conformity, group-think, and cognitive dissonance (Eichengreen 2010; Epstein and Carrick-Hagenbarth 2011, 2012; Kane 1993; Klein and Weiss 2015; Marcussen 2006, p. 189; Mayer 1993; Shiller 2008).[8] For instance, Alan Blinder's tenure as Vice Chairman of the Federal Reserve was reportedly short because he repeatedly challenged the views of senior staff (Grim 2009). Nobel laureate Paul Krugman was reportedly cut from the invite list of certain Fed conferences after he criticized the Fed (Grim 2009).

3.3.2 External Pressures

Internal pressures come from within; external pressures come from without. These external pressures include debt accommodation, political influence, and special interest groups. Given the significant influence that these channels have on the Fed, we devote a subsection to discussing each of them.

3.3.2.1 Debt Accommodation

Budget deficits are financed either with the issuance of government debt or by printing additional currency. In theory, these are distinct; in practice, they sometimes go together. Even debt-financed deficit spending can be accommodated by easier monetary policy. This is because, as more government debt is issued, the government must pay higher interest rates to attract capital from the private sector to support that debt, all else being equal. Higher interest rates will, in turn, have a tightening effect on the economy and will also raise the service of government debt (Blinder 1982; Canzoneri et al. 2011; Freedman et al. 2010). Higher interest rates can also have interaction effects with other government policies, especially if the debt issuance is large enough to put stress on the fiscal capacity of the state, making it more likely that the government will resort to inflation to pay the

---

[8] These tendencies may be related to similar tendencies in the field of macroeconomics, and, more broadly, economics (Ioannidis et al. 2017; Kirman 1992; Mankiw 2006; McCloskey and Ziliak 1996; McShane et al. 2019; Romer 2016).

debt (Reinhart et al. 2012). Accommodative monetary policy can help governments issuing debt to avoid this tightening effect on the economy and mitigate increases in the servicing costs of public debt.

While the Fed was famously freed from US Treasury control in 1951, it can still find it attractive to offset government debt issuance with accommodative (easy) monetary policy (Blinder 2000; Buchanan and Wagner 1977 [2000]). As Hein (1981, p. 5) writes,

When the federal government spends more than it takes in as revenue, the Treasury must finance the deficit by borrowing in the private marketplace (selling government securities). The increased demand for credit in financial markets, if not offset by a reduction in credit demand elsewhere or an increase in credit supply, naturally puts upward pressure on all market interest rates, Monetary authorities may then attempt to prevent the rise in interest rates from taking place. To do this, the Federal Reserve will buy government securities, thus monetizing part of the public debt by increasing the level of reserves. The increase in bank reserves, as explained above, will result in a larger money stock and, other things equal, a subsequently higher rate of inflation. Consequently, there is an indirect channel – via the response of monetary authorities to higher interest rates – by which deficits can influence the inflation rate.

Similarly, Blinder (2000, p. 1429) writes,

A large fiscal deficit (or debt) can undermine central-bank credibility in a number of ways. Most obviously, if the country has a limited (or zero) capacity to float interest-bearing debt, the central bank may be forced to monetize any budget deficits-with inflationary, or even hyperinflationary, consequences. This danger is greater if the central bank lacks independence . . . . But even if massive inflationary finance is unlikely outsized fiscal deficits and/or large accumulations of public debt (relative to GDP) put upward pressure on interest rates, which may induce a more accommodative policy from the central bank.

The empirical literature finds that effective fiscal policy often requires accommodative monetary policy (Bassetto and Sargent 2020; Bell 2000; Blinder 1982; Canzoneri et al. 2011; Freedman et al. 2010). Even in constitutional democracies, fiscal and monetary affairs are not as separate as many economists think.

There is a well-developed body of literature that suggests a link between the accumulation of public debt and accommodative monetary policy at the Fed (Allen and Smith 1983; Blinder 1983; Bradley 1985; Hamburger and Zwick 1981; Laney and Willett 1983; Niskanen 1978).[9] Increases in

---

[9] See Barro (1978), Evans (1985), Faust and Irons (1999), McMillin (1981), and McMillin and Beard (1982) for a dissenting view. Measuring this influence is, of course, plagued by

projected debt do tend to raise interest rates (Engen and Hubbard 2005; Laubach 2009), suggesting that the Fed must accommodate that effect in their prescribed policy course. This may be why Thornton (1984) originally found evidence of debt accommodation at the Fed when it was targeting interest rates.

This is a subset of the more general concern over the mutual impingement of fiscal and monetary policies. For instance, even under the Fed's new operating system, it appears as if President Trump's fiscal policies, by pushing up interest rates, were putting pressure on the floor system and thereby affecting Fed policy (Beckworth 2018a; Selgin 2018). Other policies, such as helicopter drops or the various proposals that fall under the rubric of modern monetary theory, would require even more explicit coordination between fiscal and monetary policy (Ball 2008; Bernanke 2003; Caballero and Farhi 2018; English et al. 2017; Selgin 2020; Tymoigne 2014).

3.3.2.2 Political Influence

Political influence on the Fed can also undermine monetary policy in the public interest. Political officials have a strong predisposition toward easy money for two reasons. First, the deficit-financed policies they support often are more palatable with monetary accommodation (Ehrmann and Fratzscher 2011). Second, politicians up for reelection want to boost voters' assessment of the economy, and thus the policymaker's performance in office, ahead of that election (Drazen 2000). Policymakers, in both the executive and legislative branches, have several channels through which they can exert pressure on monetary authorities.

The primary channel for the executive branch to influence the Fed is through its appointment and reappointment power (Binder and Spindel 2017; Chappell et al. 1993; Conti-Brown 2015; Ellis and Schansberg 2000; Morris 2002, ch. 5). Through their appointment authority, presidents can often ensure that they have advocates on the Board of Governors (Havrilesky and Gildea 1990; Meltzer 2009a, p. 88). The seven members of the Board of Governors are appointed by the President in fourteen-year staggered terms. It is not unusual, however, for Governors to resign before their full term, allowing a president, especially a two-term president, to appoint the majority of the Governors. Presidents have also been able to

---

the same knowledge problems as central banking detailed in Chapter 2 (Bradley 1985, p. 411; Thornton 1984, pp. 41–43).

exert substantial resignation pressure on unaccommodating board members (Hyman 1976, p. 266; Kettl 1986, p. 75; Meltzer 2009a, p. 135). Board of Governors appointees must also be confirmed by the Senate, which gives the legislative branch a veto over appointments (Waller 1992).

Presidents also have the authority, again with confirmation from the Senate, to appoint the chairman and vice chairmen for the Board of Governors to four-year terms. The chairman and vice chairmen hold substantial sway over decision-making at the Fed (Silber 2012, p. 150). In particular, the chairman holds final authority over appointments within the Fed, including presidents of the Federal Reserve Banks, and sets the agenda for the Federal Open Market Committee (comprised of the Board of Governors and five of the presidents of the Federal Reserve Banks) (Meade and Sheets 2005, p. 676; Silber 2012, p. 150). Even a strategically placed vice chairman can provide policymakers, most notably the president, with some degree of influence on the FOMC (Havrilesky 1993). For instance, Mallaby (2016, p. 448) writes that "the Reagan team ... used Manley Johnson to undermine Volcker." Alan Blinder, a member of President Clinton's Council of Economic Advisors (CEA) and occasional tutor for Chelsea Clinton, was reportedly appointed as Vice Chairman specifically to counterbalance the hawkish Greenspan and accommodate the Clinton administration's objectives (Mallaby 2016, ch. 20).

The relevant literature suggests that appointment power gives presidential administrations the ability to direct Fed policy (Auerbach 1985; Chappell et al. 1993, 2005; Ellis and Schansberg 2000; Gildea 1993; Hakes 1990; Havrilesky 1987, 1995a, ch. 9; Havrilesky and Gildea 1991, 1992; Hibbs 1977, 1987; Keech 1995; Krause 1994; Potts and Luckett 1978; Puckett 1984; Weintraub 1978; Woolley 1988).[10] This is especially prominent when it comes to policy undertaken during an election year (Bach 1971; Grier 1987, 1989; Maisel 1973, ch. 7; Maloney and Smirlock 1981; Meiselman 1986; Timberlake 1993, p. 356; Tufte 1978, ch. 2; Williams 1990), even if it is simply by accommodating fiscally induced electoral cycles (Allen 1986; Beck 1987; Drazen 2000, 2005; Hellerstein 2007; Laney and Willett 1983; Woolley 1984, ch. 6).[11]

---

[10] See Beck (1982, 1984), Caporale and Grier (1998, 2005a), Grier and Neiman (1987), Keech and Morris (1997), Morris (2002), and Wallace and Warner (1984) for a different perspective.

[11] For an alternative view, see Fand (1986), Beck (1984), Luckett and Potts (1980), and Maier (2002).

Presidents can also exert influence through indirect channels (Beck 1982, 1984; Caporale and Grier 1998, 2005b; Grier and Neiman 1987). For instance, meetings and phone calls with the president, Treasury officials, or CEA can be used to help coordinate policy efforts (Axilrod 2011, p. 211; Cargill and O'Driscoll Jr. 2013; Kettl 1986, p. 57; Meltzer 2009a, p. 88; Rubin and Weisberg 2004, p. 194). Both official and unofficial media releases, and now social media, are another avenue for policymakers to exert influence on the Fed. For instance, Havrilesky (1988), Froyen and Waud (2002), and Froyen et al. (1997) find that administrative signaling through *The Wall Street Journal* has had a measurable impact on monetary policy.

Besides the Senate's confirmation authority over nominees to the Board of Governors, Congress has other ways to influence the Fed (Binder and Spindel 2017; Cargill and O'Driscoll Jr. 2013; Grier 1991, 1996; Havrilesky 1988, 1995a; Morris 2002). For instance, Congress can impose costs on monetary policymakers through the Fed's required hearings. The chairman of the Fed is required to testify before Congress twice a year, reporting on its monetary targets and explaining deviations from previously announced targets. Oftentimes, these hearings provide an avenue for members of Congress to treat the Fed as a scapegoat for poor economic performance or to pressure the chairman to adjust their course of monetary policy.

Members of Congress can also put pressure on the Fed by threatening to explore or enact reforms to the Fed. As a creation of Congress, the Fed can be modified, or even abolished, as deemed appropriate by Congress (Axilrod 2011, p. 11; Blinder 2010, p. 125; Buchanan and Wagner 1977 [2000], p. 122). Congressional threats against the Fed have included revoking the budgetary autonomy of the Fed, shortening Board of Governors' term limits, packing the FOMC with additional appointees, changing the composition of the Board of Governors to represent different industries and groups, impeaching the chairman (and even the entire FOMC), mandating that all FOMC be politically appointed, and abolishing the FOMC (Binder and Spindel 2017; Clifford 1965, p. 345; Grier 1991, p. 206; Harrison 1991, p. 272; Havrilesky et al. 1993, p. 50; Meltzer 2009a, p. 227; Reagan 1961, p. 70; Safire 1975, p. 492; Silber 2012, pp. 203–207). While these threats have not been carried out, they are a real and constant concern (Binder and Spindel 2017; Meltzer 2009a, p. 225). These threats, as measured by legislative bills introduced to restructure the Fed, tend to reach a peak precisely when the economy is doing poorly and legislators are looking to push the Fed to do more (Binder and Spindel 2017; Havrilesky 1995a). Empirical studies of congressional pressure find a measurable influence on monetary policy through the legislative channel (Binder and Spindel 2017; Caporale and Grier 1998; Havrilesky 1993).[12]

3.3.2.3 Special Interests

As an institution with considerable power over the economy, it is no surprise that the Fed is pressured by special interest groups associated with industries that are affected by monetary policy. The financial industry has been one of the most effective groups at fostering connections with the Federal Reserve System (Government Accountability Office 2011; Reuss 1976). These connections come, in part, from the structure of the Federal Reserve System as "owned" by member banks.[13] Another major source of influence is through the "revolving door," whereby Fed employees deliver policies favorable to potential future employers in the private financial sector (Auerbach 2008, p. 55; Calabria 2012). Even small gift bribery appears to be a problem that is hard to contain at the Fed (Auerbach 2008, p. 55). Special interest groups may also lobby policymakers to pressure the Fed on their behalf (Igan et al. 2012; Kane 1980).

Empirically measuring the influence of the financial sector on Fed policy, Havrilesky (1990) and Weise (2008, 2012) find that the Fed has been responsive to signals sent by the banking industry. Epstein and Schor (2003) find that the Fed has consistently acted to maximize the profitability of both financial and nonfinancial firms. Other sectors, including manufacturing (Havrilesky et al. 1973), have also had a considerable impact on monetary policy. As the financial crisis of 2007–2008 showed, ties with the Fed can be extremely valuable during downturns (Allison 2012; Plosser 2018, p. 4; Taylor 2009, 2012; Zingales 2012).

Perhaps the most egregious example of the special interest group pressure compromising the Fed's independence was captured in the Carmen Segarra tapes (Bernstein 2014). While dealing with the regulatory role of the Fed rather than the monetary role, these secret recordings, made by an expert examiner (Segarra) working for the New York Fed and assigned to Goldman Sachs, document an inappropriate relationship between regulators and one of the organizations it was supposed to be regulating. This

---

[12] Hess and Shelton (2016) find an affect up to the 1980s, but not afterward.

[13] Member banks hold "stock," by law, in their region's Federal Reserve bank (www .federalreserve.gov/faqs/about_14986.htm). But unlike traditional equity, it does not give members voting rights or establish them as a residual claimant. Ownership in this case is more nominal than real, but it does provide a regular venue for interaction, and hence influence.

special interest group pressure helped foster a "culture ruled by group-think" (Bernstein 2014). The overly accommodative attitude of the Fed toward Goldman Sachs is a highly visible case of regulatory capture (cf. Stigler 1971), but hardly the only such case.

3.4 Historical Perspective on Incentive Problems

In the previous section, we provided a broad overview of the theory and empirical literature on pressures on the Fed. In this section, we provide a more detailed history of such pressures. We examine only the post-1951 period, as the Monetary Accord of 1951 is commonly viewed as the distinct starting point of modern Fed independence. That significant pressure continued to exist after the Accord speaks volumes about the incompatibility of discretionary central banking with monetary policy in the public interest.

William Martin, Chairman of the Fed from 1951 to 1970, was appointed to the Fed by President Truman. Despite its newly negotiated independence from the Treasury, Chairman Martin, a former Assistant Secretary of the Treasury, held that,

Independence no longer excluded consultations and exchange of information. Martin's interpretation of the 1951 Accord went further. He [Martin], and most others in the System, believed that the Federal Reserve had a responsibility to assure that Treasury bond issues did not fail. He reasoned that Congress voted the budget that the Treasury had to finance. The Federal Reserve had an obligation to help make the issues succeed in the market, provided the Treasury priced its issue at market rates. It should not refuse to accept the fiscal decision or refuse to assist in financing. Help took two forms: preventing failure of new issues and refundings, and maintaining even keel policy during Treasury operations. Even keel meant that the Federal Reserve supplied enough reserves to permit banks to purchase their share of the issue. This seems a narrow meaning of independence. When budget deficits became large and frequent, independence was severely restricted. (Meltzer 2009a, p. 261)

As Chairman, Martin came under frequent pressure to provide accommodative monetary policy (Havrilesky 1995a, p. 54). This pressure was exerted through frequent meetings with presidents, treasury secretaries, and the chairpersons of the CEA (Bach 1971, p. 91; Meltzer 2009a, p. 261). For instance, during the 1953–1954 downturn, President Eisenhower, attempting to pursue a campaign promise to avoid another depression, wrote in his diary that he "talked to the secretary of the Treasury in order to develop real pressure on the Federal Reserve Board for loosening credit still further . . . . Secretary Humphrey promised to put the utmost pressure on Chairman Martin of the Federal Reserve Board in order to get a greater money supply throughout the country" (Ferrell 1981, p. 278). While Chairman Martin initially refused to accommodate President Eisenhower, he reluctantly promised to "ease credit if the economy slowed" (Meltzer 2009a, p. 135). Facing pressure to resign, Chairman Martin ultimately provided accommodative policy (Kettl 1986, p. 88).

When the Treasury ran into issues placing securities on the market in November 1955, Chairman Martin helped support the debt (Bach 1971, p. 95; Clifford 1965, p. 313). Observing this close coordination between the Fed and the Treasury, even in the wake of the 1951 Accord, Clifford (1965, p. 321) writes,

Such quick and strong cooperative action showed that there was indeed a "revolving door" in the "fence" between the independent agencies, the Treasury and the Federal Reserve. Perhaps it could be said that really the fence was invisible and that the neighbors cultivated a common garden, but each with his own tools.

With President Eisenhower up for reelection in 1956, Eisenhower had CEA Chair Arthur Burns pressure Chairman Martin for easier monetary policy (Meltzer 2009a, p. 135). Following President Eisenhower's reelection, the Fed helped to monetize the federal debt. As Alan Greenspan, interviewed for a *Fortune* article (Burck 1959, p. 201), described, "The Fed . . . has recently been boxed in by a huge and partially monetized federal debt, which tends to produce an addition to the money supply, whose size is unrelated to the needs of private business."

When elected President in 1960, John F. Kennedy, along with the Treasury Secretary and Budget Director, also exerted influence on Chairman Martin (Havrilesky 1995a, pp. 55–58; Meltzer 2009a, p. 262). This reportedly led to Martin taking actions that were in stark contrast to his previous policy stances (Havrilesky 1995a, p. 56; Kettl 1986, pp. 93, 98–99; Meltzer 2009a, pp. 269, 317, 323). President Kennedy's administration was pushing for "Operation Twist," an attempt to decrease long-term rates while holding short-term rates steady. Despite initially opposing the initiative, Martin was successfully pressured to provide supportive monetary policy to support the program (Havrilesky 1995a, p. 57; Meltzer 2009a, p. 316; Vencill 1992, p. 203). Chairman Martin worked closely with the Treasury to coordinate the fiscal policies of President Kennedy (Meltzer 2009a, pp. 283, 287, 316, 417). For instance, regarding one particular interest rate increase, Meltzer (2009a, p. 418) writes, there is no denying administration involvement in the discount rate increase. Even if he [Martin] did not make a formal commitment, the change had been discussed with administration officials as part of a package before it was brought to the bank presidents.

Taking office in 1963, President Lyndon Johnson pushed for accommodative monetary policy to support his Great Society programs and the Vietnam War (Havrilesky 1995a, pp. 57–59; Hetzel 2008, p. 69; Meltzer 2009a, pp. 262, 443–445, 456–457; Newton 1983, p. 70).[14] Pressure also came from Congress. Hetzel (2008, p. 70) writes,

Martin confronted a president and Congress united in their hostility to interest rate increases. The situation was untenable for the Fed because it raised the possibility of a political consensus to alter the Federal Reserve Act to limit Fed independence . . . . Martin deferred a rate rise.

The Chairman of the House Committee on Banking and Currency, Wright Patman, put significant pressure on the Fed in his 1964 "A Primer on Money" report, which argued that low-interest rates, to accommodate government debt, were necessary to combat communism (Subcommittee on Domestic Finance 1964, p. 12). This appeared to be quite effective (Bach 1971, p. 124; Havrilesky 1995a, p. 60; Kettl 1986, p. 93). For instance, the FOMC's Records of Policy Actions qualified their targets with the statement, "to the extent permitted by Treasury financing" (Timberlake 1993, p. 338).

Despite holding that the Fed should not be helping to finance the Vietnam War, Chairman Martin faced "a political system hostile to interest rate increases" (Hetzel 2008, p. 71). Meeting with President Johnson, Chairman Martin agreed not to raise interest rates, allowing the monetary base to surge and generate the Great Inflation starting in 1965 (Bernanke 2013, p. 33; Hetzel 2008, pp. 71–73; Meltzer 2005, 2009a, pp. 443, 670; Weise 2012). Writing on the close connection between President Johnson and Chairman Martin, Meltzer (2009a, p. 445) writes, "Policy coordination ensnared Martin in administrative policy. He willingly sacrificed part of the Federal Reserve's independence for the opportunity to be part of the economic 'team,' make his views known to the president, and coordinate policy actions." Newton (1983, p. 113), similarly, writes, "It was obvious in 1968, even from the published statements of the Council of Economic Advisers, that the administration and the Federal Reserve System were acting totally in concert." Perhaps nothing reflects this more than the fact

---

[14] For an alternative view, see Kettl (1986, p. 102).

that in the 1967 State of the Union Address, President Johnson felt comfortable publicly pledging to "do everything in a President's power to lower interest rates and to ease money in this country" (Johnson 1967).

Once elected, President Richard Nixon moved at his first opportunity to replace Chairman Martin, who he blamed for both his previously failed presidential bid and the recession of 1969 (Greider 1987, p. 340; Wapshott 2011, p. 242). President Nixon appointed Arthur Burns as Chairman in 1970. As a close acquaintance and advisor, Nixon believed that Burns would provide accommodative policy (Meltzer 2009a, p. 583; Silber 2012, p. 71; Wells 1994, pp. 26, 42). On the day that Burns was officially appointed as Chairman, Nixon joked, "I hope that independently he will conclude that my views are the ones that should be followed" (as quoted in Havrilesky 1995a, p. 61), and directed to Burns, "please give us more money!" (as quoted in Newton 1983, p. 158).

With his mandate from President Nixon, Chairman Burns acted to consolidate Fed decision-making within his office. He spent a considerable amount of time shaping the views of the FOMC toward his own (Wells 1994, p. 44). For instance, Burns prolonged meetings to get agreement by attrition (Meltzer 2009b, p. 796). Chairman Burns also created a new rule requiring that the chairman directly approve all Fed reports (Wells 1994, p. 44). Dissenting governors were swiftly punished. For instance, in one case, Chairman Burns brought in the FBI to investigate, and in another, asked President Nixon to appoint a governor as an ambassador (Wells 1994, p. 49). Chairman Burns also expanded his authority over appointments to the presidencies of the Federal Reserve Banks by requiring that directors of the Federal Reserve Banks submit multiple names for his approval, rather than just one candidate (Meltzer 2009b, p. 830).

Despite the stagflation that emerged in 1970, Chairman Burns maintained an expansionary monetary policy in exchange for President Nixon agreeing to pass wage and price controls (Wells 1994, ch. 4, 5; Silber 2012, p. 74). President Nixon apparently told an aide that if Burns did not cooperate, he would "get it right in the chops" (Wells 1994, p. 61). To ensure that Martin continued to provide accommodative policy, President Nixon used an interview in the *Wall Street Journal* to report a firm "commitment" from Burns for easy monetary policy and threatened to "unleash" Congressman Patman, a proponent of radically reforming the Fed, if Martin broke that commitment (Havrilesky 1995a, p. 61). Strong statements such as this quickly get incorporated into market expectations and can force the Fed to act accommodatively to avoid market upsets.

Responding to these incentives, Chairman Burns privately lectured FOMC members who dared to cast dissenting votes (Silber 2012, p. 127). After Alfred Hayes, President of the Federal Reserve Bank of New York, continued to cast dissenting votes, Chairman Burns questioned his Bank's travel budget, reported media leaks to the FBI, and publicly started to search for more suitable replacements for Hayes a year ahead of his retirement (Meltzer 2009a, p. 584; Silber 2012, p. 127).

Using these tactics, Chairman Burns was able to cater monetary policy to the needs of President Nixon's administration (Greider 1987, p. 341). "Despite his constant squabbles" Kettl (1986, p. 130) writes that "Burns's policy was rarely far out of step with the Nixon administration. He largely delivered the expansive policies the president and his advisers wanted . . . and his relationship with the White House was close." According to Meltzer (2009a, pp. 583–584), "Burns was unwilling to use the independence of the Federal Reserve for its intended purpose."

The final repudiation of the gold standard in 1971 opened the door for additional pressure to be exerted on the Fed (Barro 1982, p. 104; Buchanan and Wagner 1977 [2000], p. 126). In fact, Meltzer (2009b, pp. 764–765) suggests that the decision to close the gold window may have been primarily driven by Nixon's desire to increase employment ahead of the election. If true, this was an apparently successful tactic as Chairman Burns submitted to President Nixon's pressure for monetary easement to aid his 1972 reelection bid (Abrams 2006; Kane 1974, p. 751; Rose 1974; Woolley 1984, ch. 8; Wapshott 2011, p. 255). Burns even reportedly changed the date of an FOMC meeting to ensure that monetary policy was eased early enough to have an effect, given the expected lags in monetary policy (Meltzer 2009b, p. 799).

The Nixon tapes provide substantial evidence of pressure directed toward Chairman Burns (Abrams 2006; Meltzer 2009b, p. 791; Wells 1994, ch. 4). For instance, in one meeting President Nixon told Chairman Burns "You're independent (laughter), independent (laughter). Get it [the money growth rate] up! I don't want any more angry letters from people . . .. The whole point is, get it up!" (as quoted in Meltzer 2009b, p. 796). In another meeting, Chairman Burns tells President Nixon that, "I have done everything in my power, as I see it, to help you as President, your reputation and standing in American life and history" (as quoted in Meltzer 2009b, p. 792).

Nixon also pressured Chairman Burns in letters. For instance, in a letter to Martin, President Nixon promised to replace a dissenting Governor and threatened a "major attack on the independence of the Fed" if the Fed did not provide accommodative policy (as quoted in Meltzer 2009b, p. 800). A priority of Nixon's administration was his New Economic Policy. To support this initiative, President Nixon successfully pressured the Fed to deliver easy monetary policy (Hetzel 2008, p. 89; Meltzer 2009b, p. 790; Wells 1994, ch. 6). This political pressure was an important factor in generating the inflation that emerged in 1973 (Hetzel 2008, p. 94; Meltzer 2009b, pp. 844, 856–859). Looking back on his experience with President Nixon, Chairman Burns (as quoted in Meltzer 2009a, p. 584) wrote, "Mr. Nixon tried to interfere with the Federal Reserve both in ways that were fair and in ways that by almost any standard, were unfair."

Presidential pressure on Chairman Burns eased up with the coming of the Ford Administration, possibly because the entire Board of Governors had been appointed by Republican presidents and, President Ford, facing rampant inflation, understandably had an anti-inflation agenda (Havrilesky 1995a, p. 63; Hetzel 2008, pp. 108–110; Kettl 1986, p. 132; Meltzer 2009b, p. 846). Congress, however, was not so supportive. Despite the inflation, Congress threatened the Fed to pursue a more expansionary policy (Munger and Roberts 1993, p. 91; Wells 1994, p. 132, ch. 7; Woolley 1984, pp. 144–153). Congressman Patman introduced bills that would have mandated regular audits of the Fed, required congressional approval for Fed budgets, put ceilings on Fed expenditures, required Senate confirmation of Reserve Bank president appointments, and that would have required broader labor and commercial representation on the Board of Governors (Meltzer 2009b, p. 875; Wells 1994, chs. 6, 7). While these bills were never passed, Congress did pass House Concurrent Resolution 133 in 1975, which required that the Chairman of the Fed provide Congress with money growth projections throughout the year and to explain deviations from outlined objectives (Friedman 1982, pp. 107–108; Meltzer 2009b, p. 890; Munger and Roberts 1993, p. 91; Volcker 1978).

While initially Milton Friedman was pleased when Arthur Burns, his former professor, was appointed Chairman (Friedman 1970a) due to his academic qualifications, he later summarized Burns' tenure (Friedman 1978),

We, the public, have been asking Congress to provide us with ever more goodies – yet not to raise our taxes. Congress has obliged, enlisting inflation as a hidden tax to finance the difference (and surreptitiously raise taxes by pushing more and more income into higher tax brackets). The Fed has cooperated – except when the public outcry against inflation has overcome Congressional pressure.

With newly elected President Jimmy Carter desiring more monetary accommodation for rising deficits and more coordination between the Fed and the Treasury (Cullity 1992, p. 44; Meltzer 2009b, pp. 904–905, 910, 922; Wells 1994, p. 204, ch. 9), his administration replaced Burns with Chairman G. William Miller, a proponent of monetary easement (Havrilesky 1995a, pp. 63–64; Meltzer 2009b, p. 848). Chairman Miller was apparently too accommodative, as President Carter's administration began pressuring him for tighter monetary policy (Kettl 1986, p. 170). Frustrated with Miller, President Carter offered him the position of Treasury secretary in order to replace him with Paul Volcker in 1979 (Havrilesky 1995a, p. 65; Wapshott 2011, p. 246).

Chairman Volcker famously was able to bring inflation under control with a course of tight monetary policy. While Volcker's ability to accomplish this is often used as an example of Fed independence in operation, it was anything but. As Binder and Spindel (2017, pp. 23–24) argue, "Far from a demonstration of Fed independence, the Fed's performance under Volcker's leadership indicates that support from fiscal authorities is necessary for the Fed to sustain unpopular monetary policy." This consensus, however, did not survive President Carter's 1980 reelection bid. In the run-up to this election, President Carter publicly criticized Chairman Volcker for maintaining a tight monetary policy (Havrilesky 1993, pp. 64–65; Silber 2012, p. 190; Timberlake 1993, pp. 356–357). By increasing fiscal expenditures, President Carter may have successfully cornered the Fed into delaying tighter monetary policy measures through the accommodation channel (Meltzer 2009b, pp. 1064–1065).

When elected in 1980, President Ronald Reagan pushed Volcker for tighter monetary policy to control inflation (Auerbach, 2008, pp. 151–152; Havrilesky 1995a, p. 66; Newton 1983, p. 15). With his appointment coming up in 1983, Chairman Volcker knew he had to accommodate President Reagan (Timberlake 1993, p. 356). Yet pressure came from the legislative branch for monetary easement ahead of the 1982 elections (Kettl 1986, pp. 181–182). When Volcker resisted these legislative pressures, new proposals, including to make the Fed officially part of the Treasury and to put the Secretary of the Treasury on the Board of Governors, were introduced to alter the structure of the Fed (Clymer 1982; Greider 1987, pp. 490–491, 512–514; Havrilesky 1995a, p. 112). Ironically, this gave authority to the executive branch since these proposals were only a real threat if President Reagan lent his support to them (Meltzer 2009b, p. 1109). As Havrilesky (1993, p. 174) writes, "one might argue that under Volcker during the 1979–1984 period the Federal Reserve was more or less forced to surrender to executive branch signaling because of Congressional challenges to its institutional powers." To be fair, however, Congress was able to still levy threats. Senator Byrd reportedly told Chairman Volcker that "As long as interest rates are coming down, we're not going to push it [the Balanced Monetary Policy Act of 1982]" (as quoted in Greider 1987, p. 514).

Despite Reagan's anti-inflation stance, his administration, through White House Chief of Staff James Baker, pressured the Fed for monetary easement ahead of the 1982 elections with the threat that the administration may support one of the pieces of legislation (Meltzer 2009b, p. 1109). As Meltzer (2009b, pp. 1111–1112) writes, the Fed "Caught between the two positions – political pressures, legislator threats, and fear of a crisis on one side and concern for their credibility and the need to maintain the appearance of independence on the other ... made a fist small change in policy to lower rates." Delivering monetary easement ahead of the election (Kettl 1986, pp. 181–183), Alan Meltzer (as quoted in Farnsworth 1982) observed, "Here we go again. It used to be that we would have bulges in the money supply every Presidential election year, but now we're getting them every two years for the Congressional elections as well."

Later on, in his presidency, President Reagan's inability to slow the pace of spending led to deficits that frustrated the anti-inflation goals of the Fed. Writing in the *New York Times*, economist Thomas Sargent (1983) wrote,

> Neil Wallace, an economist, has observed that monetary and fiscal authorities seem to have been playing chicken over the past two and a half years. The Federal Reserve resolved to stick to a policy that is feasible only if the budget is approximately balanced, while Congress and the executive branch together have determined prospects for taxes and spending that are feasible only if the central bank eventually becomes passive and accommodating. With such mutually infeasible prospects, all that is certain is that one side or the other must eventually give in.

While Chairman Volcker tried to pursue a tighter course of monetary policy, when it came to the presidential reelection, President Reagan's appointees to the Board of the Governors, including Vice Chairman Manuel H. Johnson, were able to mount a successful dissent against him and pursue monetary easement (Havrilesky and Katz 1992, p. 108; Silber 2012, p. 256; Winder 1992, pp. 297–298; Woodward 2000, p. 18). Frustrated with Volcker's uncooperativeness, President Reagan replaced him in 1987 with someone who had served as his unofficial advisor for years (Havrilesky 1995a, p. 69; Greider 1987, pp. 542, 570–571), Alan Greenspan. Chairman Greenspan duly delivered policies that supported President Reagan's administration (Havrilesky 1995a, pp. 174–176).

When President Clinton was elected, Greenspan flew out to meet with him to seek protection from the legislative threats to make all the FOMC members political appointees (Auerbach 2008, p. 154). As Chairman, Greenspan met regularly with the Treasury Secretary Robert Rubin and Deputy Secretary Lawrence Summers to coordinate policy (Greenspan 2007, p. 160; Rubin and Weisberg 2004, p. 9). According to Woodward (2000, p. 118), Greenspan even timed an interest rate hike so that it would not have an effect right before the election. At his reappointment, Greenspan (2007, p. 163) recalls President Clinton making a statement that "wasn't hard to read between the lines . . . he was asking for faster growth, higher wages, and new jobs." These easy monetary policies likely cleared the way for excessively loose money during the early 2000s, which contributed to the housing bubble and financial crisis (Iacoviello and Neri 2010; Rajan 2010, pp. 15, 108–117; Taylor 2009).[15]

As described in Chapter 1, the 2007–2008 financial crisis saw the unofficial and official expansion of the powers of the Fed under political influence and accommodation pressures (Beckworth 2012; Epstein and Carrick-Hagenbarth 2011; Horwitz 2012; Taylor 2009). In the heat of the crisis, independence and long-term monetary stability were sacrificed to fight the recession. As Stephen Axilrod (2011, p. 10) wrote, "as shown in the Fed's use of the discount window for emergency loans to nonbanks during the great credit crisis, the support and participation of the U.S. Treasury seemed desirable to demonstrate political unity in programs that placed the U.S. budget at risk and raised major political and social issues of fairness and equity."

Unsatisfied with the size and extent of the interventions, members of Congress took the opportunity of the crisis to introduce legislation that would have given the votes of the Federal Reserve Bank presidents to political appointees (Mishkin 2011a). Mishkin (2011b, p. 66) observed that "purchase of long-term government bonds has raised concerns that the Fed is willing to accommodate profligate fiscal policy by monetizing government debt, and this does have the potential to cast inflation expectations adrift without an anchor, which could have inflationary consequences in the future." Summarizing the actions of the Fed in response to the financial crisis, Meltzer (2009b) writes, "Under Mr. Bernanke, the Fed has sacrificed its independence and become the monetary arm of the Treasury: bailing out A.I.G., taking on illiquid securities from Bear Stearns and promising to provide as much as $700 billion of reserves

---

[15] The role of low interest rates in fueling the housing bubble is disputed in the literature. For a dissenting view, see Bernanke (2010b). Taylor (2010) critiques this rebuttal. Dokko et al. (2009) and Kuttner (2014) find a middle ground, suggesting that easy monetary policy had a modest influence.

to buy mortgages. Independent central banks don't do what this Fed has done." Similarly, John Taylor (2012, p. 92) writes,

When Bernanke replaced Greenspan in 2006, and especially in the months imme- diately before, during, and after the financial crisis in 2008, we saw monetary activism as it never had been seen before in the United States. Bernanke used the Fed's resources in a highly discretionary way to bail out creditors of financial firms. He coordinated with the administration and the Treasury to a degree that made William McChesney Martin look like a piker as he coordinated with the Johnson administration in the late 1960s. Bernanke expanded the Fed's portfolio by unpre- cedented amounts. He purchased huge amounts of mortgage-backed securities and massive amounts of Treasury securities.

The postcrisis operating system of the Fed has the potential to further reduce Fed independence by opening up its balance sheet for bailouts, infrastructure projects, and fiscal policy initiatives (Beckworth 2018b; Jordan and Luther 2019; Plosser 2018; Selgin 2018). While previously, under the corridor system, the Fed conducted open market operations to aim for an Effective Federal Funds Rate (EFFR) below its discount rate (the penalty rate for borrowing from the Fed) and above any interest paid on reserves. The introduction of Interest on Excess Reserves (IOER) created a new lower-bound rate, as no bank would accept an overnight lending rate lower than the rate the Fed was willing to pay them for maintaining excess reserves in their accounts at the Fed. In October 2008, the Fed, by setting the IOER above the FFR, transitioned from a corridor to a floor system with the IOER serving as the floor. As a result, the balance sheet of the Fed was effectively disconnected from interest rate targeting policies. One consequence is that the Fed's balance sheet can be expanded drastically to support fiscal initiatives, such as large infrastructure or transfer pro- grams, independent of interest rate policy (Selgin 2020). This is especially the case given that the IOER is set by the Board of Governors, all appoint- ees of the executive branch with confirmation by the Senate, not the entire Federal Open Market Committee, which includes representation from the Federal Reserve Bank presidents (Plosser 2018, p. 13). Mueller and Wojnilower (2016), furthermore, express concern that the discretion afforded to central bankers under the new operating system may under- mine the rule of law.

3.5 What It All Means

In this chapter, we have shown the political independence of the Fed is more myth than reality. Theory and history show that the Fed, throughout its modern history, has fallen prey to internal pressures and succumbed to external pressures. The significant incentive problems confronting monetary policymakers require us to be skeptical that the Fed can carry out its public interest mandate.

The ultimate source of the problem is the discretion granted to monetary authorities. This discretion, combined with the uncertainty inherent in macroeconomic stewardship, gives monetary policymakers too much leeway to interpret what their mandate is, how to understand the underlying conditions of the economy, and what tools and policies are properly within their purview. For these reasons, a pseudo-monetary rule that affords monetary policymakers discretion will result in these policymakers succumbing to bureaucratic inertia, political opportunism, or both. The only way to eliminate the incentive problem is to bind the hands of monetary authorities with a true monetary rule. Such a rule must not be modifiable by the Fed and would require an external enforcement mechanism. Absent these two conditions, purported rules are no more than pseudo-rules. Continued adherence to pseudo-rules means we will continue to suffer the adverse effects of incentive misalignments in monetary policy.

References

Abrams, Burton (2006). How Richard Nixon Pressured Arthur Burns: Evidence from the Nixon Tapes. *Journal of Economic Perspectives*, 20(4), 177–188.

Alchian, Allen (1950). Uncertainty, Evolution, and Economic Theory. *Journal of Political Economy*, 58(3), 211–221.

Allen, Stuart and Michael Smith (1983). Government Borrowing and Monetary Accommodation. *Journal of Monetary Economics*, 12(4), 605–616.

Allen, Stuart (1986). The Fed and the Electoral Cycle: Note. *Journal of Money, Credit and Banking*, 18(1), 88–94.

Allison, John (2012). *The Financial Crisis and the Free Market Cure: How Destructive Banking Reform Is Killing the Economy*. McGraw-Hill.

Auerbach, Robert (1985). Politics and the Fed. *Contemporary Economic Policy*, 3(5), 43–58.

(1991). Institutional Preservation at the Federal Reserve. *Contemporary Economic Policy*, 9(3), 46–58.

(2008). *Deception and Abuse at the Fed: Henry B. Gonzalez Battles Alan Greenspan's Bank*. University of Texas Press.

Axilrod, Stephen H. (2011). *Inside the Fed*. The MIT Press.

Bach, George (1971). *Making Monetary and Fiscal Policy*. Brookings Institution.

Ball, Laurence (2008). Helicopter Drops and Japan's Liquidity Trap. *Monetary and Economic Studies*, 26(December), 87–106.

(2016). Ben Bernanke and the Zero Bound. *Contemporary Economic Policy*, 34(1), 7–20.

Ballhaus, Rebecca, Andrew Restuccia, and Paul Kiernan (2019). Trump Calls for a Big Fed Rate Cut, Again Criticizes Central Bank Chairman. *The Wall Street Journal*, August 19. Available online (accessed August 20, 2019), www.wsj.com/articles/ trump-calls-for-a-big-fed-rate-cut-again-criticizes-central-bank-chairman-11566230832

Barro, Robert (1978). Comment from an Unreconstructed Ricardian. *Journal of Monetary Economics*, 4(3), 569–581.

(1982). United States Inflation and the Choice of Monetary Standard. In Robert E. Hall (Ed.), *Inflation: Causes and Effects*. University of Chicago Press, pp. 99–110.

Barron, C. W. (1914). *The Federal Reserve Act*. Boston New Bureau Company.

Bassetto, Marco and Thomas J. Sargent (2020). Shotgun Wedding: Fiscal and Monetary Policy. NBER Working Paper No. 27004. Available online (accessed May 27, 2020), www.nber.org/papers/w27004

Beck, Nathaniel (1982). Presidential Influence on the Fed in the 1970s. *American Journal of Political Science*, 26(3), 415–445.

(1984). Domestic Political Sources of American Monetary Policy: 1955–1982. *Journal of Politics*, 46(3), 786–817.

(1987). Elections and the Fed: Is There a Political Monetary Cycle? *American Journal of Political Science*, 31(1), 194–216.

Becker, Gary. (2007). *Economic Theory* (2nd Edition). Routledge.

Beckworth, David (Ed.) (2012). *Boom and Bust Banking: The Causes and Cures of the Great Recession*. The Independent Institute.

Beckworth, David (2018a). Donald Trump's Real Influence on Fed Policy. *Alt-M*. August 15. Available online (accessed May 28, 2020), www.alt-m.org/2018/08/ 15/donald-trumps-real-influence-on-fed-policy/

(2018b). The Great Divorce: The Federal Reserve's Move to a Floor System and the Implications for Bank Portfolios. Mercatus Center at George Mason University. Available online (accessed September 4, 2019), www.mercatus.org/system/files/ beckworth-great-divorce-mercatus-research-v6.pdf

Bell, Stephanie (2000). Do Taxes and Bonds Finance Government Spending? *Journal of Economic Issues*, 34(3), 603–620.

Bernanke, Ben (2002). On Milton Friedman's Ninetieth Birthday. Remarks at the Conference to Honor Milton Friedman. University of Chicago, Chicago. November 8. Available online (accessed July 10, 2019), www.federalreserve.gov/ BOARDDOCS/SPEECHES/2002/20021108/

(2003). "Constrained Discretion" and Monetary Policy. Remarks before the Money Marketeers of New York University, New York. February 3. Available online (accessed May 31, 2019), www.federalreserve.gov/boarddocs/speeches/2003/ 20030203/default.htm#fn4

(2010a). Central Bank Independence, Transparency, and Accountability. Speech at the Institute for Monetary and Economic Studies International Conference at the Bank of Japan, Tokyo, Japan. Available online (accessed May 16, 2019), www .federalreserve.gov/newsevents/speech/bernanke20100525a.htm

(2010b). Monetary Policy and the Housing Bubble. Speech given at the Annual Meeting of the American Economic Association. January 3, Atlanta, GA.

Available online (accessed June 1, 2020), www.federalreserve.gov/newsevents/speech/bernanke20100103a.htm

(2013). *The Federal Reserve and the Financial Crisis*. Princeton University Press.

Bernanke, Ben, Thomas Lauback, Frederic Mishkin, and Adam Posen (2001). *Inflation Targeting: Lessons from the International Experience*. Princeton University Press.

Bernanke, Ben and Frederic Mishkin (1997). Inflation Targeting: A New Framework for Monetary Policy? *Journal of Economic Perspectives*, 11(2), 97–116.

Bernstein, Jake (2014). Inside the New York Fed: Secret Recordings and a Culture Clash. ProPublica. September 26. Available online (accessed November 7, 2019), www.propublica.org/article/carmen-segarras-secret-recordings-from-inside-new-york-fed

Binder, Sarah and Mark Spindel (2017). *The Myth of Independence: How Congress Governs the Federal Reserve*. Princeton University Press.

Blinder, Alan (1982). Issues in the Coordination of Monetary and Fiscal Policy. Monetary Policy Issues in the 1980s [Symposium Sponsored by the Fed Bank of Kansas City]. Available online (accessed May 29, 2020), www.kansascityfed.org/publicat/sympos/1982/S82.pdf

(1983). On the Monetization of Deficits. In Laurence H. Meyer (Ed.), *The Economic Consequences of Government Deficits*. Economic Policy Conference Series, volume 2. Springer, pp. 39–73.

(2000). Central-Bank Credibility: Why Do We Care? How Do We Build It? *The American Economic Review*, 90(5), 1421–1431.

(2010). How Central Should the Central Bank Be? *Journal of Economic Literature*, 48 (1), 123–133.

(2019). A New Tactic in Trump's War on the Fed. *The Wall Street Journal*. July 15.

Boettke, Peter J. and Christopher J. Coyne (2009). Context Matters: Institutions and Entrepreneurship. *Foundations and Trends in Entrepreneurship*, 5(3), 135–209.

Boettke, Peter J. and Daniel Smith (2013). Federal Reserve Independence: A Centennial Review. *Journal of Prices & Markets*, 1(1), 31–48.

Bordo, Michael and Edward Prescott (2019). Federal Reserve Structure, Economic Ideas, and Monetary and Financial Policy. The National Bureau of Economic Research Working Paper No. 26098. Available online (accessed August 1, 2019), www.nber.org/papers/w26098#fromrss

Boyes, William, Williams Stewart Mounts, and Clifford Sowell (1988). The Federal Reserve as a Bureaucracy: An Examination of Expense-Preference Behavior. *Journal of Money, Credit and Banking*, 20(2), 181–190.

Bradley, Michael (1985). Federal Deficits and the Conduct of Monetary Policy. *Journal of Macroeconomics*, 6(4), 411–431.

Buchanan, James (2008). Same Players, Different Game: How Better Rules Make Better Politics. *Constitutional Political Economy*, 19(3), 171–179.

Buchanan, James and Richard Wagner (1977 [2000]). *Democracy in Deficit*. Liberty Fund, Inc.

Burck, Gilbert (1959). A New Kind of Stock Market. *Fortune*, March, 120–121, 199, 201.

Caballero, Ricardo and Emmanuel Farhi (2018). The Safety Trap. *Review of Economic Studies*, 85(1), 223–274.

Calabria, Mark (2012, March 27). Wall Street's Seat at the Fed? *Cato@Liberty*. Available online (accessed June 1, 2020), www.cato-at-liberty.org/wall-streets-seat-at-the-federal-reserve/

Canzoneri, Matthew, Robert Cumby, and Behzad Diba (2011). The Interaction between Monetary and Fiscal Policy. In Benjamin M. Friedman and Michael Woodford (Eds.), *Handbook of Monetary Economics*, volume 3B. North-Holland, pp. 935–999.

Caplan, Bryan (2009, March). Two Mea Culpas. *EconLog*. Library of Economics and Liberty. Available online (accessed May 28, 2020), http://econlog.econlib.org/archives/2009/03/two_mea_culpas.html

(2012, February 18). The Mystery of Bernanke Solved, *EconLog*. Library of Economics and Liberty. Available online (accessed May 28, 2020), http://econlog.econlib.org/archives/2012/02/the_mystery_of_2.html

Caporale, Tony and Kevin Grier (1998). A Political Model of Monetary Policy with Application to the Real Fed Funds Rate. *Journal of Law and Economics*, 41(2), 409–428.

(2005a). How Smart Is My Dummy? Time Series Tests for the Influence of Politics. *Political Analysis*, 13(1), 77–94.

(2005b). Inflation, Presidents, Fed Chairs, and Regime Shifts in the U.S. Real Interest Rate. *Journal of Money, Credit and Banking*, 37(6), 1153–1163.

Cargill, Thomas and Gerald O'Driscoll Jr. (2013). Federal Reserve Independence: Reality or Myth? *Cato Journal*, 33(3), 417–435.

Chappell, Henry, Thomas Havrilesky, and Rob Roy McGregor (1993). Partisan Monetary Policies: Presidential Influence through the Power of Appointment. *The Quarterly Journal of Economics*, 108(1), 185–218.

Chappell, Henry, Rob Roy McGregor, and Todd Vermilyea (2005). *Committee Decisions on Monetary Policy: Evidence from Historical Records of the Federal Open Market Committee*. The MIT Press.

Clifford, Jerome (1965). *The Independence of the Fed System*. University of Pennsylvania Press.

Clymer, Adam (1982). Kennedy Urges End to Federal Reserve Autonomy. *New York Times*. April 7.

Condon, Christopher (2019). Here's a Timeline of All Trump's Key Quotes on Powell and the Fed. *Bloomberg*. June 11. Available online (accessed July 1, 2019), www.bloomberg.com/news/articles/2019-06-11/all-the-trump-quotes-on-powell-as-fed-remains-in-the-firing-line

Conti-Brown, Peter (2015). The Institutions of Federal Reserve Independence. *Yale Journal on Regulation*, 32(2), 257–310.

Cullity, John (1992). Arthur F. Burns (1904–1987). In Bernard S. Katz (Ed.), *Biographical Dictionary of the Board of Governors of the Federal Reserve*. Greenwood Press, pp. 38–49.

Dokko, James, Brian Doyle, Michael Kiley, Jinill Kim, Shane Sherlund, Jae Sim, and Skander Van den Heuvel (2009). Monetary Policy and the Housing Bubble. Finance and Economics Discussion Series No. 49. Washington, DC: Board of Governors of the Federal System. December 22. Available online (accessed June 8, 2020), www.federalreserve.gov/pubs/feds/2009/200949/200949pap.pdf

Drazen, Allan (2000). The Political Business Cycle after 25 Years. *NBER Macroeconomics Annual*, 15, 75–117.

(2005). "Lying Low" during Elections: Political Pressure and Monetary Accommodation. University of Maryland Working Paper. Available online (accessed June 8, 2020), http://econweb.umd.edu/~drazen/Lying%20Low102005ee.pdf

Dudley, Bill (2019). The Fed Shouldn't Enable Donald Trump. *Bloomberg Opinion*. August 27. Available online (accessed September 4, 2019), www.bloomberg.com/opinion/articles/2019-08-27/the-fed-shouldn-t-enable-donald-trump

Ehrmann, Michael and Marcel Fratzscher (2011). Politics and Monetary Policy. *Review of Economics and Statistics*, 93(3), 941–960.

Eichengreen, Barry (2010, March 26). The Last Temptation of Risk. *The National Interest* (May–June). Available online (accessed July 10, 2019), http://nationalinterest.org/article/the-last-temptation-of-risk-3091

Ellis, Michael and Eric Schansberg (2000). The Determinants of Tenures on the Federal Reserve Board of Governors: Should I Stay or Should I Go? *Applied Economics*, 32 (2), 231–237.

Engen, Eric and Glenn Hubbard (2005). Federal Government Debt and Interest Rates. In Mark Gertler and Kenneth Rogoff (Eds.), *NBER Macroeconomics Annual*, volume 19. The MIT Press, pp. 83–160.

English, William, Christopher Erceg, and David Lopez-Salido (2017). Money-Financed Fiscal Programs: A Cautionary Tale. Hutchins Center Working Paper No. 31.

Epstein, Gerald and Jessica Carrick-Hagenbarth (May 2011). Avoiding Group Think and Conflicts of Interest: Widening the Circle of Central Bank Advice. *Central Banking Journal*, 21(4), 61–68.

(2012). Dangerous Interconnectedness: Economists' Conflicts of Interest, Ideology and Financial Crisis. *Cambridge Journal of Economics*, 36(1), 43–63.

Epstein, Gerald and Juliet Schor (2003). Corporate Profitability as a Determinant of Restrictive Monetary Policy: Estimates for the Postwar United States. In Thomas Mayer (Ed.), *The Political Economy of American Monetary Policy*. Cambridge University Press, pp. 49–62.

European Central Bank. (2011). Protocol on the Statute of the European System of Central Banks and of the European Central Bank. Available online (accessed May 28, 2020), www.ecb.europa.eu/ecb/legal/pdf/en_statute_2.pdf

Evans, Paul (1985). Do Large Deficits Produce High Interest Rates? *The American Economic Review*, 75(1), 68–87.

Fand, David I. (1986). Fed Hegemony and Monetary Surprises. *Cato Journal*, 6(2), 581–586.

Farnsworth, Clyde H. (1982). Monetarists Divided on Fed's Stand. *New York Times*, October 12. Section D, p. 1, Column 3.

Faust, Jon and John Irons (1999). Money, Politics, and the Post-War Business Cycle. *Journal of Monetary Economics*, 43(1), 61–89.

Federal Reserve (2020). Review of Monetary Policy Strategy, Tools, and Communications. Updated May 12, 2020. Available online (accessed May 27, 2020), www.federalreserve.gov/monetarypolicy/review-of-monetary-policy-strategy-tools-and-communications.htm

Ferrell, Robert (Ed.) (1981). *The Eisenhower Diaries*. W. W. Norton.

Freedman, Charles, Michael Kumhof, Douglas Laxton, Dirk Muir, and Susanna Mursula (2010). Global Effects of Fiscal Stimulus during the Crisis. *Journal of Monetary Economics*, 57(5), 506–526.

Friedman, Milton (1970a). A New Chairman at the Fed. *Newsweek*. February 2.

(1970b). Burns and Guidelines. *Newsweek*, 86. June 15.

(1978). Burns on the Outside. *Newsweek*. January 9.

(1982). Monetary Policy: Theory and Practice. *Journal of Money, Credit and Banking*, 14(1), 98–118.

Friedman, Milton and Anna Schwartz (1963). *A Monetary History of the United States, 1863–1960*. Princeton University Press.

Froyen, Richard, Thomas Havrilesky, and Roger Waud (1997). The Asymmetric Effects of Political Pressures on US Monetary Policy. *Journal of Macroeconomics*, 19(3), 471–493.

Froyen, Richard and Roger Waud (2002). The Determinants of Fed Policy Actions: A Re-Examination. *Journal of Macroeconomics*, 24(3), 413–428.

Gandrud, Christopher and Cassandra Grafström (2012). Does Presidential Partisanship Affect Fed Inflation Forecasts? APSA 2012 Annual Meeting Paper. Available online (accessed June 8, 2020), https://papers.ssrn.com/sol3/papers.cfm?abstract_id=2105301

Gildea, John A. (1993). Explaining FOMC Members' Votes. In Thomas Mayer (Ed.), *The Political Economy of American Monetary Policy*. Cambridge University Press, pp. 211–228.

Gode, Dhananjay and Shyam Sunder (1993). Allocative Efficiency of Markets with Zero-Intelligence Traders: Market as a Partial Substitute for Individual Rationality. *Journal of Political Economy*, 101(1), 119–137.

Government Accountability Office (2011). Federal Reserve Bank Governance: Opportunities Exist to Broaden Director Recruitment Efforts and Increase Transparency. United States Government Accountability Office. Available online (accessed July 16, 2019), www.sanders.senate.gov/imo/media/doc/d1218%20(2).pdf

Grier, Kevin B. (1987). Presidential Elections and Fed Policy: An Empirical Test. *Southern Economic Journal*, 54(2), 475–486.

(1989). On the Existence of a Political Monetary Cycle. *American Journal of Political Science*, 33(2), 376–389.

Grier, Kevin (1991). Congressional Influence on U.S. Monetary Policy: An Empirical Test. *Journal of Monetary Economics*, 28(2), 201–220.

(1996). Congressional Oversight Committee Influence on U.S. Monetary Policy Revisited. *Journal of Monetary Economics*, 38(3), 571–579.

Grier, Kevin and Howard Neiman (1987). Deficits, Politics and Money Growth. *Economic Inquiry*, 25(2), 201–214.

Grim, Ryan (2009, October 23). Priceless: How the Fed Bought the Economics Profession. *Huffington Post*. Available online (accessed June 1, 2020), www.huffingtonpost.com/2009/09/07/priceless-how-the-federal_n_278805.html

Greenspan, Alan (1988, February 2). Testimony before the United States Senate Committee on Banking, Housing and Urban Affairs. Available online (accessed May 28, 2020), https://fraser.stlouisfed.org/files/docs/historical/greenspan/Greenspan_19880202.pdf

(2007). *The Age of Turbulence*. The Penguin Press.

Greider, William (1987). *Secrets of the Temple: How the Federal Reserve Runs the Country*. Random House.

Hamburger, Michael and Burton Zwick (1981). Deficits, Money and Inflation. *Journal of Monetary Economics*, 7(1), 141–150.

Hakes, David (1990). The Objective and Priorities of Monetary Policy under Different Fed Chairmen. *Journal of Money, Credit and Banking*, 22(3), 327–337.

Harris, Ethan (2008). *Ben Bernanke's Fed*. Harvard University Press.

Harrison, William (1991). Fed District Directors: Support System for a Public Institution. *Journal of Economics and Business*, 43(3), 271–282.

Havrilesky, Thomas (1987). A Partisanship Theory of Fiscal and Monetary Regimes. *Journal of Money, Credit and Banking*, 19(3), 308–325.

(1988). Monetary Policy Signaling from the Administration to the Federal Reserve. *Journal of Money, Credit and Banking*, 20(1), 83–101.

(1990). The Influence of the Federal Advisory Council on Monetary Policy. *Journal of Money, Credit and Banking*, 22(1), 37–50.

(1993). The Politicization of Monetary Policy: The Vice Chairman as the Administration's Point Man. *Cato Journal*, 13(1), 137–142.

(1995a). *The Pressures on American Monetary Policy* (2nd Edition). Kluwer Academic Publishers.

Havrilesky, Thomas and John Gildea (1990). Packing the Board of Governors. *Challenge*, 33(2), 52–55.

(1991). The Policy Preferences of FOMC Members as Revealed by Dissenting Votes: Comment. *Journal of Money, Credit and Banking*, 23(1), 130–138.

(1992). Reliable and Unreliable Partisan Appointees to the Board of Governors. *Public Choice*, 73(4), 397–417.

Havrilesky, Thomas and Bernard S. Katz (1992). Alan Greenspan (1926–). In, Bernard S. Katz (Ed.), *Biographical Dictionary of the Board of Governors of the Fed*. Greenwood Press, pp. 103–113.

Havrilesky, Thomas, Henry Chappell, John Gildea, and Rob McGregor (1993). Congress Threatens the Fed. *Challenge*, 36(2): 50–57.

Havrilesky, Thomas, William Yohe, and David Schirm (1973). The Economic Affiliations of Directors of Federal Reserve Banks. *Social Science Quarterly*, 54(4), 608–622.

Hein, Scott (1981). Deficits and Inflation. *Review of the Federal Reserve Bank of St. Louis*, 63(3), 3–10.

Hellerstein, Rebecca (2007). Is There a Dead Spot? New Evidence on FOMC Decisions before Elections. *Journal of Money, Credit and Banking*, 39(6), 1411–1427.

Hess, Gregory and Cameron Shelton (2016). Congress and the Federal Reserve. *Journal of Money, Credit and Banking*, 48(4), 603–633.

Hetzel, Robert (2008). *The Monetary Policy of the Federal Reserve: A History*. Cambridge University Press.

Hetzel, Robert and Ralph Leach (2001). The Treasury-Federal Reserve Accord: A New Narrative Account. *Federal Reserve Bank of Richmond Economic Quarterly*, 87(1), 33–55.

Hibbs, Douglas (1977). Political Parties and Macroeconomic Policy. *American Political Science Review*, 71(4), 1467–1487.

(1987). *The American Political Economy: Macroeconomics and Electoral Politics.* Harvard University Press.

Hogan, Thomas, Linh Le, and Alexander William Salter (2015). Ben Bernanke and Bagehot's Rules. *Journal of Money, Credit and Banking,* 47(2–3), 333–348.

Horwitz, Steven (2012). Causes and Cures of the Great Recession. *Economic Affairs,* 32 (3), 65–69.

Hyman, Sidney (1976). *Marriner S. Eccles: Private Entrepreneur and Public Servant.* Stanford University Press.

Iacoviello, Matteo and Stefano Neri (2010). Housing Market Spillovers: Evidence from an Estimated DSGE Model. *American Economic Journal: Macroeconomics,* 2(2), 125–164.

Igan, Deniz, Prachi Mishra, and Thierry Tressel (2012). A Fistful of Dollars: Lobbying and the Financial Crisis. *NBER Macroeconomics Annual,* 26(1), 195–230.

Ioannidis, John, T. Stanley, and Chris Doucouliagos (2017). The Power of Bias in Economics Research. *The Economic Journal,* 127(605), F236–F265.

Johnson, Lyndon (1967). State of the Union Address. January 10, 1967, Washington, DC. Available online (accessed August 5, 2019), https://millercenter.org/the-presi dency/presidential-speeches/january-10-1967-state-union-address

Jordan, Jerry and William Luther (2019). Central Bank Independence and the Federal Reserve's New Operating Regime. AIER Sound Money Project Working Paper No. 2019-07.

Kane, Edward (1974). The Re-politicization of the Fed. *Journal of Financial and Quantitative Analysis,* 9(5), 743–752.

(1980). Politics and Federal Reserve Policymaking: The More Things Change the More they Remain the Same. *Journal of Monetary Economics,* 6(2), 199–211.

(1993). Bureaucratic Self-Interest as an Obstacle to Monetary Reform. In Thomas Mayer (Ed.), *The Political Economy of American Monetary Policy.* Cambridge University Press, pp. 283–298.

Keech, William (1995). *Economic Politics: The Costs of Democracy.* Cambridge University Press.

Keech, William and Irwin Morris (1997). Appointments, Presidential Power, and the Federal Reserve. *Journal of Macroeconomics,* 19(2), 253–267.

Kettl, Donald (1986). *Leadership at the Fed.* Yale University Press.

Kirman, Alan (1992). Whom or What Does the Representative Individual Represent? *Journal of Economic Perspectives,* 6(2), 117–136.

Klein, Aaron and Olivia Weiss (2015). Reform the Fed? Get Rid of Groupthink. Bipartisan Policy Center Blog. April 7. Available online (accessed July 10, 2019), https://bipartisanpolicy.org/blog/reform-the-fed-get-rid-of-groupthink/

Krause, George (1994). Fed Policy Decision Making: Political and Bureaucratic Influences. *Journal of Political Science,* 38(1), 124–144.

Kuttner, Kenneth (2014). Low Interest Rates and Housing Bubbles: Still No Smoking Gun. In Willem H. Buiter, (Ed.), *The Role of Central Banks in Financial Stability: Has It Changed?* World Scientific, pp. 159–185.

Laney, Leroy and Thomas Willett (1983). Presidential Politics, Budget Deficits, and Monetary Policy in the United States; 1960–1976. *Public Choice,* 40(1), 53–69.

Laubach, Thomas (2009). New Evidence on the Interest Rate Effects of Budget Deficits and Debt. *Journal of the European Economic Association,* 7(4), 858–885.

Luckett, Dudley G. and Glenn T. Potts (1980). Monetary Policy and Partisan Politics: Note. *Journal of Money, Credit and Banking*, 12(3), 540–546.

Luther, William (2019). Stephen Morre, Herman Cain, and the Myth of Independence. American Institute for Economic Research. Thursday, April 11. Available online (accessed July 1, 2019), www.aier.org/article/sound-money-project/stephen-moore-herman-cain-and-myth-independence

Maier, Philipp (2002). Rhetoric and Action: What Are Central Banks Doing During Elections? *Public Choice*, 112(3/4), 235–258.

Maisel, Sherman J. (1973). *Managing the Dollar: An Inside View by a Recent Governor of the Fed Board.* W. W. Norton & Company, Inc.

Mallaby, Sebastian (2016). *The Man Who Knew: The Life and Times of Alan Greenspan.* Penguin Press.

Maloney, Kevin J. and Michael L. Smirlock (1981). Business Cycles and the Political Process. *Southern Economic Journal*, 48(2), 377–392.

Mankiw, Gregory (2006). The Macroeconomist as Scientist and Engineer. *Journal of Economic Perspectives*, 20(4), 29–46.

Marcussen, Martin (2006). Transnational Governance Network of Central bankers. In Marie-Lauri Djelic and Kerstin Sahlin-Andersson (Eds.), *Transnational Governance Institutional Dynamics of Regulation.* Cambridge University Press, pp. 180–204.

Mayer, Thomas (1993). Minimizing Regret: Cognitive Dissonance as an Explanation of FOMC Behavior. In Thomas Mayer (Ed.), *The Political Economy of American Monetary Policy.* Cambridge University Press, pp. 241–254.

McCloskey, Deirdre and Stephen Ziliak (1996). The Standard Error of Regressions. *Journal of Economic Literature*, 34(1), 97–114.

McMillin, Douglas (1981). A Dynamic Analysis of the Impact of Fiscal Policy on the Money Supply: Note. *Journal of Money, Credit and Banking*, 13(2), 221–226.

McMillin, Douglas and Thomas Beard (1982). "Deficits, Money and Inflation": Comment. *Journal of Monetary Economics*, 10(2), 273–277.

McShane, Blakeley, David Gal, Andrew Gelman, Christian Robert, and Jennifer Tackett (2019). Abandon Statistical Significance. *The American Statistician*, 73(suppl. 1), 235–245.

Meade, Ellen and Nathan Sheets (2005). Regional Influences on FOMC Voting Patterns. *Journal of Money, Credit and Banking*, 37(4), 661–677.

Meiselman, David I. (1986). Is There a Political Monetary Cycle? *Cato Journal*, 6(2), 563–586.

Meltzer, Allan H. (2005). Origins of the Great Inflation. *Federal Reserve Bank of St. Louis Review*, 87(2, Part 2), 145–176.

(2009a). *A History of the Fed*, volume 2, Book 1, 1951–1969. The University of Chicago Press.

Meltzer, Alan H. (2009b). Inflation Nation. *The New York Times.* May 3. Available online (accessed July 21, 2020), www.nytimes.com/2009/05/04/opinion/04meltzer.html

Meyer, Laurence (2004). *A Term at the Fed: An Insider's View.* Collins.

Mishkin, Frederic S. (2011a). Politicians Are Threatening the Fed's Independence. *The Wall Street Journal.* September 29. Available online (accessed May 22, 2020), www.wsj.com/articles/SB10001424052970204831304576597200646525870

(2011b). Over the Cliff: From the Subprime to the Global Financial Crisis. *Journal of Economic Perspectives*, 25(1), 49–70.

Morris, Irwin (2002). *Congress, the President, and the Federal Reserve*. University of Michigan Press.

Mueller, Paul and Joshua Wojnilower (2016). The Federal Reserve's Floor System: Immediate Gain for Remote Pain? *Journal of Private Enterprise*, 31(2), 15–40.

Munger, Michael, and Brian Roberts. (1993). The Federal Reserve and Its Institutional Environment: A Review. In Thomas Mayer (Ed.), *The Political Economy of American Monetary Policy*. Cambridge University Press, pp. 83–98.

Newton, Maxwell (1983). *The Fed: Inside the Federal Reserve, the Secret Power Center that Controls the American Economy*. Times Books.

Niskanen, William (1978). Deficits, Government Spending, and Inflation: What Is the Evidence? *Journal of Monetary Economics*, 4(3), 591–602.

North, Douglass (1991). Institutions. *Journal of Economic Perspectives*, 5(1), 97–112.

Nozick, Robert (1974). *Anarchy, State, and Utopia*. Basic Books, Inc.

Ostrom, Elinor (2005). *Understanding Institutional Diversity*. Princeton University Press.

Plosser, Charles (2018). The Risks of a Fed Balance Sheet Unconstrained by Monetary Policy. In Michael Bordo, John Cochrane, and Amit Seru (Eds.), *The Structural Foundations of Monetary Policy*. Hoover Institution Press, pp. 1–16.

Potts, Glenn and Dudley Luckett. (1978). Policy Objectives of the Fed System. *Quarterly Journal of Economics*, 92(3), 525–534.

Puckett, Richard (1984). Federal Open Market Committee Structure and Decisions. *Journal of Monetary Economics*, 14(1), 97–104.

Rajan, Raghuram. (2010). *Fault Lines: How Hidden Fractures Still Threaten the World Economy*. Princeton University Press.

Reagan, Michael (1961). The Political Structure of the Fed System. *American Political Science Review*, 55(1), 64–76.

Reinhart, Carmen, Vincent Reinhart, and Kenneth Rogoff (2012). Public Debt Overhangs: Advanced-Economy Episodes since 1800. *Journal of Economic Perspectives*, 26(3), 69–86.

Reuss, Henry (1976). Fed Directors: A Study of Corporate and Banking Influence. Staff Report for the Committee on Banking, Currency and Housing. House of Representatives.

Rolnick, Arthur (1985). Research Activities and Budget Allocations among Fed Banks: Comment. *Public Choice*, 45(2), 193–195.

Romer, Paul (2016). The Trouble with Macroeconomics. Working Paper. Available online (accessed July 10, 2019), https://paulromer.net/trouble-with-macroeconomics-update/WP-Trouble.pdf

Rose, Sanford (1974). The Agony of the Federal Reserve. *Fortune*, July.

Rubin, Robert E. and Jacob Weisberg (2004). *In an Uncertain World: Tough Choices from Wall Street to Washington*. Random House.

Safire, William (1975). *Before the Fall: An Inside View of the Pre-Watergate Whitehouse*. Doubleday & Company, Inc.

Salter, Alexander William and William Luther (2019). Adaptation and Central Banking. *Public Choice*, 180(3–4), 243–256.

Salter, Alexander William and Daniel Smith (2019). Political Economists or Political Economists? The Role of Political Environments in the Formation of Fed Policy under Burns, Greenspan, and Bernanke. *Quarterly Review of Economics and Finance*, 71(1), 1–13.

Sargent, Thomas (1983). Confrontations over Deficits. *New York Times*, August 12.

Selgin, George (2016). Real and Pseudo Rules. *Cato Journal*, 36(2), 279–296.

(2018). *Floored!: How a Misguided Fed Experiment Deepened and Prolonged the Great Recession*. Cato Institute.

(2019). The Fed's Chicago Shindig. *Alt-M*. June 26. Available online (accessed July 10, 2019), www.alt-m.org/2019/06/26/the-feds-chicago-shindig/

(2020). *The Menace of Fiscal QE*. Cato Institute.

Shiller, Robert (2008, November 1). Challenging the Crowd in Whispers, Not Shouts. *New York Times*. Available online (accessed May 15 2020), www.nytimes.com/2008/11/02/business/02view.html?_r=1&pagewanted=print

Shughart II, William and Robert Tollison (1983). Preliminary Evidence on the Use of Inputs by the Fed System. *The American Economic Review*, 73(3), 291–304.

Silber, William (2012). *Volcker: The Triumph of Persistence*. Bloomsbury Press.

Smialek, Jeanna (2019). Trump's Feud with the Fed Is Rooted in Presidential History. *The New York Times*. June 24. Available online (accessed June 27, 2019), www.nytimes.com/2019/06/24/business/economy/federal-reserve-trump.html?smid=nytcore-ios-share

Smith, Adam (1776 [1976]). *An Inquiry into the Nature and Causes of the Wealth of Nations*. Liberty Fund, Inc.

Smith, Daniel J. and Peter J. Boettke (2015). An Episodic History of Modern Federal Reserve Independence. *The Independent Review: A Journal of Political Economy*, 20(1), 99–120.

Stigler, George (1971). The Theory of Economic Regulation. *Bell Journal of Economics and Management Science*, 2(1), 3–21.

Subcommittee on Domestic Finance, Committee on Banking and Currency (1964). A Primer on Money. House of Representatives 88th Congress, 2nd Session.

Taylor, John (2009). *Getting off Track: How Government Actions and Interventions Caused, Prolonged, and Worsened the Financial Crisis*. Stanford University Press.

(2010). The Fed and the Crisis: A Reply to Ben Bernanke. *The Wall Street Journal*. January 10. Available online (accessed May 15 2020), https://web.stanford.edu/~johntayl/2010_pdfs/Fed-Crisis-A-Reply-to-Ben-Bernanke-WSJ-Jan-10-2010.pdf

(2012). *First Principles: Five Keys to Restoring America's Prosperity*. W. W. Norton.

Thornton, Daniel (1984). Monetizing the Debt. *Economic Synopses, Federal Reserve Bank of St. Louis Review*, 66 (December), 30–43.

Timberlake, Richard (1993). *Monetary Policy in the United States: An Intellectual and Institutional History*. University of Chicago Press.

Timiraos, Nick (2019). Fed Chief Wedged between a Slowing Economy and an Angry President. *The Wall Street Journal*. August 18. Available online (accessed May 15 2020), www.wsj.com/articles/fed-chief-wedged-between-a-slowing-economy-and-an-angry-president-11566166246

Toma, Mark (1982). Inflationary Bias of the Fed System: A Bureaucratic Perspective. *Journal of Monetary Economics*, 10(2), 163–190.

Toma, Eugenia Froedge and Mark Toma (1985a). Research Activities and Budget Allocations among Fed Banks. *Public Choice*, 45(2), 175–191.

  (1985b). Research Activities and Budget Allocations among Fed Banks: Reply. *Public Choice*, 45(2), 197–198.

Tuccille, Jerome (2002). *Alan Shrugged*. John Wiley & Sons, Inc.

Tufte, Edward R. (1978). *Political Control of the Economy*. Princeton University Press.

Tymoigne, Eric (2014). Modern Money Theory, and Interrelations between the Treasury and Central Bank: The Case of the United States. *Journal of Economic Issues*, 48(3), 641–662.

Vencill, Daniel (1992). William McChesney Martin, Jr. (1906–). In Bernard S. Katz (Ed.), *Biographical Dictionary of the Board of Governors of the Federal Reserve*. Greenwood Press, pp. 192–210.

Volcker, Paul (1978). The Role of Monetary Targets in an Age of Inflation. *Journal of Monetary Economics*, 4(2), 329–339.

Volcker, Paul, Alan Greenspan, Ben Bernanke, and Janet Yellen (2019). America Needs an Independent Fed. *The Wall Street Journal*. August 5. Available online (accessed August 6, 2019), www.wsj.com/articles/america-needs-an-independent-fed-11565045308

Wallace, Myles and John Warner (1984). Fed Policy and Presidential Elections. *Journal of Macroeconomics*, 6(1), 79–88.

Waller, Christopher J. (1992). A Bargaining Model of Partisan Appointments to the Central Bank. *Journal of Monetary Economics*, 29(3), 411–428.

Wapshott, Nicholas. (2011). *Keynes Hayek: The Clash that Defined Modern Economics*. W. W. Norton.

Weintraub, Robert (1978). Congressional Supervision of Monetary Policy. *Journal of Monetary Economics*, 4(2), 341–362.

Weise, Charles (2008). Private Sector Influences on Monetary Policy in the United States. *Journal of Money, Credit and Banking*, 40(2–3), 449–462.

  (2012). Political Pressures on Monetary Policy during the US Great Inflation. *American Economic Journal: Macroeconomics*, 4(2), 33–64.

Wells, Wyatt C. (1994). *Economist in an Uncertain World: Arthur F. Burns and the Federal Reserve 1970–1978*. Columbia University Press.

Wessel, David. (2018). Report: Alternatives to the Fed's 2 Percent Inflation Target. Hutchins Center on Fiscal and Monetary Policy at Brookings. Available online (accessed May 25, 2020), www.brookings.edu/wp-content/uploads/2018/06/ES_20180607_Hutchins-FedInflationTarget.pdf

White, Lawrence (2005). The Federal Reserve System's Influence on Research in Monetary Economics. *Econ Journal Watch*, 2(2), 325–354.

Williams, John T. (1990). The Political Manipulation of Macroeconomic Policy. *The American Political Science Review*, 84(3), 767–795.

Williamson, Stephen (2019). The Fed's Operating Framework: How Does It Work and How Will It Change? *Cato Journal*, 39(2), 303–316.

Winder, Robert C. (1992). Martha Romayne Seger (1932–). In Bernard S. Katz (Ed.), *Biographical Dictionary of the Board of Governors of the Federal Reserve*. Greenwood Press, pp. 295–299.

Woodward, Bob (2000). *Maestro: Greenspan's Fed and the American Boom.* Simon & Schuster.

Woolley, John (1984). *Monetary Politics: The Fed and the Politics of Monetary Policy.* Cambridge University Press.

—— (1988). Partisan Manipulation of the Economy: Another Look at Monetary Policy with Moving Regression. *The Journal of Politics,* 50(2), 335–360.

Zingales, Luigi (2012). *A Capitalism for the People: Recapturing the Lost Genius of American Prosperity.* Basic Books.

When Firefighters Are Arsonists

4.1 Do Financial Crises Weaken the Case for Rules?

A sympathetic reader may grant us many of the arguments we have made thus far. Despite the supposed independence of central banks, monetary policy is subject to a host of incentive problems, many of which stem from de facto political influence. Monetary policy also suffers from a serious information problem. This is more than the technical difficulties of implementing monetary policy: It is a true knowledge problem, in that much of the knowledge necessary for the maintenance of monetary equilibrium (allocatively neutral demand stabilization) cannot be divorced from the market process that generates this knowledge. The argument for genuine monetary rules, as compared to constrained discretion, seems stronger than initially supposed.

But now we encounter what many regard as the Achilles' heel of monetary rules. Such rules may be able to cope well enough with economic fluctuations during ordinary times. But precisely because these rules are adequate to deal with *ordinary* macroeconomic events, they are by their nature unable to cope with *extraordinary* macroeconomic events. Chief among these are financial crises. While the ultimate source of financial crises is fiercely debated, there is a consensus among monetary and financial economists that such crises represent a severe breakdown in the ordinary, well-functioning channels between monetary policy and credit markets.

The 2007–2008 crisis was such an event. The seminal account remains Gorton (2010), who argues that the panic had the same general form as a traditional banking crisis, which happened to take place among non-(commercial) banking financial institutions. The transition from information insensitivity to information sensitivity of crucial financial instruments (both the ordinary, such as commercial loans, and the exotic, such as collateralized debt obligations backed by subprime mortgages) is a watershed moment in a developing panic. Once agents have an incentive to acquire private information regarding the balance sheets underpinning these securities, the assumption that financial institutions' assets are of sufficient value to back their liabilities no longer holds. The retreat to safer assets can place severe pressure on financial institutions, in terms of both liquidity and solvency. Should this process continue unchecked, the entire financial *system* may become insolvent. This has obvious deleterious consequences for economic activity: The malaise is never contained solely within credit and other financial markets but spills over into the market for final goods and services as well, since virtually all nonfinancial firms require a sound financial system to conduct their daily operations. Recessions that follow financial crises tend to be severe, in terms of both the drop in output and rise in unemployment (e.g., Jordà et al. 2013; Paul 2019; Reinhart and Rogoff 2009; see also Bordo and Haubrich 2017). Financial crises are incredibly difficult to predict. And while they often exhibit similar systemic-level patterns, how crises play out often depends on the specifics of the monetary financial institutions in place.

Because of this, we cannot bind the monetary authority to hard and fast rules. If we do not allow central banks wide leeway to combat financial panics, the contagion from such panics can cause the entire financial system to come to a screeching halt. Furthermore, there is significant theoretical support for the argument that financial turbulence affects output and employment through pathways other than the typical money supply/aggregate demand channel. Ben Bernanke (1981, 1983) famously argued that bank failures during the Great Depression contributed to the severity of that recession, not merely due to the contraction of the money supply but also due to the erosion of credit intermediation channels between banks. Goodhart (1985, 1987) echoes Bernanke's emphasis on the importance of relationships between borrowers and lenders. And Solow (1982) argued that central banks have a unique responsibility to maintain the integrity of the financial system. This interesting mix of supply- and demand-side considerations suggests that repeated interactions between financial market counterparties constitute valuable capital that economizes on transaction costs, in particular information costs.

Building on these foundations, the recent literature on "macroprudential" policy (e.g., Bernanke 2011; Galati and Moessner 2013; Hanson et al. 2011; Lim et al. 2011) takes the implications of the uniqueness and potential destructiveness of financial panics to their logical conclusions.

Bernanke (2011, p. 1) usefully summarizes the differences between this new literature and previous approaches to financial stability:

Ultimately, the goal of macroprudential supervision and regulation is to minimize the risk of financial disruptions that are sufficiently severe to inflict significant damage on the broader economy. The systemic orientation of the macroprudential approach may be contrasted with that of the traditional, or "microprudential," approach to regulation and supervision, which is concerned primarily with the safety and soundness of individual institutions, markets, or infrastructures.

In other words, a macroprudential approach to financial regulation and oversight focuses on properties of the financial system as a whole rather than specific financial institutions. Its toolkit includes countercyclical capital requirements, debt maturity regulation, and the extension of existing bank regulations to the "shadow banking" sector, which featured so prominently during the recent crisis (Galati and Moessner 2013; Hanson et al. 2011). Under this framework, the solution to the omnipresent specter of financial panic is more discretionary oversight. Central banks around the world, including the Fed, have greatly expanded the scale and scope of not only traditional monetary policy activities but oversight and regulatory activities as well. As such, they are well positioned to implement the kind of continuing supervision necessary to prevent nascent financial turmoil from developing into full-blown panic. Even if a monetary policy rule is a good idea for ordinary times, the challenge of the extraordinary means that discretion is not only a desirable but a necessary feature of any central bank. Thus, the insistence on constraining rules in financially turbulent times is not only counterproductive but dangerous.

In contrast, we hold that financial crises do not weaken the case for rules. If anything, crises *strengthen* the case for rules. Principles and rules should take priority during a crisis. As Hayek (1971) notes, when "we decide each issue solely on what appears to be its individual merits, we always overestimate the advantages of central direction. Our choice will regularly appear to be one between a certain known and tangible gain and the mere probability of the prevention of some unknown beneficial action by unknown persons." Although Hayek was defending principle against expediency in the abstract, his remarks encapsulate what is wrong with policy responses to financial crises.

First, we deny that financial crises require us to abandon price-theoretic thinking. We are against "triage economics" (Boettke and Palagashvili 2015), by which we mean the view that crises impel us to adopt fundamentally different theoretical paradigms and policymaking tools. Financial crises may have extraordinary consequences, but appreciating these consequences does not require discarding the economic way of thinking. By interpreting the events that constitute a crisis through the lens of ordinary economics – in a word, the basic tools of price theory – we can see that financial crises are often the predictable (in the sense of causally intelligible) result of bad incentives in the monetary and financial systems (Boettke and Luther 2010). Second, even assuming arguendo that financial crises present extraordinary challenges, it does not follow that those challenges are best met with extraordinary policy interventions. However much we may wish it otherwise, economic policy is not crafted and implemented in a vacuum. Policy is, by its nature, *political*, even when crafted by clever and public-spirited experts with economics PhDs. We need to take seriously the realization that, once we account for the kinds of stabilization policy that emerge from *actually existing* political processes, a "hidebound" approach that emphasizes rules rather than discretion may be the least socially costly response.

These are strong claims, and they require an equally strong defense. But before we can get to them, we need to spend a little time reviewing the orthodox strategy for handling financial panics, as well as how the Fed interpreted and applied those strategies during the darkest days of the 2007–2008 crisis. This will provide the necessary context for understanding just what we lose when we embrace a crisis mindset. Sound economic policy requires always applying the economic way of thinking, which means we cannot ignore the long-term institutional consequences of policy in favor of short-term stabilization consequences, no matter how urgent the latter seem. To the perpetual cry in the face of crisis, "We must do something!," the economist has a duty to remind those urgent to stem the tide that they must take account of both the seen and the unseen consequences of their behaviors (Bastiat 1850).

4.2 Financial Crises and the Lender of Last Resort

Both defenders of rules and supporters of discretion can agree on one thing: Conditional upon having a central bank, a wise response to financial crises will adhere to the last-resort lending principles made famous by Walter Bagehot in his analysis of the British money market, *Lombard Street*. While the idea behind the lender of last resort originated with Henry Thornton (1802), Bagehot (1873) provided the first systematically coherent account. Money typically takes the form of bank liabilities, which is an important link between the health of banks' balance sheets and overall liquidity.[1] This, in turn, affects the various monetary aggregates, and hence (in the short run) overall economic activity. Central banks are responsible for the quantity of money within the economic system, which implies they are uniquely capable of extending emergency loans to commercial banks during nascent panics. If done correctly, emergency lending can help banks that have become illiquid (short-term liabilities exceed short-term assets) but are still solvent (assets exceed liabilities). Without such lending, there is a serious risk that a liquidity problem, which is ultimately the central banks' responsibility, can evolve into an insolvency problem, over which central banks have much less control.

There are crucial institutional differences between central banking in Bagehot's day and our own. It may even be a misnomer to call the late nineteenth-century Bank of England a central bank, if by "central bank" we mean something that bears the same institutional properties as today's Fed. While the Bank of England enjoyed legal tender status for its notes, was the official bank of the British government, and eventually acquired a monopoly of note issue, it was in many ways a private institution. It existed under the constraints of a commodity money system and residual claimancy for the Bank of England's shareholders (Goodfriend 2012). Today, the Fed has a monopoly on the production of base money, unconstrained by specie, and its "shareholders" exercise few, if any, of the traditional prerogatives associated with residual claimancy and ownership.

These differences are important, especially when doing historical comparisons. But they do not undermine the *principles* bequeathed by Bagehot, which can be divorced from the institutional environment he first suggested and creatively reapplied in our own circumstances. Interestingly, Bagehot was not a fan of (proto-)central banking. He much preferred the Scottish system of "free banking" (cf. White 1995, 1999), in which banks were generally free of statutory regulation. Instead, banks were governed primarily by the general body of property, contract, and tort law. He expressed these sentiments forcefully in *Lombard Street*:

Nothing can be truer in theory than the economical principle that banking is a trade and only a trade, and nothing can be more surely established by a larger experience than that a Government which interferes with any trade injures that trade. The best thing undeniably that a Government can do with the Money Market is to let it take care of itself. (1873: IV.1)

---

[1] Importantly, the base money regime of the Bank of England was radically different than that of contemporary central banks. We discuss this further subsequently.

But given the existence of the Bank of England and its unique privileges, Bagehot preferred it to act in the public interest by discounting loans in instances of financial turmoil: "Theory suggests, and experience proves, that in a panic the holders of the ultimate Bank reserve (whether one bank or many) should lend to all that bring good securities quickly, freely, and readily. By that policy they allay a panic; by every other policy they intensify it" (VII.21). Bagehot recognized that this policy could be abused by irresponsible commercial banks who took on excessive amounts of risk. In order to disincentivize overly risky behavior by banks, he recommended lending freely at a penalty rate of interest – that is, higher than the market rate. If banks were aware ex ante that they would have to pay a premium for emergency liquidity, they would be more likely to refrain from activities that create the need for such liquidity in the first place. In this way, Bagehot anticipated moral hazard problems in modern financial systems: "In former quiet times the influence, or the partial influence, of that rule [of lending at low rates in times of crisis] has often produced grave disasters. In the present difficult times an adherence to it is a *recipe* for making a large number of panics" (XII.19, emphasis in original). Hence, a responsible lender of last resort must make "very large loans at very high rates" (ch.II.48).

Bagehot emphasized two other principles that underpin last-resort lending theory to this day. First, the lender of last resort, in addition to lending only to solvent banks, must do so only on good and familiar collateral. Loans "should be made on everything which in common times is good 'banking security'" (VII.72), but "the bank, or banks, holding the ultimate reserve should refuse bad bills or bad securities" (VII.59). Just as the penalty rate discourages ex ante opportunism, the good collateral requirement discourages ex post fraud. The good collateral requirement makes it very difficult for insolvent institutions to swim when by rights they should sink. After all, if their collateral were good, they would not be insolvent.

Second, the last-resort lending policy should be publicly announced in advance, to better anchor the expectations of financiers. "The public have a right to know," Bagehot insists, "whether the Bank of England – the holders of our ultimate bank reserve – acknowledge this duty, and are ready to perform it" (VII.21). If this policy is not credibly announced beforehand, "both our liability to crises and our terror at crises will always be greater than they would otherwise be" (VII.75). The logic is straightforward: If the central bank commits to lending at penalty rates solely on good collateral in difficult times, banks have an incentive not to engage in the kinds of behaviors that turn prosperous times into difficult times.

Bagehot's rules thus function in concert. Each pillar is supported by the two others. Failure to adhere to any one of the rules undermines the efficacy of the rest. Since Bagehot wrote, these principles have been restated and reformulated but never improved upon. Perhaps the best modern summary is Alan Meltzer's (1986, p. 83). Meltzer offers four rules of thumb that reflect Bagehot's principles and can be applied in the context of fully developed central banks:

1. Central banks should embrace their role as lenders of last resort.
2. Central banks should lend on "collateral that is marketable in the ordinary course of business."
3. Central banks ought to lend freely and fully, but at a rate above the market interest rate, in order to discourage moral hazard.
4. Central banks should publicly and credibly commit to this policy *before* a financial crisis begins.

There is a fascinating contrast between the accepted canons of lender of last resort *theory* and the actual behavior of lenders of last resort in *practice*. Among the developed world's central banks, the Fed is arguably the worst offender. Even before the 2007–2008 crisis, the Fed has never meaningfully adhered to Bagehot's principles, despite their overwhelming acceptance by economists. George Selgin (2012, p. 307) ably sums up the historical record of the Fed's emergency policies: "The Fed, for its part, appears unable to resist lending to insolvent banks." For example, in 1974, the Fed allowed Franklin National access to the discount window but did not charge a penalty rate. At one time Franklin National was the nation's twentieth-largest bank, with total deposits of $1.45 billion (Bordo 1990, p. 26). In 1984, the Fed extended emergency loans to Continental Illinois. The bank's managers argued that, because of its size and interconnectedness with other financial institutions, Continental Illinois could not be allowed to fail without risking a financial crisis. This was a watershed moment. It was the first time that bank managers' arguments for the systemic importance of their institutions, and by implication the risk of financial contagion, was accepted as a rationale for bailing out a commercial bank. Most scholars point to the Continental Illinois bailout for a relatively concrete point at which "too big to fail" becomes a de facto operating principle, which also meant, unfortunately, the institutionalization of moral hazard (cf. Miller and VanHoose 2007, pp. 233–234).

Also, the Fed was instrumental in securing a bailout for Long-Term Capital Management in 1998. While the liquidity injection came from private sources, the Fed's intermediary and coordinating role was noteworthy because the recipient was not a commercial bank but a hedge fund. The history of the Fed's bailout policies, capably analyzed in Robert Hetzel's (2008, ch. 16; 2012, ch. 9) works, suggests that these policies, at best, were in uncomfortable tension with the accepted best practices of last-resort lending.

4.3 Bernanke *contra* Bagehot? The Fed's Response to the 2007–2008 Crisis

But what about the most recent crisis? Perhaps the Fed, learning from its past behavior, more closely implemented Bagehot's rules this time around. Admittedly, the Fed did lend freely. The bailouts were unprecedented in magnitude (cf. Broz 2012; Fleming 2012), as befit the severity of the crisis. Nevertheless, the counterargument fails. Unless emergency lending is limited to illiquid yet solvent firms, this lending is a vice, not a virtue. The chief problem was that the *scope* of the Fed's practices was too wide. The *scale* cannot fix this fundamental error. It is clear the Fed rescued insolvent firms, picking winners and losers with no clear discriminating criteria. Ex-Fed Chairman Paul Volcker stated that "The Federal Reserve judged it necessary to take actions that extend to the very edge of its lawful and implied powers, transcending certain long-embedded principles and practices" (Volcker 2008, p. 2). Furthermore, the US Government Accountability Office (2011, p. 1) held that "the scale and nature of this assistance amounted to an unprecedented expansion of the Federal Reserve System's traditional role as a lender-of-last-resort to depository institutions." Yet despite this break from last-resort lending orthodoxy, Bernanke claimed repeatedly and publicly that the Fed's policies actually embodied that orthodoxy. In what follows we explore Bernanke's remarks on Fed policy, with particular emphasis on how he saw the Fed's actions as consistent with Bagehot's rules. We then demonstrate that the Fed's crisis response violated several of Bagehot's strictures.

On March 27, 2012, Ben Bernanke gave a lecture at George Washington University. The topic was the Fed's response to the financial crisis. During this talk, Bernanke asserted the Fed's policies were consistent with Bagehot's principles for responsible last-resort lending. Bernanke (2012, p. 10) noted that "in the financial panic, the central bank has to lend freely according to Bagehot's rules to halt runs and to try to stabilize the financial system." This required creating "a whole bunch of other programs, special liquidity and credit facilities that allowed us to make loans to other kinds of financial institutions, again, on the Bagehot principle that providing liquidity to firms that are suffering from loss of funding is the best way to calm a panic" (Bernanke 2012, p. 14). The main point of his remarks was, despite the unprecedented activities undertaken by the Fed, its policies nonetheless represented sound Bagehotian wisdom: "Once again, the Federal Reserve, responding in the way that Bagehot would have had us respond, established special programs. Basically, we stood as backstop lenders, we said: 'Make your loans to these companies, and we'll be here ready to backstop you if there's a problem rolling over these funds'" (Bernanke 2012, p. 19).

Both before and after this lecture, Bernanke repeated the claim that the Fed was a responsible lender of last resort according to Bagehot's principles. Bernanke (2008a, 2008b) presents a view of liquidity provision by central banks that is distinctly Bagehotian. And Bernanke (2010, p. 8) contains an explicit endorsement of Bagehot's principles on all major points, asserting that "in the recent episode, central banks around the world followed the dictum set forth by Bagehot in 1873: To avert or contain panics, central banks should lend freely to solvent institutions, against good collateral." As a final example, at the Fed's centennial celebration, Bernanke contended that the Fed under his leadership "responded as the 19th Century essayist Walter Bagehot had advised, by serving as liquidity provider of last resort to financial firms and markets" (Bernanke 2013).

Thus, Bernanke clearly saw the Fed's crisis response as a legitimate application of Bagehot's rules. But when we explore these policies in a little more depth, we realize that there are many problems with his claims (Hogan et al. 2015). First, the Fed did not clearly adhere to the prescription that emergency loans should be provided only at a penalty rate. Immediately prior to the crisis, the Fed's discount window rates were above the federal funds rate, which is consistent with the penalty rate rule. Up until July 2007, the discount rate was 6.25 percent, 100 basis points above the federal funds rate. But in late 2007, as the crisis unfolded, the Fed reduced the spread between these two rates, and extended emergency loans to a period of 30, and eventually 90, days. By March 18, 2008, the discount rate was 2.5 percent, only 25 basis points above the federal funds rate. It is important to note that this radically understates the Fed's discounting *activities*, since the traditional discount window was little used during the crisis (Selgin 2012, p. 310). Instead, the Fed created several facilities – the Term Auction Facility (TAF), the Primary Dealer and Other Broker-Dealer Credit Facility, and the Term Security Lending Facility (TSLF) – which in various ways skirted the bounds of acceptable last-resort lending behavior.

The second of these was essentially another discount window, for the advantage of primary dealers, with rates equal to those at the traditional window. But, unlike the traditional window, this facility provided significant volumes of loans, on risky assets besides. By December 2010, the largest borrowers were Citigroup, Goldman Sachs, Merrill Lynch, and Morgan Stanley. Each borrowed approximately $2 trillion, and total lending through this facility reached nearly $9 trillion (Selgin 2012, p. 311; Sheridan 2011, pp. 13–14). As for the TAF, funds were auctioned off, with the interest rate determined over the course of the auctions rather than being set at an explicit penalty rate. TAF also allowed investment banks to access the discount window, and TSLF allowed several private organizations that regularly served as the Fed's counterparties to unload (temporarily) their risky assets onto the Fed's balance sheet, in exchange for safe assets from the Fed.

Whether the Fed followed the penalty rate rule is thus, at best, murky. But its bailout policies were clearly contrary to the rule that specifies emergency liquidity should be extended to illiquid firms only. To preserve the health of the financial system, the Fed "felt obliged to rescue several primary dealers, *and to do so at the expense of solvent banks*" (Selgin 2012, p. 310, emphasis added).[2] The creation of Maiden Lane, an LLC under the purview of the New York Fed, to facilitate JPMorgan Chase's takeover of Bear Stearns was the first sign of the Fed's overstepping the bounds of last-resort lending orthodoxy.[3] The Fed also had a hand in Congress' passing of the Troubled Asset Relief Program (TARP), which provided $700 billion for direct bailouts: Timothy Geithner, who was then president of the New York Fed, played a crucial political-entrepreneurial role in facilitating this program (Stewart 2009). Given that politically engaged banks were more likely to receive TARP funds, received larger TARP support, and were

---

[2] On the issue of primary dealers, Selgin (2012, p. 311) continues,

> Because the Fed sterilized most of its subprime asset purchases, by reducing its Treasury holdings by over $250 billion and by having the Treasury increase its deposits at the Fed by about $300 billion, the purchases actually reduced the availability of liquid funds to solvent banks. In short, in propping up an operating system that was supposed to help it to act according to Bagehot's advice, the Fed found itself honoring that advice only in the breach.

[3] Volcker (2008, p. 2) condemned the Fed's response to the Bear Stearns episode: "What appears to be in substance a direct transfer of mortgage and mortgage-backed securities of questionable pedigree from an investment bank to the Federal Reserve seems to test the time honored central bank mantra in time of crisis – 'lend freely at high rates against good collateral' – to the point of no return."

aided faster than politically unengaged banks (Blau et al. 2013), the Fed's hand in this program is particularly concerning.

In September 2008, AIG received a bailout through the creation of structured investment vehicles (Maiden Lane II and III) similar to that used to implement the Bear Stearns bailout. The Fed continued to set up a plethora of new facilities and programs – the Commercial Paper Funding Facility, the Asset-Backed Commercial Paper Program, Money Market Mutual Fund Liquidity Facility, and the Term Asset-Backed Securities Loan Facility – to continue its efforts to stabilize key private institutions' balance sheets. Admittedly, the line between liquidity injections and direct credit allocation can be murky, especially in a crisis (Goodfriend 2011). But these behaviors are firmly on the side of resource allocation rather than market stabilization (Hummel 2012, pp. 186–189).

The Fed violated Bagehotian doctrine most flagrantly by trying to save insolvent firms. This was perhaps most obvious with the Citigroup and AIG bailouts: "The Fed ignored the classical advice never to accommodate unsound borrowers when it helped bail out insolvent Citigroup and AIG" (Humphrey 2010, p. 359). In conjunction with the FDIC and the Treasury, the Fed guaranteed $306 billion of Citigroup's loans and injected $20 billion into the company through TARP, with another $25 billion to follow (Federal Reserve et al. 2008). But market perceptions of Citigroup, in terms of its financial soundness, were decidedly unfavorable: "The market has voted and considers Citi (in terms of its common stock) insolvent. For some reason the government feels that with more taxpayer money and time the company's solvency problem will resolve itself" (Zwikel 2009). The same was true of AIG. The New York Fed granted AIG an $85 billion emergency loan in exchange for a 79.9 percent equity interest for the government (Federal Reserve 2008). But for these policies, AIG would have gone bankrupt (cf. Isidore 2013). Lender of last resort policy is supposed to be aimed at saving *solvent but illiquid* banks. Bernanke correctly noted that Bagehot's rules recommend lending freely. But they do *not* recommend lending indiscriminately, which is what the Fed did. The Fed's rescue of insolvent banks was categorically un-Bagehotian.

Equally unjustifiable on Bagehotian grounds was the Fed's various rounds of quantitative easing. In brief, the Fed targeted unusual assets on distressed firms' balance sheets in order to keep those firms solvent. The first round (QE1) involved purchasing mortgage-backed securities ($400 million), as well as commercial paper and other distressed assets ($250 million) from Bear Stearns and AIG. The second round (QE2), announced in November 2010, contained $600 million in Treasury securities purchases, which was less worrisome. But a few years later, the third round (QE3), announced in September 2012, committed to mortgage-backed securities purchases totaling $40 billion per month. Because the program was open-ended, this round earned the name of "QE infinity." Purchases eventually halted in October 2014, at which point the Fed's balance sheet totaled $4.5 trillion. Gokhale (2012), although writing before QE3, none-theless recognizes the essence of the QE programs: "The Fed's unpreced-ented earlier rounds of quantitative easing ... were designed to accommodate impaired assets with financial institutions, purchasing and holding them until a recovery could begin." This goes beyond assistance to illiquid but solvent firms, with allocative goals for firms' balance sheets, as well as particular asset classes. Bagehot's rules, as principles, are open to a degree of interpretation with respect to the bounds of acceptable assistance to distressed firms. But the Fed's policies, whatever else their virtues, were simply not within these bounds.

What about the quality of collateral? Here too the Fed's behavior falls short of Bagehot's prescriptions. Bernanke (2012, p. 14) admits that the Fed's actions were without precedent because its emergency activities "took place in a different institutional context than just the traditional banking context." In other words, the Fed extended loans and other support to institutions other than commercial banks. It is important to remember Bagehot's rules do not permit lending on *any* collateral; it must be collat-eral that is "marketable in the ordinary course of business" (Meltzer 1986, p. 83).[4] This was not an accurate characterization of mortgage-backed securities and other assets at the time, which were widely regarded to be wildly inflated in price, or else too difficult to price with any reasonable degree of objectivity. "I would like to know what those damn things are worth," Bernanke himself remarked (Torres and Lanman 2007). While it is

---

[4] Section 13(3) of the Federal Reserve Act authorizes emergency lending to nonbanks in the event of financial distress. It states that,

> Such policies and procedures shall be designed to ensure that any emergency lending program or facility is for the purpose of providing liquidity to the financial system, and not to aid a failing financial company, and that the security for emergency loans is sufficient to protect taxpayers from losses and that any such program is terminated in a timely and orderly fashion. The policies and procedures established by the Board shall require that a Federal reserve bank assign, consistent with sound risk management practices and to ensure protection for the taxpayer, a lendable value to all collateral for a loan executed by a Federal reserve bank under this paragraph in determining whether the loan is secured satisfactorily for purposes of this paragraph.

well-known that many securities become more difficult to market during crises, this is usually a liquidity problem, rather than a problem with the assets themselves. And liquidity is precisely what central banks are well positioned to provide. But, in this case, the Fed's activities are better understood not as an attempt to prevent liquidity from drying up, but to rescue firms deemed too important to fail, even though these firms made leveraged purchases of dubious assets.

Lastly, all of the earlier discussed occurred in an unpredictable and ad hoc manner. As in previous crises (cf. Meltzer 2009, p. 29), there was no clear announcement regarding how the Fed would behave in the event of financial turbulence. For instance, Bernanke et al. (2019, p. 109) write, "None of us was ever sure what would work, what would backfire, or how much stress the system could handle . . .. We had to feel our way through the fog, sometimes changing our tactics, sometimes changing our minds, with enormous uncertainty about the outcomes."

According to Bagehot's rules, the last-resort lender's "duty did not stop with the actual provision of liquidity in times of crisis, but also included advance notice that it would lend freely in any and all future crises" (Humphrey 2010, p. 347). The Bagehotian prescription requiring public and credible commitment was thus also violated. The salient issue was, at the time, the incomprehensibility of the bailout decisions: first Bear Stearns received a bailout, then Lehman was allowed to fail, followed by a bailout for AIG. Bernanke et al. (2019, pp. 61–63) contend that the decision to bail out Bear Stearns and AIG, while allowing Lehman to fail, was defensible. They argue that Lehman did not have a willing buyer nor sufficient collateral, and that they lacked Congressional authority to do what was necessary in Lehman's case. Ball (2018a, 2018b) and Posner (2015) dissent. Ball (2018a) is particularly blunt in his assessment of what explains the nonbailout of Lehman: "Many emails and memos document the discussions among Fed and Treasury officials in the days before the bankruptcy, and they make it clear that the discussions had nothing to do with the Fed's legal authority or Lehman's collateral. Instead, Lehman's fate was determined by officials' views of the political and economic consequences of a Lehman rescue or a Lehman bankruptcy."[5]

---

[5] Ball's argument is a distillation of his more extensive scholarly work (Ball 2018b). He devotes multiple chapters pushing back against the explanation given by Bernanke et al. (2019), that they failed to rescue Lehman for concerns over collateral and legality. Ball (2018b, ch. 12) ultimately concludes Lehman was permitted to fail due to fears of political backlash and mistakenly underestimating its systemic importance.

Ultimately, the debate over Lehman's viability (or lack thereof) is of secondary importance. What matters is public expectations, which were left adrift by the lack of a clear and consistent policy. Market actors were understandably confused, and confusion only makes panics worse.[6] "In no case has it [the Fed] spelled out beforehand its underlying rationale. In no case has it stated what criteria and indicators trigger its decisions, nor promised that it would rely on the same triggers in all future crises" (Humphrey 2010, p. 360). By refusing to announce and adhere to anything resembling a prespecified rule for crisis lending, the Fed again failed to follow an important part of last-resort lending orthodoxy.

To sum up: The Fed did lend freely during the financial crisis. But it lent freely in inappropriate ways. It engaged in too many other rescue operations, such as the outright purchase of questionable assets, that exceed the bounds of Bagehot's rules. There was no meaningful penalty in its loan rates. Not only did it actively step beyond Bagehot's rules to help commercial banks avoid the penalty rate, but it specifically introduced the TAF to "overcome the stigma" (Bernanke et al., 2019, p. 42) of borrowing from the discount window. It went out of its way to save insolvent firms, often to the detriment of merely illiquid firms. And it contributed to an overall environment of uncertainty by carrying out each of the earlier discussed functions without publicly issued guidance. Whatever else can be said for Fed policymakers under Bernanke's leadership, they were not following in Bagehot's footsteps. While Bernanke (2012) initially claimed that the Fed's bailouts were consistent with Bagehot, more recently, writing with Geithner and Paulson, Jr. (Bernanake et al. 2019), he admits to going "Beyond Bagehot."[7]

4.4 Firefighting Today, Arson Tomorrow

We must be careful not to confuse the two important questions that arise from the Fed's response to the financial crisis. The first question is, did the Fed's activities actually stabilize markets? Answering this question is a delicate task in counterfactual history. Clearly, it is plausible the Fed's actions prevented the financial crisis from having even worse real

---

[6] As Bernanke et al. (2019, p. 62) admit, they may have contributed to the chaotic atmosphere in markets post-Lehman: "We helped contribute to the confusion about our motives with some statements we made after Lehman's collapse, when we did not want to rattle the market by admitting we had been powerless to save a systemic firm."

[7] See also Bernanke (2015, p. 410).

economic effects. The policy of Ben Bernanke, Fed chairman, can be viewed as an extreme application of the scholarship of Ben Bernanke (1981, 1983), academic economist. Bernanke's understanding of the Great Depression was that the breakdown in intermediation relationships between banks contributed to the severity of that crisis. As such, Bernanke's policies during the financial crisis, which make much more sense as an attempt to rescue the private financial organizations that served as the Fed's counterparties in the course of monetary policy implementation than they do as orthodox last-resort lending, were reasonable.

However, there is an argument to be made that the Fed's response made the crisis worse, not better. Miron (2009, p. 14) argues that "the bailout might have exacerbated the credit crunch," and Hett and Schmidt (2016) provide evidence that the bailouts weakened investors' incentives to monitor banks' risk, and thus weakened market discipline. More recently, Hogan (2018, 2019) and Selgin (2018) contend that the Fed's sterilization policy (interest on excess reserves) was a crucial factor driving the slow recovery. Koyama and Johnson (2014, pp. 56–57, citations omitted) argue that,

The first two instances of quantitative easing taken by the Federal Reserve (QE1 and QE2) were not accompanied by any clear indication of what target the Fed was attempting to hit. The Fed announced how much and what type of securities they intended to purchase, but not what their ultimate policy goal was. As a result, while both programs resulted in some increase in inflation expectations and the value of stocks, markets were left guessing about how long the programs would continue, and what future Fed policy would be in the aftermath. This policy uncertainty is exacerbated by the numerous counterproductive comments made by the Fed that these policies did not represent an attempt to move inflation significantly above 2% and the discretionary nature of the extension to QE1 and Operation Twist. With QE3 the Federal Reserve announced purchases of $75 billion dollars of securities a month until "labor markets improved substantially" in an attempt to give more forward guidance to markets. However, the ambiguous meaning of when the Fed would consider labor markets to have substantially improved, or how much inflation the Fed would be willing to tolerate before pulling back meant that markets were still left guessing what future monetary policy would like, essentially only moving us slightly away from discretion and towards a truly rule based policy if at all.

The bottom line is that it is not self-evident that the Fed's policies prevented what otherwise would have been an even more serious recession.

This is an interesting and important question. But the second question is more interesting and important still. Given that the Fed's policies under Bernanke simply make no sense as an application of Bagehot's rules, why did Bernanke feel the need at the time to defend Fed policy specifically on the grounds of orthodox last-resort lending? The one thing we can be sure of is that the Fed's response was *not* orthodox. If we need more evidence of this, we need to consult none other than … Ben Bernanke. As Bernanke (2015) writes, "… I believed we needed insurance in the form of a larger than usual cut in the federal funds rate" (p. 162), "extraordinary times justified extraordinary measures …" (p. 294), and that "we went beyond Bagehot by using our lending authority to rescue large institutions on the brink of collapse …" (p. 410). Alongside former Treasury Secretaries Timothy Geithner and Henry Paulson, Bernanke writes in a recent memoir of the crisis that the bailout policies were in fact unprecedented in both scale and scope. For instance, Bernanke et al. (2019) write, "It was the most aggressive federal intervention in financial markets since the Depression …" (p. 60) and that "We had hoped that demonstrating the government's willingness to take extraordinary actions to prevent chaotic failures would calm the markets …" (p. 60).

The earlier discussion reveals something hidden and pernicious in the argument that discretion is required in monetary policy, if for no other reason than central bankers need discretion to combat financial turmoil. The implicit story behind the pro-constrained discretion regime is that financial crises are not within the purview of "ordinary" economics. Because of the unique dangers and challenges posed by financial crises, those responsible for stewarding the money and credit system must be permitted a wide berth. Given these assumptions, discretionary authority amid financial turbulence makes sense. But we do not grant the premise. The standard tools of microeconomics, applied to both market *and non-market* actors, explains both the institutional underpinnings of these crises, as well as the strange policy responses to them. Bad incentives confronting both private and public organizations explain bad outcomes. While there may be such a thing as an extraordinary financial crisis, there is no such thing as extraordinary *explanations* for a crisis, in terms of the underlying economics.

4.4.1 The Ordinary Explains the Extraordinary

From our perspective, one of the most important ideas to communicate is that, while there may be macroeconomic phenomena such as fluctuations in GDP, swings in unemployment, and bouts of inflation and disturbances from deflation, there are only microeconomic explanations and solutions. Economic theory is price-theoretic economics, grounded in individual choice in the face of constraints.[8] Monetary policy is an applied branch of economic theory, in which the logic of choice is played out in the context of money and banking, financial institutions, and the various incentives wrapped in price signals. When macroeconomic volatility and disturbances occur, the root cause is to be found in agents' incentives and information as they pursue their best strategies, given their circumstances.

Alfred Marshall (1890, bk. 1, ch. 1) argued that "Economics is a study of mankind in the ordinary business of life." We do not need to imbue economic actors with extraordinary cognitive skills, nor do we have to assume saintly motives to see how the working of the price system will guide individuals toward productive specialization and mutually beneficial exchange. Adam Smith's famous passage about the butcher, the brewer, and the baker in *The Wealth of Nations* (1776, p. 18) is preceded by a discussion of cooperation and coordination among strangers. "In civilized society," Smith writes, we "stand at all times in need of the co-operation and assistance of great multitudes" yet our "whole life is scarce sufficient to gain the friendship of a few persons."

How this anonymous cooperation is accomplished is one of the most important lessons that classical and modern economics taught. In the face of scarcity, individuals must choose; in making their choices they negotiate trade-offs; in negotiating trade-offs they need tools to aid them in their task; and those tools within the context of commercial life come in the form of the high-powered incentives associated with private property rights, the information provided by free price movements, the lure of profits, and the disciplining effect of loss. When the basic institutions of property, prices, and profit-and-loss are interfered with, economic action and the weighing of trade-offs does not cease. It is instead conducted with the guidance of dysfunctional incentives and distorted information, with the unhappy result of miscoordination of economic plans through time. Investment plans do not mesh with future consumption demands.

In the context of finance, macroeconomic disturbances against the trend can result from the manipulation of money and credit. Such manipulation is necessary (but not sufficient) to explain the 2007–2008 crisis. The primary concern of economists such as Ludwig von Mises and F. A. Hayek was on the havoc caused by monetary mischief. They developed a monetary theory of the business cycle which was firmly price-theoretic.

---

[8] Price theory is the study of "market adjustment and adaptation under alternative institutional arrangements" (Boettke and Canedla 2017). See also Jaffe et al. (2019) and Weyl (2019).

Their theory focused analytical attention on how distortions in the market for loanable funds would mislead investors into making errors. When these errors are revealed, economic actors must recalculate their plans. What makes the Mises–Hayek story so important is that, because capital is lumpy and investment is irreversible, errors have real costs. The economic system cannot adjust instantaneously to changes in tastes, technology, and resource availability. Instead, capital and labor must be reallocated and the most productive use of resources must be rediscovered. The market variables of prices, profits-and-losses, and resource ownership must be continually adjusted until brought into alignment with the underlying variables of tastes, technology, and resource availability. This is why in the Mises–Hayek story, the boom is the distortion, while the bust is the correction. Errors are revealed and corrected, and the transition begins toward a more sustainable path to economic activity.

Our point is a very basic one: scarcity, trade-offs, and the need for economic actors to negotiate trade-offs does not disappear following economic disruptions, small or large. As economists, we are committed to price-theoretic explanations even for phenomena as daunting as financial crises. No matter how extraordinary the circumstances, to render intelligible the multitude of adjustments and adaptations being made by the actors inside the economy, we need to emphasize the ordinary economics of incentive alignment and the efficient utilization of information.

Our argument, in this chapter and throughout this book, is that basic economic reasoning can help uncover the anatomy of financial crises. In fact, we argue that financial crises are in part caused by the previous "emergency" economic measures that were adopted with the promise of bringing short-term relief while ignoring long-term consequences on economic growth.[9] In this chapter, we emphasize how the responses to the 2007–2008 financial crisis are also an illustration of choosing "triage economics" measures, which ignore the *principles* of economics. We contend that the emotions of an economic crisis give rise to economic policy ideas that would not be justified by a calmer analysis. In other words, crises enable political actors to disregard the teachings of economics when we most need to remember those teachings. But after the crisis recedes, the debilitating consequences of the policies remain. The rule-of-law approach we advocate stresses the general liberal principles of justice, in the context

---

[9] This is similar to Calomiris and Haber (2014), who argue that credit crunches often have political, rather than market, origins.

of a realist political economy.[10] Liberalism seeks to establish a social system that is absent any political privileges and thus devoid of discrimination and the rejection of domination. Liberalism, in the writings of Adam Smith to F. A. Hayek, is a "system of principles" that provides a bulwark against seemingly pragmatic, but in reality short-sighted, approaches to public policy (Hayek 1960). As we see it, the arguments for discretion, including constrained discretion, concede far too much to expediency.

4.4.2 Firefighters Today, Arsonists Tomorrow

The view that financial crises are extraordinary, "sunspot"-like events leads naturally to the view that we need a special kind of economics, as well as economic policy, to combat them. As explained earlier, once this first principle is conceded, the rest of the activist policies pursued by central banks following the 2007–2008 crisis follow as a matter of course. In challenging both the feasibility and desirability of "triage" economics, we hope to call the discipline back to time-tested price-theoretic principles. It is precisely when the world is at its most complicated that we need the simple yet extraordinarily powerful tools of basic economics. It cannot be emphasized enough that in economics, "simple" does *not* mean "simplistic."

---

[10] In *Law, Legislation and Liberty* (1973, pp. 56–61), Hayek argues that the "necessity" of various drastic economic policies is a consequence of earlier responses that bequeathed a legacy of dysfunctional incentives and distorted information. Freedom, as a consequence, always tends to lose out to coercion by the governing authorities. Only by following general rules, rather than discretion, can freedom be preserved. Hayek (1973, pp. 56–67) argues that,

> Since the value of freedom rests on the opportunities it provides for unforeseen and unpredictable actions, we will rarely know what we lose through a particular restriction of freedom. Any such restriction, any coercion other than the enforcement of general rules, will aim at the achievement of some foreseeable particular result, but what is prevented by it will usually not be known. The direct effects of any interference with the market order will be near and clearly visible in most cases, while the most indirect and remote effects will mostly be unknown and will therefore be disregarded.

One of the first rules of basic economics is that the bad economics only focuses on the direct and immediate consequences of any action or policy, while good economics takes into account the indirect and long-run consequences of those actions and policies. Long-run growth, in other words, should not be sacrificed for short-run relief in policy deliberations, but in practice such sacrifices are made because of the calculations of political actors, which include the decision of which economic theories to choose in designing public policies.

In times of crises it is too often assumed we need extraordinary and complex theories but what we really need is cool-headed and basic economic principles. For example, this proposition was true in the immediate period of post-communism, when perhaps the best tool to understand the shortage economy, along with the various unintended consequences and institutions and practices that had evolved because of the administrative pricing system both within and outside of the "planned economy," was the persistent and consistent application of supply-and-demand analysis. This holds in all crises situations. Incentives matter, information is necessary, and institutions structure the environment within which we interact in our commercial and noncommercial lives. Of course, incentives and information are tricky, but that is the beauty of the persistent and consistent application of the economic way of thinking: It provides the set of theoretical eyeglasses that brings into sharp relief the confusing and blurry reality of the world outside the window. Simple economics, by which we mean the application of the basic principles of economics, is able to raise the ordinary man to the heights of observational genius, but without economics, even a genius is reduced to foolishness (Buchanan 1966). When we forget and discard the basic principles of economics, we make the very crisis we wish to solve worse.

But there is another problem related to the ad hoc conceptualization of financial crises as qualitatively distinct events we must explore. The problem is this: Once policymakers, including ones with advanced economics training, decide that extraordinary policy must be employed to combat extraordinary turmoil, they expose the crisis response to the inevitable vagaries of politics. While there are notable and welcome exceptions, economists who study financial crises have spent too much time on highly technical issues, such as the transmission mechanisms between the financial sector and the real economy, and not enough time incorporating basic political economy considerations into their analyses. Because of this, both academic and policy-engaged economists severely misrepresent the likely consequences of financial stabilization policy.

In the late 1970s, James Buchanan and Richard Wagner (1977 [2000]) wrote a controversial book with the provocative title, *Democracy in Deficit: The Political Legacy of Lord Keynes*. Their target was not responses to financial crises, nor monetary policy, but rather the orthodox Keynesian apparatus as existed before that apparatus fell out of academic favor. The following quote makes clear their intended contribution:

This book is an essay in political economy rather than in economic theory. Our focus is upon the *political institutions through which economic policy must be implemented*, policy which is, itself, ultimately derived from theory, good or bad. And central to our argument is the principle that the criteria for good theory are necessarily related to the political institutions of the society ... This necessary linkage between the basic political structure of society and the economic theory of policy has never been properly recognized by economists, despite its elementary logic and its overwhelming empirical apparency. (1977 [2000], pp. 4–5, emphasis added)

Just so. Buchanan and Wagner received much hostile criticism for this work, but their fundamental argument has yet to be appreciated by the profession. It does not matter how strong the theoretical justification for economic policy is if that policy is ineptly implemented in actual political processes by real legislators, civil servants, policy advisors, and interest groups. Buchanan and Wagner wrote at a time of ballooning deficits (although by comparison to today's, they seem almost trivial!), high inflation, and rising unemployment, challenging Keynesian orthodoxy on the grounds that it was not incentive-compatible for public agents in a democratic republic. Keynesian economics had discarded the "old-time fiscal religion," which insisted on balanced budgets, except temporarily during wartime. It is, of course, true that Keynes prescribed not perpetual deficits, but a budget that balanced over the course of the business cycle. This requires deficit spending during recessions but accumulating budget surpluses during an expansion. But again, this is not incentive-compatible for civil servants and interest groups, who, according to "concentrated benefits, dispersed costs" logic, push for perpetually higher spending, nor legislators, who make the ultimate spending decisions and due to electoral logic are always trying to increase public largesse for their constituents. Again, it was completely irrelevant whether the Keynesian program of aggregate demand management was sound in the abstract, because there is no such thing as economic policy abstracted from politics. Buchanan and Wagner correctly insisted that economic theory, including the theory of economic policy, must consider the political process through which any proffered policies must pass. Once this concession is made, the range of policy prescriptions changes radically.

Our point is precisely the same as the one made by Buchanan and Wagner, but in the context of central bank policy, which includes responses to financial crises. The chief failing of the policy response to the 2007–2008 crisis was not realizing this essential point. By the admission of many of the key actors, their chief concern was protecting the financial system no matter the cost in terms of overturning previously established rules or the costs of ensuing moral hazard problems. As Bernanke et al. (2019, p. 8) write, "The top priority in an epic crisis should always be to end it, even though that will likely create some moral hazard .... When panic strikes, policymakers need to do everything in their power to quell it, regardless of the political ramifications, regardless of their ideological convictions, regardless of what they've said or promised in the past." Their goal was the same as Colonel Chamberlain's at Little Round Top: "Hold the ground at all hazards." But this heroic bayonet charge in the face of overwhelming odds conceals a tragic reality: Any victory achieved by neglecting the political consequences of economic policy is a pyrrhic victory. Policymakers in response to financial crises see themselves as firefighters, but because they do not adequately consider the systemic effects of their emergency scramble on the political-economic system, they inadvertently become arsonists.

Whether amid a crisis or not, banking and finance are inherently political, as Calomiris and Haber (2014) recognize. Financial intermediation requires the creation and enforcement of a specific and complex set of property rights, which is the government's prerogative. But governments also have strategic incentives to renege on that protection or engage in marginal changes to the content of those property rights in service of its own interests. Calomiris and Haber refer to this interaction as the "Game of Bank Bargains." The government

is not a disinterested, independent party ... The most obvious conflict of interest is that this group regulates banks ... but also looks to banks as a source of public finance. That is, it simultaneously regulates the banks and borrows from, or taxes, them. It therefore has an incentive to fashion a regulatory environment that favors government's (or government actors') access to finance at the expense of fashioning an environment conducive to a stable and efficient banking system. (Calomiris and Haber 2014, p. 34)

Here Calomiris and Haber place emphasis on regulation (and, implicitly, rent extraction) for the purposes of public finance, but their insight applies just as well to the regulatory framework overseen by central banks. In both scenarios, there is a wide berth for both private and public agents to pursue personally profitable but socially costly policies, due to their ability to reap concentrated benefits while diffusing the associated costs onto less influential groups, such as taxpayers (cf. Calomoris and Haber 2014, pp. 37–38). The political logic also holds in times of crisis. Remember that the Fed went out of its way during the crisis to preserve the balance sheets of the primary dealers, its main agents in implementing monetary policy. This was a continuation of 30+ years of bailout policy that further institutionalized moral hazard in the banking system. Saving the primary dealers was in the Fed's interests, to continue its maintenance of control over the monetary financial system. Certainly, there are public interest explanations for these policies. But remembering Buchanan and Wagner, it is in the nature of policy, even when crafted in the public interest, to be captured and rerouted toward various private interests when the political foundations of the policymaking and implementing process are overlooked.

How can it be that policies motivated by public interest, especially when crafted and implemented by men and women of integrity, advance purposes so contrary to their original intent? The answer is that it is not the *intentions* of the policymakers that matter, but the *adaptive value* of policy in a context where success requires placating various private interest groups, whose interests often diverge from that of the public at large. Intentions are a characteristic of individuals and organizations, but it is the systemic effects, in the forms of various filters that weed out some patterns of behavior and promote others, that drive outcomes. Alchian (1950) first developed the filtering argument in the context of markets. It does not matter whether firms consciously intend to maximize profits or not. The market acts as a filter, which rewards firms that make profits and punishes those that do not. Hence it is reasonable to model firms as profit maximizers, not due to the desires of firms, but due to the institutional filter of the market process. But once we introduce politics, the properties that are promoted or discouraged by the filter change significantly. We cannot assume that policy crafted in the public interest will, when it makes it through the filter, continue to function as intended.

Salter and Luther (2019) apply this filtering argument to central bank behavior, specifically the institutional environment in which central banks possess significant discretionary power. Regarding the response of Bernanke's Fed to the financial crisis, Salter and Luther (2019, p. 253, emphasis in original, quote attributions omitted) argue:

We do not deny that Bernanke did what he thought was best for the public's interest. Moreover, we acknowledge that, as a first-rate macroeconomist and monetary historian, he had good reasons for doing what he did. Nonetheless, we maintain that the actions of the Bernanke Fed had adaptive value [for reasons unrelated to public interest]. Those actions preserved the power, influence, and resources of the Fed's decision makers. . . . The Fed relies on its primary dealers to implement monetary policy. If the primary dealers fail, then the monetary transmission mechanism fails. Hence, the Fed "felt obliged to rescue several primary dealers, and to do so at the expense of solvent banks." Failing to take such action, in the view of Fed decision makers, would risk losing control of monetary policy. One should not expect central bankers to undertake a limited response, such as that dictated by Bagehot's rules, in such a situation.

To be clear, we are not claiming that a more constrained course of action would not have worked. Rather, we are saying that *it does not matter if it would have worked*. Central bank decision makers are unlikely to adhere to a doctrine that limits their responses when they perceive existential threats to the financial system. Indeed, being selected as a central banker practically requires a willingness to take any and all actions necessary for the continued operation of a financial system wherein the central bank is a dominant player. By his own admission, Bernanke "did not want to be remembered as the person whose decisions had led to the Fed's destruction." We contend that such a view is not unique to Bernanke. Because such actions have adaptive value, it is part of what it means to be a central banker.

To sum up: Among other errors, the argument that central bank discretion is necessary to combat financial crises overlooks crucial institutional considerations. Discretion is supposedly necessary to craft policy tailored to the particulars of a crisis. But the flexibility associated with discretion is a curse, not a blessing. Unfortunately, discretion ensures stabilization policy will be compromised when it is formulated and implemented in a political environment, which all policy is. Once we consider the "political institutions through which economic policy must be implemented," we recognize that allowing discretion opens us up to a world not of benevolent technocrats managing the financial system, but a world of institutionalized moral hazard and ever-expanding "mandate creep" for activist-central banks. Discretion does not allow central bankers to serve as firefighters. Instead it unwittingly turns them into arsonists.

4.5 What Can Be Done?

We must face the facts: In today's world of activist-central banks with wide discretionary powers, the relatively limited response to crises necessitated by Bagehot's rules are not incentive-compatible. Once, it appears they were. For example, the Bank of England arguably behaved as a Bagehotian lender of last resort during the 1890 Baring crisis, working in concert with the Bank of France and important private clearinghouses (Schwartz 1987, p. 19). Goodfriend (2012) argues that the Bank of England, because it still retained many of the features of a private, for-profit bank in the late nineteenth century, had incentives to follow Bagehot's rules: Stabilizing the financial system by engaging in limited lending enhanced shareholder profits, but the indiscriminate bailouts practiced by today's central banks did not.

But the Fed has never behaved as Bagehot thought a last-resort lender should. The episodes mentioned in this chapter demonstrate that the Fed has consistently and persistently erred on the side of extensive bailouts. The result is a financial system replete with moral hazard. Given the continued existence of the Fed, what can we do to prevent such behavior in the future? Ordinary monetary policy can be constrained by a strict rule. What about extraordinary monetary policy? Can central banking practices be modified so that, no matter the temptation of the moment, monetary policymakers will hold fast to time-tested principles?

The answer may lie in a somewhat dated theory of monetary policy during crises. The view known as the Richmond Fed doctrine – also called the Goodfriend–King doctrine due to those authors' endorsement of the policy in an influential paper (Goodfriend and King 1988) – holds that the central bank should limit itself to the creation and supply of high-powered money to the market, even during financially turbulent times. In addition to Goodfriend and King, other prominent endorsers of this paradigm include Friedman (1960), Kaufman (1991), and Schwartz (1992). Sterilized discount window lending (or similar policies) are unnecessary (cf. Bordo 1990); it is unclear at best that the central bank can provide emergency *credit* more efficiently than can private banks and other financial organizations. In fact, the supply of emergency credit, especially in discrete forms that insulate receipt organizations from reputational consequences, as was explicitly done during the financial crisis (Bernanke et al. 2019, p. 42),[11] actually hampers the transmission of information and distorts market incentives.

The central bank's comparative advantage is providing the market with ample *liquidity* and then allowing the market to allocate that liquidity according to banks' willingness to pay. Rather than wade into the thorny issue of deciding the boundary between illiquid and insolvent, the central bank commits to creating an underlying framework for the market such that the market answers that question through its ordinary allocative processes. This view has a significant added benefit: If central banks are restrained from emergency lending, they cannot indulge in the temptation

---

[11] Also relevant is the Fed's operating system transition from a corridor to a floor system. By disrupting the fed funds interbank lending market, the Fed reduced "an important promoter of interbank monitoring, as well as an important source of information about individual bank's health" (Selgin 2018, p. 44).

to give insolvent but politically important banks loans, thus stemming moral hazard (Flannery 1996, p. 805).

The Richmond Fed doctrine fits well with our anti-triage economics approach to financial crises. The proper way to respond to extraordinary turbulence in financial markets remains ordinary monetary policy. Crises already generate a tremendous amount of uncertainty for investors and businesses. Allowing monetary authorities to engage in extraordinary interventions only adds to that uncertainty. This is especially true if one properly accounts for the knowledge problems discussed in Chapter 2. The new firefighting approach of central bankers tries to quell the recessionary fires with anything and everything, even if we do not understand the causes of the crisis or the tools we wish to use. This is precisely what gets us into trouble.

Monetary rules, however, can be crafted to cope with changes in the demand for high-powered money. As such, this kind of rule can cope with the predictable spike in high-powered money demand that we would expect during a turbulent "flight to liquidity." Undoubtedly, if this approach is employed, some – perhaps many – banks and other financial organizations would fail, and there would still be spillover from the financial economy to the real economy in the form of decreased output and increased unemployment. On paper, this perhaps makes the Richmond Fed approach less attractive than Bagehot's rules, or the wide-ranging response of the Fed during the 2007–2008 crisis. But it is precisely against such "on paper" abstractions, divorced from political economy considerations, that we have argued are illegitimate. Given the institutional environment we have – a central bank that is, in every meaningful sense, a public organization – the least bad response may be a true monetary rule that forces the central bank to follow the Richmond Fed prescriptions (Salter 2016). It is also worth remembering that once it becomes widely known that the Richmond Fed doctrine has become the "rule of the game," the diminution of moral hazard will make it much less likely that a financial crisis arises in the first place.

Ultimately, financial crises do not weaken the case for rules. They strengthen the case for rules. Once we realize that crises are not examples of a categorically different kind of economics and that the best of intentions behind discretionary stabilization policy frequently become thwarted by political reality, we see that the challenge of the extraordinary is not crafting the right policy response package. It is reigning in our desire to "do something," instead of adhering to the difficult, but effective, principles of generality, predictability, and robustness required by genuinely lawful monetary institutions

References

Alchian, Armen (1950). Uncertainty, Evolution, and Economic Theory. *Journal of Political Economy*, 58(3), 211–221.

Bagehot, Walter (1873). Lombard Street: A Description of the Money Market. Henry S. King and Co. Available online (accessed May 27, 2020), www.econlib.org/library/Bagehot/bagLomCover.html

Ball, Laurence (2018a). Ten Years On, the Fed's Failings on Lehman Brothers Are All Too Clear. *The Guardian*. Monday, September 3. Available online (accessed September 26, 2019), www.theguardian.com/commentisfree/2018/sep/03/federal-reserve-lehman-brothers-collapse

(2018b). *The Fed and Lehman Brothers*. Cambridge University Press.

Bastiat, Frédéric (1850). *Economic Sophisms and "What Is Seen and What Is Not Seen."* Liberty Fund, Inc.

Bernanke, Ben (1981). Bankruptcy, Liquidity, and Recession. *The American Economic Review*, 71(2), 155–159.

(1983). Nonmonetary Effects of the Financial Crisis in the Propagation of the Great Depression. *The American Economic Review*, 73(3), 257–276.

(2008a). Federal Reserve Policies in the Financial Crisis. Remarks by Chairman Ben S. Bernanke, Board of Governors of the Federal Reserve System. December 1. Available online (accessed May 27, 2020), www.federalreserve.gov/newsevents/speech/bernanke20081201a.htm

(2008b). Liquidity Provision by the Federal Reserve. Remarks by Chairman Ben S. Bernanke at the Federal Reserve Bank of Atlanta Financial Markets Conference, Sea Island, GA. May 13. Available online (accessed May 27, 2020), www.federalreserve.gov/newsevents/speech/bernanke20080513.htm

(2010). On the Implications of the Financial Crisis for Economics. Remarks by Chairman Ben S. Bernanke at the Conference Co-sponsored by the Bendheim Center for Finance and the Center for Economic Policy Studies, Princeton, NJ. September 24. Available online (accessed May 27, 2020), www.federalreserve.gov/newsevents/speech/bernanke20100924a.pdf

(2011). Implementing a Macroprudential Approach to Supervision and Regulation. Speech given at the Forty-Seventh Annual Conference on Bank Structure and Competition, Chicago. May 5. Available online (accessed May 28, 2020), www.bis.org/review/r110509b.pdf

(2012). The Federal Reserve's Response to the Financial Crisis, Lecture 3. Lecture given at George Washington University School of Business. March 27. Available online (accessed May 27, 2020), www.federalreserve.gov/newsevents/files/chairman-bernanke-lecture3-20120327.pdf

(2013). Opening Remarks by Chairman Ben S. Bernanke at the Ceremony Commemorating the Centennial of the Federal Reserve Act. Washington, DC. December 16. Available online (accessed May 27, 2020), www.federalreserve.gov/newsevents/speech/bernanke20131216a.htm

(2015). *The Courage to Act: A Memoir of a Crisis and Its Aftermath.* W. W. Norton & Company.

Bernanke, Ben, Timothy Geithner, and Henry Paulson (2019). *Firefighting: The Financial Crisis and Its Lessons*. Penguin Books.

Blau, Benjamin, Tyler Brough, and Diana Thomas (2013). Corporate Lobbying, Political Connections, and the Bailout of Banks. *Journal of Banking and Finance*, 37(8), 3007–3017.

Boettke, Peter (2010). Simple Economics Is NOT Necessarily Simple-Minded Economics. Coordination Problem. February 22. Available online (accessed May 28, 2020), www.coordinationproblem.org/2010/02/simple-economics-is-not-neces sarily-simpleminded-economics.html

Boettke, Peter and Rosolino Candela (2017). Price Theory as a Prophylactic against Popular Fallacies. *Journal of Institutional Economics*, 13(3), 725–752.

Boettke, Peter and William Luther (2010). The Ordinary Economics of an Extraordinary Crisis, (with William Luther). In Steven Kates (Ed.), *Macroeconomic Theory and Its Failings: Alternative Perspectives on the World Financial Crisis*. Edward Elgar Publishing, pp. 14–25.

Boettke, Peter and Liya Palagashvili (2015). The Comparative Political Economy of a Crisis. *Advances in Austrian Economics*, 20, 235–263.

Bordo, Michael (1990). The Lender of Last Resort: Alternative Views and Historical Experience. *Federal Reserve Bank of Richmond Economic Review*, 76(1), 18–29.

Bordo, Michael and Joseph Haubrich (2017). Deep Recessions, Fast Recoveries, and Financial Crises: Evidence from the American Record. *Economic Inquiry*, 55(1), 527–541.

Broz, Lawrence (2012). The Federal Reserve as Global Lender of Last Resort, 2007–2011. Working paper presented at Governing the Federal Reserve, Nuffield College, Oxford University. October 4–5. http://ssrn.com/abstract= 2105302

Buchanan, James (1966 [2001]). Economics and Its Scientific Neighbors. In *The Collected Works of James M. Buchanan*, volume 17. Liberty Fund, Inc.

Buchanan, James and Richard Wagner (1977 [2000]). *Democracy in Deficit: The Political Legacy of Lord Keynes*. Liberty Fund, Inc.

Calomiris, Calomiris and Steven Haber (2014). *Fragile by Design: The Political Foundations of Scarce and Unstable Credit*. Princeton University Press.

Federal Reserve (2008). Press Release. September 16. Available online (accessed May 27, 2020), www.federalreserve.gov/newsevents/press/other/20080916a.htm

Federal Reserve, Federal Deposit and Exchange Corporation, and U.S. Department of the Treasury (2008). Joint Press Release. November 23. Available online (accessed May 27, 2020), www.federalreserve.gov/newsevents/press/bcreg/20081123a.htm

Flannery, Mark (1996). Financial Crises, Payment System Problems, and Discount Window Lending. *Journal of Money Credit and Banking*, 28(4), 804–824.

Fleming, Michael (2012). Federal Reserve Liquidity Provision during the Financial Crisis of 2007–2009. Federal Reserve Bank of New York, Staff Report No. 563. Available online (accessed May 27, 2020), http://ssrn.com/abstract=2126214

Friedman, Milton (1960). *A Program for Monetary Stability*. Fordham University Press.

Galati, Gabriele and Richhild Moessner (2013). Macroprudential Policy: A Literature Review. *Journal of Economic Surveys*, 27(5), 846–878.

Gokhale, Jagadeesh (2012). Is QE3 about Bernanke's Employment? *Real Clear Markets*. October 5. Available online (accessed May 27, 2020), www.realclearmarkets.com/ articles/2012/10/05/is_qe3_about_bernankes_employment_99916.html

Goodfriend, Marvin (2011). Central Banking in the Credit Turmoil: An Assessment of Federal Reserve Practice. *Journal of Monetary Economics*, 58(1), 1–12.

(2012). The Elusive Promise of Independent Central Banking. Keynote Lecture, 2012 BOJ-IMES Conference. Institute for Monetary and Economic Studies, Bank of Japan. Available online (accessed May 27, 2020), www.imes.boj.or.jp/research/papers/english/me30-3.pdf

Goodfriend, Marvin and Robert King (1988). Financial Deregulation, Monetary Policy, and Central Banking. *Federal Reserve Bank of Richmond Economic Review* (May/June), 1–33.

Goodhart, Charles (1985). *The Evolution of Central Banks*. London School of Economics and Political Science.

(1987). Why Do Banks Need a Central Bank? *Oxford Economic Papers*, 39(1), 75–89.

Gorton, Gary (2010). *Slapped by the Invisible Hand: The Panic of 2007*. Oxford University Press.

Government Accountability Office (2011). Federal Reserve System: Opportunities Exist to Strengthen Policies and Processes for Managing Emergency Assistance. Report to Congressional Addressees. July. Available online (accessed May 23, 2020), www.gao.gov/products/GAO-11-696

Hanson, Samuel, Anil Kashyap, and Jeremy Stein (2011). A Macroprudential Approach to Financial Regulation. *Journal of Economic Perspectives*, 25(1), 3–28.

Hayek, Friedrich August (1960). *The Constitution of Liberty*. University of Chicago Press.

(1971). Principles or Expediency? In F. A. Hayek, Friedrich von Hayek, Henry Hazlitt, Leonard R. Read, Floyd Arthur Harper, and Gustavo Velasco (Eds.), *Toward Liberty: Essays in Honor of Ludwig von Mises on the Occasion of His 90th Birthday, September 29, 1971*, volume 1. Institute for Humane Studies, pp. 29–49.

(1973). *Law, Legislation and Liberty*, volume 1. University of Chicago Press.

Hett, Florian and Alexander Schmidt (2016). Bank Rescues and Bailout Expectations: The Erosion of Market Discipline during the Financial Crisis. *Journal of Financial Economics*, 126(3), 635–651.

Hetzel, Robert (2008). *The Monetary Policy of the Federal Reserve: A History*. Cambridge University Press.

(2012). *The Great Recession: Market Failure or Policy Failure?* Cambridge University Press.

Hogan, Thomas (2018). Bank Lending and Interest on Excess Reserves. Working Paper. Available online (accessed May 15, 2020), https://papers.ssrn.com/sol3/papers.cfm?abstract_id=3118462

(2019). Post-Crisis Decline in Bank Lending. Baker Institute Issue Brief. Available online (accessed May 15, 2020), www.bakerinstitute.org/research/post-crisis-decline-bank-lending/

Hogan, Thomas, Linh Le, and Alexander William Salter (2015). Ben Bernanke and Bagehot's Rules. *Journal of Money, Credit, and Banking*, 47(2–3), 333–348.

Hummel, Jeffrey Rogers (2012). Ben Bernanke versus Milton Friedman: The Federal Reserve's Emergence as the U.S. Economy's Central Planner. In David Backworth (Ed.), *Boom and Bust Banking: The Causes and Cures of the Great Recession*. Independent Institute, pp. 165–210.

Humphrey, Thomas (2010). Lender of Last Resort: What It Is, Whence It Came, and Why the Fed Isn't It. *Cato Journal*, 30(2), 333–364.

Jaffe, Sonia, Robert Minton, Casey B. Mulligan, and Kevin Murphy (2019). *Chicago Price Theory*. Princeton University Press.

Kaufman, George (1991). The Lender of Last Resort: A Contemporary Perspective. *Journal of Financial Services Research*, 5(2), 95–110.

Koyama, Mark and Blake Johnson (2014). Monetary Stability and the Rule of Law. *Journal of Financial Stability*, 17, 46–58.

Lim, Cheng Hoon, Alejo Costa, Francesco Columba, P. Kongsamut, Akira Otani, M. Saiyid, Torsten Wezel, and Xiaoyong Wu (2011). Macroprudential Policy: What Instruments and How to Use Them? Lessons from Country Experiences. IMF Working Papers, pp. 1–85, 2011. Available at SSRN (accessed May 27, 2020), https://ssrn.com/abstract=1956385

Marshall, Alfred (1890). *Principles of Economics*. EconLog Economics Library. Available online (accessed May 27, 2020), www.econlib.org/library/Marshall/marP.html?chapter_num=2#book-reader

Meltzer, Allan (1986). Financial Failures and Financial Policies. In George Kaufman and Roger Kormendi (Eds.), *Deregulating Financial Service: Public Policy in Flux*. Ballinger Publishing Company, pp. 79–96.

——— (2009). Reflections on the Financial Crisis. *Cato Journal*, 29, 25–30.

Miller, LeRoy Roger and David VanHoose (2007) *Money, Banking, and Financial Markets*. South-Western.

Miron, Jeffrey (2009). Bailout or Bankruptcy? *Cato Journal*, 29(1), 1–17.

Jordà, Òscar, Moritz Schularick, and Alan Taylor (2013). When Credit Bites Back. *Journal of Money, Credit, and Banking*, 45(s2), 3–28.

Isidore, Chris (2013). Bernanke to be Grilled in AIG Suit. *CNN Money*. July 29. Available online (accessed May 27, 2020), http://money.cnn.com/2013/07/29/news/companies/greenberg-bernanke-aig/

Paul, Pascal. (2019). A Macroeconomic Model with Occasional Financial Crises. *Journal of Economic Dynamics and Control*, 112, 103830.

Posner, Eric (2015). Bernanke's Biggest Blunder, *Slate.com*. October 29. Available online (accessed September 26, 2019), https://slate.com/news-and-politics/2015/10/bernanke-memoir-says-fed-couldnt-help-lehman-brothers.html

Reinhart, Carmen and Kenneth Rogoff (2009). *This Time Is Different: Eight Centuries of Financial Folly*. Princeton University Press.

Salter, Alexander William (2016). Robust Political Economy and the Lender of Last Resort. *Journal of Financial Services Research*, 50(1), 1–27.

Salter, Alexander William and William Luther (2019). Adaptation and Central Banking. *Public Choice*, 180(3–4), 243–256.

Schwartz, Anna J. (1987). Real and Pesudo-Financial Crises. In Money in Historical Perspectives, National Bureau for Economic Research, pp. 271–288. Available online, https://econpapers.repec.org/bookchap/nbrnberch/7506.htm

Schwartz, Anna (1992). The Misuse of the Fed's Discount Window. *Federal Reserve Bank of St. Louis Review*, 74(5), 58–69.

Selgin, George (2012). L Street: Bagehotian Prescriptions for a 21st-Century Money Market. *Cato Journal*, 32, 303–332.

(2018). *Floored!: How a Misguided Fed Experiment Deepened and Prolonged the Great Recession*. Cato Institute.

Sheridan, Brian (2011). Lender of Last Resort: An Examination of the Federal Reserve's Primary Dealer Credit Facility. University of Note Dame Working Paper. Available online (accessed May 28, 2020), https://economics.nd.edu/assets/41471/brian_sheridan_lender_of_last_resort.pdf

Smith, Adam (1776). *An Inquiry into the Nature and Causes of the Wealth of Nations*. W. Strahan and T. Cadell.

Solow, Robert (1982). On the Lender of Last Resort. In Charles Kindleberger and Jean-Pierre Laffargue (Eds.), *Financial Crises: Theory, History and Policy*. Cambridge University Press, pp. 237–248.

Stewart, James (2009). Eight Days: The Battle to Save the American Financial System. *The New Yorker*, 85, 58–81.

Thornton, Henry (1802). *An Inquiry into the Nature and Effects of the Paper Credit of Great Britain*. Reprinted with an Introduction by F. A. Hayek. Rinehart.

Torres, Craig and Scott Lanman (2007). Bernanke Says Housing to Remain "Drag" on U.S. Growth (Update 3). *Bloomberg Online*. October 15. Available online (accessed May 15, 2020), www.bloomberg.com/apps/news?pid=newsarchive&sid=a_6erMJbqHYs&refer=home

Volcker, Paul (2008). Remarks to the Economic Club of New York. Grand Hyatt Hotel, New York. April 8. Available online (accessed July 21, 2020): www.econclubny.org/documents/10184/109144/2008VolckerTranscript.pdf

Weyl, E. Glen (2019). Price Theory. *Journal of Economic Literature*, 57(2), 329–384.

White, Lawrence (1995). *Free Banking in Britain: Theory, Experience, and Debate, 1800–1845* (2nd Edition). Institute for Economic Affairs.

(1999). *The Theory of Monetary Institutions*. Blackwell Publishers.

Zwikel, Andy (2009). Why Doesn't Insolvency Equal Bankruptcy? *Seeking Alpha*. March 6. Available online (accessed May 15, 2020), http://seekingalpha.com/article/124519-why-doesnt-insolvency-equal-bankruptcy

On the Shoulders of Giants

Monetary Policy Insights of the Classically Liberal Nobel Laureates

5.1 Introduction

To the classically liberal political economists of the nineteenth century, sound money was a vital component of responsible economic policy. Many of these thinkers, such as Jean-Baptiste Say and Walter Bagehot, thought that the market mechanism itself could contribute to a robust monetary framework (Arnon 1987; Jacoud 2013; West 1997). Others, such as Robert Torrens and Thomas Tooke, believed lawful money could be more effectively provided by a centralized monetary authority controlled by government (Arnon 2010). Importantly, those on both sides realized the question was one of comparative institutional effectiveness.

This perspective has since fallen by the wayside. Monetary economics scholarship related to the theory and practice of central banking has become unrecognizable since this initial promising era. Most research now focuses on improving data collection and further refining models. Political economy considerations, including the knowledge and incentive problems addressed in Chapters 2 and 3, often enter the analysis as an afterthought, if at all. An alternative literature, however, focuses on examining the monetary framework itself. It places comparative institutional analysis in the analytical foreground and technical considerations in the analytical background, hearkening back to a tradition of economics when the discipline was still referred to as "political economy." This literature explores how alternative monetary frameworks relate to monetary stability. Importantly, the heroic information and incentive assumptions on the behalf of central bankers are relaxed in order to compare the operation of realistic alternatives. This requires taking seriously both information and incentive imperfections on the part of both private and public agents.

The scholars working in this line of inquiry, while not denying the importance of refining technical monetary models, recognize that technical optimality in the world of models is often in conflict with strategic considerations in the world of politics. Since, in practice, political considerations tend to thwart technical considerations, optimal monetary theory is often rendered nonoperational within the existing framework of discretionary central banking. Focusing instead on the fundamental institutions of monetary policy, carefully considering questions of incentive alignment and information generation, is a more fruitful research program for advancing sound money.

In this chapter, we start by discussing how modern monetary scholarship, while it sometimes incorporates elements of political economy as a secondary consideration, fails the *robustness test*: It does not account for knowledge and incentive problems in a serious way. Then, we discuss the scholarly progression of notable classical liberal scholars and Nobel laureates F. A. Hayek, Milton Friedman, and James M. Buchanan, focusing on their quest for sound money. These scholars, although not disinterested in the abstract operation of monetary systems, believed that the ultimate consideration was whether a monetary system could function reasonably well in a world fraught with information and incentive problems. Each became increasingly frustrated when economists at the helm of the Fed compromised sound money as the policymakers struggled with knowledge problems and succumbed to institutional incentives that directed them away from monetary stability. This experience gradually led Hayek and Friedman to reject technical and empirical considerations unless they were convincingly integrated within a comparative institutions approach to money. Buchanan, partly from building on Hayek and Friedman's scholarship, worked within the comparative monetary framework from the very beginning, but even within that framework, his ideas developed significantly over time.

Hayek, Friedman, and Buchanan ultimately concluded that our existing monetary framework was insufficient for achieving sound money in a world typified by knowledge and incentive problems. Each also believed that radical reforms were necessary. Despite their agreement on this point, they offered different institutional solutions for securing sound money. Hayek turned toward competing private currencies, Friedman to binding rules, and Buchanan to constitutionalizing money. We believe that tracing the intellectual progression of these classical liberal scholars as they wrestled with the problem of securing sound money over their academic careers offers valuable insight into the importance of putting first things first when it comes to monetary scholarship. These first things are not refinements of abstract models, although this practice certainly deserves a seat at the table. Instead, the first things are institutional features that determine what incentives agents face and what information they have at their disposal. Without engaging basic institutional questions, even the most sophisticated monetary economics research cannot contribute to the quest for sound money.

Before turning to the intellectual development of their ideas, we first explain why we believe modern monetary scholarship, even when it includes some political economy concerns, ultimately fails the robustness test. This *robust political economy* standard is the yardstick for scholarship at the intersection of politics and economics.[1] In their own way, Hayek, Friedman, and Buchanan focused their attention in monetary scholarship on a robust political economy of monetary institutions. This is precisely why we can continue to draw on their work to understand what is wrong with contemporary monetary institutions, as well as how they might be fixed.

5.2 How Modern Monetary Scholarship Fails the Robustness Test

The preponderance of contemporary monetary scholarship fails to address the knowledge and incentive problems inherent in central banking, instead focusing on purely technical aspects of monetary policy (e.g., Abbate and Thaler 2019; Alpanda and Zubairy 2019; Paciello 2012; Rogers et al. 2018). At best, a subset of the literature attempts to address political economy considerations narrowly, rather than addressing fundamental institutional considerations (e.g., Airaudo and Olivero 2019; Berger et al. 2011; Lanne and Lütkepohl 2008; Mishkin 2009; Tillmann forthcoming). This means proposed improvements still rely on the illusory benevolence and epistemic superiority of central bankers vis-à-vis the economic agents they are attempting to influence.

Mainstream attempts to meet political economy challenges in monetary policy yield two proposed solutions. The first solution is to appoint central bankers based on their preexisting stances on monetary policy (Herrendorf and Lockwood 1997; Lohmann 1992; Lossani et al. 1998; Rogoff 1985;

---

[1] A monetary system is robust if its underlying rules make the system general and predictable. While robustness is conceptually separable from generality and predictability, it is practically dependent upon these latter characteristics. We discuss generality and predictability at greater length in Chapter 6.

Romer and Romer 1997). The second solution is to implement nonconstitutional monetary rules that guide or confine monetary discretion (Barro and Gordon 1983a, 1983b; Bassetto 2019; Bernanke and Mishkin 1997; Bernanke et al. 1999; Cukierman and Meltzer 1986).

The literature developing these solutions reflect important findings in monetary policy scholarship. The insights therein are valuable. For instance, the monetary surprise literature (e.g., Barro and Gordon 1983a, 1983b; Cukierman and Meltzer 1986) provides an important model of an incentive problem facing monetary authorities. Their solutions, however, ultimately fail the robustness test because they do not do justice to the full range of information and incentive problems faced by monetary authorities. This means that, in practice, the efficacy of these solutions is curtailed and may even be counterproductive.

Appointing central bankers based on their preexisting stances requires the heroic assumption that the political and bureaucratic incentives inherent in central banking will not influence central bankers to alter or repudiate their preexisting views. Yet, there is no guarantee that central bankers' true beliefs will be reflected in the monetary policy process once we take a realistic appraisal as to the political incentives inherent in that process. As discussed in Chapter 3, the evidence demonstrates that even PhD economists at the helm of the Fed have succumbed to political and bureaucratic pressures (e.g., Salter and Smith 2019). In addition, as discussed in Chapter 2, the knowledge problem looms large in the background; this approach does not even attempt to address this often-underrated difficulty associated with forming and implementing monetary policy. And, as we argued in Chapter 3, it is this indeterminacy, which opens the door for deleterious influence via internal and external channels. Assuming that appointing someone with appropriate credentials can mitigate these difficulties is avoiding the problem, not solving it.

Nonbinding monetary rules also assume away some of the most pressing knowledge and incentive problems. Monetary heuristics or guidelines are no substitute for true rules. While recognizing some aspects of incentive and knowledge problems, and thus offering lukewarm support for rules, the monetary literature addressing political economy often explicitly permits abandoning these monetary rules in difficult circumstances. For instance, Meltzer (2014, p. 160), in arguing for enforceable rules, states that "any rule must have a provision that permits the rule to be set aside." Ricardo Reis (2013), while admitting some forms of incentive and knowledge problems, and thus the possible benefits of mandates, argues that technical problems require giving monetary authorities discretion.

Allowing for discretion on the part of monetary authorities, especially during extraordinary times, is only efficacious if we assume monetary policymakers have a "God's-eye" view of the macroeconomy, possessing information that market actors cannot access. They do not, as we demonstrated in Chapter 2. This difficulty is especially pronounced during extraordinary times when uncertainty peaks. Monetary guide rails and other "pseudo-rules" (cf. Selgin 2016) also depend on the assumption that monetary authorities would not deviate from these guide rails except under the appropriate circumstances and to the right degree. These kinds of rule substitutes have no bite, and so cannot discipline policymakers when the stakes are highest. Not surprisingly, monetary pseudo-rules lacking enforcement mechanisms have been ineffective in constraining the actions of monetary authorities (Salter 2014; Taylor 2007, 2009; White 2007).

Furthermore, both of these literatures assume that a stable objective function exists for central bankers. In other words, they tend to view central bankers as disinterested technicians trying to advance an agreed-upon conception of social welfare. Political economy problems are thus collapsed into the relatively easy task of choosing a central banker with policy stances approximate to the given objective function, followed by constraining them with the appropriate (nonbinding) guideline to achieve that objective. As Reis (2013, p. 26) writes, "Choosing the central banker is a complementary way to pick an objective function for the central bank." One of the seminal pieces in the literature views policymakers as "attempting to maximize an objective that reflects 'society's' preferences on inflation and unemployment" (Barro and Gordon 1983b, p. 591). If that assumption holds, then it is fairly straightforward to find, appoint, and incentivize a central banker of the appropriate policy beliefs to enforce the right policy, or, to create a monetary rule that achieves it. This approach trivializes the political difficulties inherent in monetary policy.

However, no stable objective function for central bankers exists.[2] Assuming an objective function on the part of central banks is just as problematic as assuming or attempting to aggregate a social welfare function for society at large (Arrow 1950; Buchanan 1954; Sen 1977). We cannot make recourse to social maximands. Instead we must take seriously

---

[2] Another view is that the objective function is predicated on the underlying monetary constitution (cf. Buchanan and Brennan 1980). In other words, the existence of an objective function depends on a *true* monetary rule being in place. But in this case, the label "objective function" is misleading, since this environment is inherently at odds with discretionary policy.

that group decisions emerge out of individual decision-makers interacting subject to some decision rule (Brennan and Buchanan 1985; Buchanan 1964; Munger and Munger 2015). This insight applies to all public organizations, which includes central banks. Positing a stable objective function for central banks assumes away the possibility of agency problems and committee conflicts of the kind that the literature on public choice has demonstrated are the norm, not the exception, in nonmarket contexts.

Our critique of the earlier solutions can be put succinctly: They fail the test of robust political economy. The project of robust political economy adopts a comparative institutional framework: comparing alternative institutional frameworks under the real-world stress of both knowledge and incentive problems (Boettke and Leeson 2004; Levy 2002; Pennington 2011). We call those institutions "robust" that work well even in the presence of less-than-ideal information and incentive conditions. In contrast, institutional arrangements that work well only when we make generous assumptions concerning information and incentives are fragile. In the context of monetary policy, most of the literature fails to consider whether these proposed solutions work well even when central bankers, and the market actors whom they attempt to influence, are less-than-perfectly informed and have incentives that are less-than-perfectly aligned with the welfare of the general public. Failure to incorporate robustness concerns makes these solutions means–ends inconsistent; solutions that look good on paper are, in the real world, too fragile to achieve the desired ends. To put it bluntly, they are nonoperational.

While, as described earlier, we hold that mainstream literature misses elements of both knowledge and incentive problems, we think that the "objective function" approach is especially problematic in terms of the knowledge problem. The objective function approach necessarily overlooks how the institutions governing public choice in central banks affect the generation and dissemination of knowledge. Information production and diffusion are governed by the institutions within which decision-makers interact. By focusing on the epistemic properties (Hayek 1945; Lavoie 1985; Pennington 2011; Sowell 1980) of public choice within central banks, we can better understand (a) how central bankers come to formulate their goals, (b) how monetary policies, when carried out, succeed or fail at achieving those goals, and (c) the feedback process between means and ends, which determines how the rational choice calculus of central bankers unfolds in the future. Epistemic issues are typically given less attention and weight in the literature than issues relating to misaligned incentives. But if anything, focusing on what can be known and how knowledge unfolds is even more important in monetary policy, since as a nonmarket decision procedure it necessarily eschews the real-time knowledge generated by the market process. In order to understand the promises and perils of discretionary central banking, it is not enough to understand only the incentives central bankers face; we must understand the knowledge dynamics in their environment as well.

It is worth noting separately that nonrobust monetary scholarship has a hard time explaining why we have a central bank in the first place. The Fed was originally intended to be a formalization of the interbank clearing process of the old US National Banking System. Advocates of the Federal Reserve Act explicitly denied the Fed would behave as a central bank, as American public opinion was firmly against the creation of such an institution. Shortly after the Fed came into being, however, it began experimenting with its powers in a way that we now recognize as the antecedents of modern monetary policy. Because the standard incentive problem treatments take the form of either static or dynamic games with prespecified objective functions (goals), the literature cannot explain the bureaucratic "mandate creep" that gave rise to the Fed *as a central bank* (Binder and Spindel 2017; Conti-Brown 2016). Only by drawing upon well-established insights from public choice and political economy can we achieve a unified account of the incentive and knowledge problems that are not only inherent in modern central banking (Boyes et al. 1988; Otahal 2011; Wagner 1986) but gave rise to a central bank in the first place.[3]

5.3 The Quest for a Robust Monetary Framework

How, then, should we do monetary economics scholarship? What does a research program that puts robust political economy at its center, in the context of monetary theory and policy, look like? Fortunately, we do not have to speculate or draw up a research plan de novo. F. A. Hayek, Milton Friedman, and James M. Buchanan each wrestled with these questions throughout their careers, and their scholarship provides a much-needed counterbalance to the institutionally antiseptic scholarship that currently dominates the literature.

---

[3] Some examples of scholarship that recognizes the need for micro-level historical context to understand what information and incentives central bankers confront include Grier (1987), Meiselman (1986), Morris (2002, p. 123), Romer and Romer (1994), and Summers (1991).

In this section, we detail the intellectual development of Nobel laureates F. A. Hayek, Milton Friedman, and James M. Buchanan as they sought to understand how best to advance the classical liberal tenant of sound money in a free society. This kind of scholarship is frequently dismissed for its supposed ideological undertones. Such an attitude misunderstands the nature of economic science in general, as well as the relationship between positive and normative economics in particular. Hayek, Friedman, and Buchanan should not be read as assuming a libertarian or "cowboy capitalist" economic ordering is the correct one, and then making whatever reasoning steps are required to arrive at that conclusion. Instead, each was dedicated to exploring how macroeconomically effective monetary institutions could be constructed in a way that maintained society's fundamental public character of democratic self-governance. If their proposals are radical, it is only because in their estimation the existing institutional landscape does violence to macroeconomic stability, constitutional governance, or both. It is no scholarly vice to consider, in addition to whether proposed institutional alternatives are means–ends consistent, whether the ends themselves are appropriate for the kind of society that citizens envision themselves upholding. We defend the *kind of analysis*, rather than the particular conclusions, of Hayek, Friedman, and Buchanan as an example of political economy at its finest: uncompromising in terms of its core price-theoretic logic, while unafraid of the possibilities afforded by alternative institutional arrangements. It is not their scholarship that is too broad to be scientific, it is the mainstream that is too narrow to live up to the promise of what political economy can contribute to human knowledge.

5.3.1   F. A. Hayek

Hayek's early forays into monetary scholarship reflect an attempt to improve monetary policy within the central banking framework that existed at the time. Hayek (1924 [1999], ch. 1; 1925; 1937) focuses strictly on advancing technical and empirical refinements to achieve monetary stability. For example, Hayek (1925 [1999], p. 115) writes that the "most urgent goal is to find the right indicator for determining at which precise moment credit restrictions should be put into effect." While he acknowledged some concerns for knowledge and incentive problems, Hayek (1994 [2007], p. 72) held that "there was every reason to expect that, with a better understanding of the problems, we should some day [sic] be able to use these powers successfully."

Hayek rejected the notion that we should consider any other institutional arrangements for money other than a central bank (Hayek 1960, p. 324; White 1999, p. 763). Hayek's (1960) justification for this was threefold. First, he held that since money played such a vital role in the economy, nonmarket provision had a comparative advantage in creating generality, predictability, and robustness. Second, he held that market forces could not restrict or ease credit appropriately in response to economic fluctuations. Third, Hayek believed that monetary policy should be coordinated with fiscal policy.

Over the course of his life, Hayek would refine his views. Much of this was due to decades of conversation within the scholarly monetary economics community, as well as accumulated experience with how central banking worked in practice. In an essay based on a lecture delivered at the Geneva Gold and Monetary Conference, Hayek (1976a, p. 14) reflected his growing disillusion regarding the ability of central banks to achieve monetary stability, writing,

I do not want to question that a very intelligent and wholly independent national or international monetary authority might do better than an international gold standard, or any other sort of automatic system. But I see not the slightest hope that any government, or any institution subject to political pressure, will ever be able to act in such a manner.

In other words, Hayek began to suspect the claim that ideal central banking could outperform ideal market provision of money was a red herring. What mattered most is whether *actual* central banking could outperform *actual* market provision.

Hayek's (1976a, p. 16) growing skepticism included the belief that even trained economists could not be entrusted with the monetary authority. In his subsequently published *Denationalisation of Money* (Hayek 1976b), Hayek observed that central banks invariably produced, or at minimum contributed to, inflation, fiscal profligacy, and economic nationalism. This was due to both knowledge and incentive problems inherent in central banking. For instance, Hayek (1976b, p. 80) argues that

A single monopolistic governmental agency can neither possess the information which should govern the supply of money nor would it, if it knew what it ought to do in the general interest, usually be in a position to act in that manner. Indeed, if, as I am convinced, the main advantage of the market order is that prices will convey to the acting individuals the relevant information, only the constant observation of the course of current prices of particular commodities can provide information on the direction in which more or less money ought to be spent. Money is not a tool of policy that can achieve particular foreseeable results by control of its quantity.

In part due to the knowledge problems, central bank independence could not keep special interests and political pressures at bay, leading to a long-run bias in favor of easy money and credit. Low-interest rates created overinvestment and generated the possibility for subsequent booms and busts. The centralized control of money enabled and reinforced Keynesian policies, allowing the unprecedented growth in the size of government. The only solution, for Hayek, was to allow competition in currency, arguing that

We have always had bad money because private enterprise was not permitted to give us a better one. In a world governed by the pressure of organized interests, Evolving views on monetary policy the important truth to keep in mind is that we cannot count on intelligence or understanding but only on sheer self-interest to give us the institutions we need. Blessed indeed will be the day when it will no longer be from the benevolence of the government that we expect good money but from the regard of the banks for their own interest. (1976b, p. 100)

In the second edition of *Denationalisation of Money*, Hayek (1978) expanded further on this, adding a subchapter on "The abolition of central banks." Hayek argued that we should allow the market to set interest rates just like any other price in the market, free of government manipulation.[4] One of the most important arguments for markets in money, he argued, was that the kind of currency that would emerge via competition is unknowable. If we could out-guess the market, we would not need the market. The issue must be put to the market test (Hayek 1978, p. 66). Ultimately, Hayek (1981 [1999]) ended up focusing his monetary research on investigating how competition in currency via the market would operate.[5] Early in his scholarly career, Hayek firmly believed that a central bank was an essential component of a free society. As an economist, he sought refinements of existing monetary models to assist central bankers in achieving sound money. But by the end of his career, he openly rejected his previous views and instead argued that, given the inherent knowledge and incentive problems in central banking, we needed to explore alternative institutions in a comparative institutional framework. He concluded that a market of competing currencies was the most robust system for achieving sound money.

---

[4] Though Hayek notes that even without a central bank, the government would still have some influence over interest rates via government debt.

[5] There are important differences between Hayek's currency competition and the modern literature on "free banking" (cf. Selgin 2015; White 1999).

5.3.2 Milton Friedman

Friedman (1948, p. 246)[6] also began his scholarly career in monetary economics within the framework of existing monetary institutions, holding that, "Government must provide a monetary framework for a competitive order since the competitive order cannot provide one for itself." Friedman (1948, p. 247), however, did embrace one drastic institutional reform even from his early days, proposing a 100 percent reserve banking system to reduce the discretionary monetary powers of the central bank.[7]

Friedman (1958, p. 254) recognized the need for sound money since a fluctuating price level could become a source of economic disturbance that negatively affected economic growth. With this recognition, Friedman (1960 [1992]) dedicated an entire book to achieving sound money, *A Program for Monetary Stability*. Friedman (1960 [1992], p. 23), beginning to recognize the omnipresent political pressures on and within monetary institutions, started to question the predominant research program focusing on equipping monetary authorities with the latest technical and empirical skills. He instead asked whether scholars should focus on designing institutions to constraint monetary authorities:

The central problem is not to construct a highly sensitive instrument that can continuously offset instability introduced by other factors, but rather to prevent monetary arrangements from themselves becoming a primary source of instability. What we need is not a skilled monetary driver of the economic vehicle continuously turning the steering wheel to adjust to the unexpected irregularities of the route, but some means of keeping the monetary passenger who is in the back seat as ballast from occasionally leaning over and giving the steering wheel a jerk that threatens to send the car off the road.

Friedman (1960 [1992], p. 100) explored institutional solutions to these political economy concerns, such as a binding 4 percent growth rate target for the money stock and ending gold reserve requirements. Yet, while Friedman (1962b, p. 219) sought ways to monitor and restrain central bankers, he persisted in his belief that a central bank was necessary "to provide a stable monetary framework for a free economy" (Friedman 1962a, p. 38). Nevertheless, Friedman's concern for monetary robustness

---

[6] For more in-depth treatments of Friedman's contributions to monetary economics, see Nelson and Schwartz (2008), Nelson (2007), and Lothian (2009). See Selgin (2008) for a historical analysis, and critique, of Friedman's views on monetary policy as they progressed.

[7] See Burns (2016) on the development of the limited banking "Chicago Plan" and its influence on Friedman.

emerged as a distinct criterion within his proposed solutions. Perhaps Friedman's (1962b, pp. 50–51) views at this time can be best summarized by this passage:

It may be that these mistakes were excusable on the basis of the knowledge available to men at the time – though I happen to think not. But that is really beside the point. Any system which gives so much power and so much discretion to a few men that mistakes – excusable or not – can have such far-reaching effects is a bad system. It is a bad system to believers in freedom just because it gives a few men such power without any effective check by the body politic – this is the key political argument against an "independent" central bank. But it is a bad system even to those who set security higher than freedom. Mistakes, excusable or not, cannot be avoided in a system which disperses responsibility yet gives a few men great power, and which thereby makes important policy actions highly dependent on accidents of personality. This is the key technical argument against an "independent" bank. To paraphrase Clémenceau, money is much too serious a matter to be left to the Central Bankers.

Constraining monetary authorities, while maintaining a central bank, could be achieved by three ways: (1) through the adoption of a commodity standard, (2) through an independent central bank, and (3) legislated rules (Friedman 1962b). Of these three options, Friedman ruled out returning to a commodity standard as undesirable. He held that a truly independent central bank was impossible given the pressures put on it during times of uncertainty and the strength of special interest groups, especially financiers. This left "the only feasible device currently available for converting monetary policy into a pillar of a free society rather than a threat to its foundations" as legislative rules that mandated a specified growth in the money stock (Friedman 1962a, p. 55; see also Friedman 1968, p. 17).

Friedman's popular writing at this time, however, tended to blame monetary instability on technical failures rather than political economy issues (Friedman 1966, 1967a, 1967c, 1970b, 1971). For instance, in a 1969 column, Friedman writes that "inflation is made in Washington" because "they have taken the behavior of interest rates rather than of the quantity of money as their guide – and this mistake has led them far astray from their intended path." This was the basis for his praise when his mentor Arthur Burns was appointed chairman of the Fed in 1970. Friedman (1970a), believing that monetary failures were primarily technical, held that Burns' training and expertise would finally bring sound monetary policy.

But this emphasis on the technical difficulties of monetary policy eventually gave way to robustness concerns once again. The failure of Arthur Burns to adopt sound monetary policy led Friedman to doubt whether the serious monetary problems were really technical (Friedman 1974, p. 23). In other words, he realized that putting the right people in charge of the central bank was not a robust solution to political economy problems. Even if we solved the technical issues, Friedman (1972) wrote that "we would probably experience a four-year cycle, with unemployment reaching its trough in years divisible by four and inflation reaching its peak in the succeeding year."[8] Friedman (1978) also saw the pressures exerted by the adoption of Keynesian deficit spending as an obstacle to monetary stability:

We, the public, have been asking Congress to provide us with ever more goodies – yet not to raise our taxes. Congress has obliged, enlisting inflation as a hidden tax to finance the difference (and surreptitiously raise taxes by pushing more and more income into higher tax brackets). The Fed has cooperated – except when the public outcry against inflation has overcome Congressional pressure.[9]

Thus, Friedman recognized that the mutual impingement of monetary and fiscal concerns posed a serious danger to economic stability, and perhaps even democratic self-governance itself. In a drastic turn, Friedman began to question the very need for a central bank and even suggested that a computer, by automating monetary policy, would provide a more robust solution to the political economy problems (Bennett 1980; Friedman 2007; *San Francisco Chronicle 1987*; Silber 2012, p. 194).[10] Frustrated with the incentive problems faced by central banks, Friedman (1982, p. 118) wrote that:

The only two alternatives that do seem to me feasible over the longer run are either to make the Federal Reserve a bureau in the Treasury under the Secretary of the Treasury, or to put the Federal Reserve under direct congressional control. Either involves terminating the so-called independence of the system. But either would establish a strong incentive for the Fed to produce a stabler [sic] monetary environment than we have had.

It is clear that Friedman by this point had switched from working on the tactics of monetary policy (the technical and empirical problems) to exploring comparative monetary institutions on the basis of their robustness to political economy concerns (Friedman 1984, 1992). Through this lens, Friedman increasingly saw the weaknesses of the existing monetary system and the advantages of alternative systems, even suggesting that the

---

[8] Research on political business cycles, to the extent they exist, suggest that they are induced monetarily (Drazen 2000).

[9] Also see Friedman (1967b).

[10] Paul Volcker and Arthur Burns argue that Friedman was using the computer as a metaphor (Silber 2012, p. 194).

"United States would be better off if the Federal Reserve had never been established" (Rainie and White 1981). Friedman's (1984, 1984 [2014], p. 634) full range of alternatives included constitutional rules, combining the central bank with the Treasury Department, transitioning to a gold standard, competitive note issue, and holding high-powered money to a zero-growth rate.[11] Only drastic reforms of this nature had the potential to "end the arbitrary power of the Federal Reserve System to determine the quantity of money and would do so without establishing any comparable locus of power ..." (Friedman 1984, p. 51). Even though he had reservations, Friedman (1984, p. 47) came to approve of "Hayek's proposal to remove restrictions on the issuance of private moneys to compete with government moneys."[12] To Friedman and co-author Anna Schwartz:

Even granted the market failures that we and many other economists had attributed to a strictly laissez-faire policy in money and banking, the course of events encouraged the view that turning to government as an alternative was a cure that was worse than the disease, a least with existing government policies and institutions. Government failure might be worse than market failure. (1986, p. 39)

From early in his career, Friedman recognized the tension between monetary discretion and strictly binding rules. His initial scholarship focused on improving the tactics of monetary policy to navigate a politically feasible path between these two extremes. Over his lifetime, however, he became less confident in the ability of the central bank, under intense political pressure, to achieve this. He ultimately rejected the ability of discretionary monetary authorities to be able to achieve sound money, even if the technical and informational problems were solved.

5.3.3 James M. Buchanan

Unlike Hayek and Friedman, James M. Buchanan started his scholarly analysis of monetary policy squarely within the comparative institutional framework. He never focused on technical refinements or other abstract improvements in monetary models. His perpetual concern was comparing alternative monetary regimes in real, not ideal, settings.

[11] Friedman (1984, p. 46) writes regarding the gold standard, "I regard ... a real gold standard ... as constituting an improvement rather than a deterioration in our monetary arrangements. And that alternative, which is by no means ideal, has minuscule political support." See Friedman (1961) on his distinction between real and pseudo gold standards.

[12] Friedman and Schwartz (1986, pp. 40–46), however, exhibited more skepticism toward denationalizing money, instead favoring central banks constrained by rigid rules.

For Buchanan (1962), monetary regimes should be judged based on their ability to generate predictable outcomes for economic actors. Buchanan (1962, p. 164) divided the possible institutional solutions into two categories. The first category attempted to achieve monetary predictability through the top-down direction. The second category relied on a bottom-up approach. Importantly, both of these categories had to adopt symmetric behavioral and epistemic assumptions. Buchanan rejected as an assumption the belief that public actors were wiser or more virtuous than private actors and vice versa. Buchanan favored monetary institutions that enabled bottom-up market forces to contribute to monetary stability. For instance, Buchanan's ideal monetary system would be based on a commodity that tracked the average level of prices. The role of the monetary authority would be to buy and sell that commodity at prespecified prices. Market forces would then be unleashed to arbitrage deviations between the actual price level and the prespecified price level, automatically providing the incentives for price stability.

In addition, Buchanan held that constitutional rules would be necessary to protect the system from political interference. The adoption of Keynesian ideas in politics, especially the acceptance of perpetual deficits, made Buchanan even more skeptical of monetary arrangements that involved top-down elements (Buchanan and Wagner 1977 [2000], p. 124). Brennan and Buchanan (1980 [2000], p. 153) argued that a constitutional mandate should specify the appropriate target level of inflation. They were cognizant of the limits of constitutions when it came to money, however, arguing that, "there is no way that the power to create money can be divested of its revenue implications by a money rule alone. This may be viewed as a persuasive argument for relying on possibly imperfect market alternatives, and denying government the power to create money under any circumstance at all" (Brennan and Buchanan 1980 [2000], p. 155). In other words, Brennan and Buchanan recognized a rule without bite was no rule at all.

For Buchanan (1983, p. 146; see also 1986 [2001]), scholarship focusing on improvements within the existing monetary framework would inevitably be "mired in the muck of modern politics." These views became more pronounced following the financial crisis. Buchanan (2009, p. 155) wrote that, "Critical evaluation and assessment suggests that the structure of the whole monetary economy is flawed, which points toward genuine constitutional revolution rather than either a change in participants or piecemeal adjustments in the regulatory apparatus." But Buchanan's skepticism of the robustness of both government and market forces for monetary stability remained the basis of his argument for constitutional control of money.

Even more consistently than Hayek or Friedman, Buchanan conducted monetary research within a robust political economy framework. While initially he explored a broader range of possible institutional alternatives to our given monetary structure, he gradually became convinced that the only solution was to constitutionalize money. What the constitutionalization of money entails – especially the relationship between constitutional money and true monetary rules – is sufficiently important that we explore it in greater depth in the next chapter.

5.4 Imaginative Frontiers of Monetary Political Economy

Monetary scholarship in the central banking era has largely focused on improving the implementation of monetary policy within the existing institutional framework. This means scholars primarily investigate technical and empirical refinements to improve the policies implemented by discretionary monetary authorities. While there is a place for this kind of research, it is ultimately of limited value because it treats information and incentive problems far too casually. Lasting progress in monetary theory and policy requires putting robustness concerns front and center.

The intellectual evolution of Hayek and Friedman, as well as the more consistent research program of Buchanan, highlight the proper concerns of monetary policy scholarship. These classical liberal scholars, instead of limiting themselves to minor refinements of existing monetary models and procedures, viewed comparative institutional analysis, embedded within a robust political economy framework, as the best research avenue for achieving monetary stability. Each of them adopted the view that knowledge and incentive problems rendered discretionary central banks incapable of reliably delivering sound money. Given their realization of the importance that sound money played in a free society, their explorations of radical alternatives to our existing monetary system were fully justified. Hayek turned toward denationalization. Friedman turned toward rigid monetary rules, perhaps even fully algorithmic policy. Buchanan advocated for constitutionalizing money.

The concern for robustness in Hayek, Friedman, and Buchanan's works is not coincidental. Their classically liberal intellectual heritage helped them realize that democratic self-governance, lawful public authority, and macroeconomic stability were complements, not substitutes. The common thread running throughout their scholarly works is the importance of the *rule of law* in all public institutions, including monetary institutions. Sacrificing true rules in favor of discretion, in the hopes that enlightened monetary policymakers can improve on macroeconomic outcomes, inadvertently destroys the macroeconomy's means of stabilization. In the next chapter, we elaborate on the ideal of the rule of law, both within the classical liberal tradition and as applied to contemporary monetary issues. In doing so we help carry forward Hayek, Friedman, and Buchanan's common project, which has been unfortunately neglected.

References

Abbate, Angela and Dominik Thaler (2019). Monetary Policy and the Asset Risk-Taking Channel. *Journal of Money, Credit and Banking*, 51(8), 2115–2144.

Airaudo, Marco and María Pía Olivero (2019). Optimal Monetary Policy with Countercyclical Credit Spreads. *Journal of Money, Credit and Banking*, 51(4), 787–829.

Alpanda, Sami and Sarah Zubairy (2019). Household Debt Overhand and Transmission of Monetary Policy. *Journal of Money, Credit and Banking*, 51(5), 1265–1307.

Arnon, Arie (1987). Banking between the Invisible and Visible Hands: A Reinterpretation of Ricardo's Place within the Classical School. *Oxford Economic Papers*, 39(2), 268–281.

(2010). *Monetary Theory and Policy from Hume and Smith to Wicksell*. Cambridge University Press.

Arrow, Kenneth (1950). A Difficulty in the Concept of Social Welfare. *Journal of Political Economy*, 58(4), 328–346.

Barro, Robert and David Gordon (1983a). Rules, Discretion and Reputation in a Model of Monetary Policy. *Journal of Monetary Economics*, 12(1), 101–122.

(1983b). A Positive Theory of Monetary Policy in a Natural Rate Model. *Journal of Political Economy*, 91(4), 589–610.

Bassetto, Marco (2019). Forward Guidance: Communication, Commitment, or Both? *Journal of Monetary Economics*, 108, 69–86.

Bennett, Robert (1980). The Talk of New Orleans: Agonies of World Banking. *New York Times*, Section 3, p. 1, Column 4, June 8.

Berger, Helge, Michael Ehrmann, and Marcel Fratzscher (2011). Monetary Policy in the Media. *Journal of Money, Credit and Banking*, 43(4), 689–709.

Bernanke, Benjamin, Thomas Laubach, Frederic Mishkin, and Adam Posen (1999). *Inflation Targeting: Lessons from the International Experience*. Princeton University Press.

Bernanke, Benjamin and Frederic Mishkin (1997). Inflation Targeting: A New Framework for Monetary Policy? *Journal of Economic Perspectives*, 11(2), 97–116.

Binder, Sarah and Mark Spindel (2017). *The Myth of Independence: How Congress Governs the Federal Reserve*. Princeton University Press.

Boettke, Peter and Peter T. Leeson (2004). Liberalism, Socialism, and Robust Political Economy. *Journal of Markets and Morality*, 7(1), 99–111.

Boyes, William, William Stewart Mounts, and Clifford Sowell (1988). The Federal Reserve as a Bureaucracy: An Examination of Expense-Preference Behavior. *Journal of Money, Credit and Banking*, 20(2), 181–190.

Brennan, Geoffrey and James Buchanan (1980 [2000]). *The Power to Tax: Analytical Foundations of a Fiscal Constitution*. Liberty Fund, Inc.

(1985). *The Reason of Rules*. Cambridge University Press.

Buchanan, James M. (1954). Social Choice, Democracy, and Free Markets. *Journal of Political Economy*, 62(2), 114–123.

(1962). Predictability: The Criterion of Monetary Constitutions. In Leland Yeager (Ed.), *In Search of a Monetary Constitution*. Harvard University Press, pp. 155–183.

(1964). What Should Economists Do? *Southern Economic Journal*, 30, 213–222.

(1983). Monetary Research, Monetary Rules, and Monetary Regimes. *Cato Journal*, 3 (Spring/Summer), 143–146.

(1986). The Relevance of Constitutional Strategy. *Cato Journal*, 6(2), 513–517.

(2009). Economists Have No Clothes. *Perspectives in Moral Science*, 0, 151–156.

Buchanan, James M. and Richard Wagner (1977 [2000]). *Democracy in Deficit: The Political Legacy of Lord Keynes*. Liberty Fund, Inc.

Conti-Brown, Peter (2016). *The Power and Independence of the Federal Reserve*. Oxford University Press.

Cukierman, Alex and Allan Meltzer (1986). A Theory of Ambiguity, Credibility, and Inflation under Discretion and Asymmetric Information. *Econometrica*, 54(5), 1099–1128.

Drazen, Allan (2000). The Political Business Cycle after 25 Years. *NBER Macroeconomics Annual*, 15, 75–117.

Friedman, Milton (1948). A Monetary and Fiscal Framework for Economic Stability. *The American Economic Review*, 38(3), 245–264.

(1958). The Supply of Money and Changes in Prices and Output. In Patman Wright (Ed.), *The Relationship of Prices to Economic Stability and Growth*. Government Printing Office, pp. 241–256.

(1960 [1992]). *A Program for Monetary Stability*. Fordham University Press.

(1961). Real and Pseudo Gold Standards. *The Journal of Law & Economics*, 4, 66–79.

(1962a). *Capitalism and Freedom*. University of Chicago Press.

(1962b). Should There Be an Independent Monetary Authority? In Leland Yeager (Ed.), *In Search of a Monetary Constitution*. Harvard University Press, pp. 219–243.

(1966). Inflationary Recession. *Newsweek*. October 17, p. 92.

(1967a). Current Monetary Policy. *Newsweek*. January 9, p. 59.

(1967b). Fiscal Responsibility. *Newsweek*. August 7, p. 68.

(1967c). Current Monetary Policy. *Newsweek*. October 30, p. 80.

(1968). The Role of Monetary Policy. *The American Economic Review*, 58(1), 1–17.

(1969). The Inflationary Fed. *Newsweek*. January 20, p. 78.

(1970a). A New Chairman at the Fed. *Newsweek*. February 2, p. 68.

(1970b). Monetary Overheating. *Newsweek*. July 6, p. 75.

(1971). Money – Tight or Easy. *Newsweek*. March 1, p. 80.

(1972). The Case for a Monetary Rule. *Newsweek*. February 7, p. 67.

(1974). Letter on Monetary Policy. *Federal Reserve Bank of St. Louis Review*, 56(3), 20–23.

(1978). Burns on the Outside. *Newsweek*. January 9, pp. 52–53.

(1982). Monetary Policy: Theory and Practice. *Journal of Money, Credit and Banking*, 14(1), 98–118.

(1984). Monetary Policy for the 1980s. In John H. Moore (Ed.), *To Promote Prosperity*. Hoover Institution, pp. 23–60.

(1984 [2014]). Monetary Policy Structures. In House Republican Committee (Ed.), *Candid Conversations on Monetary Policy*. House Republican Research Committee, pp. 32–50. Reprinted in: *Cato Journal*, 34(3), 631–656.

(1992). *Money Mischief*. Harcourt Brace & Company.

(2007). M. Friedman @ rest. *The Wall Street Journal*. January 22.

Friedman, Milton and Anna Schwartz (1986). Has Government Any Role in Money? *Journal of Monetary Economics*, 17(1), 37–62.

Grier, Kevin B. (1987). Presidential Elections and Fed Policy: An Empirical Test. *Southern Economic Journal*, 54(2), 475–486.

Hayek, Friedrich August (1924 [1999]). A Survey of Recent American Writing: Stabilization Problems in Gold Exchange Standard Countries. In Stephen Kresge (Ed.), *Good Money, Part I. The Collected Works of F. A. Hayek*. Liberty Fund Inc., pp. 39–70.

(1925 [1999]). Monetary Policy in the United States after the Recovery from the Crisis of 1920. In Stephen Kresge (Ed.), *Good Money, Part I. The Collected Works of F. A. Hayek*. Liberty Fund Inc., pp. 71–152.

(1937). *Monetary Nationalism and International Stability*. Longman, Green.

(1944 [2007]). *The Road to Serfdom*. Bruce Caldwell (Ed.). The University of Chicago Press.

(1945). The Use of Knowledge in Society. *The American Economic Review*, 35(4), 519–530.

(1960). *The Constitution of Liberty*. The University of Chicago Press.

(1976a). *Choice in Currency*. Institute for Economic Affairs.

(1976b). *Denationalisation of Money*. The Institute of Economic Affairs.

(1978). *Denationalisation of Money: The Argument Refined*. The Institute of Economic Affairs.

(1981 [1999]). The Future Unit of Value. In Stephen Kresge (Ed.), *Good Money Part II. The Collected Works of F. A. Hayek*, pp. 238–252.

Herrendorf, Berthold and Ben Lockwood (1997). Rogoff's "Conservative" Central Banker Restored. *Journal of Money, Credit, and Banking*, 29(4), 476–495.

Jacoud, Gilles (2013). *Money and Banking in Jean-Baptiste Say's Economic Thought*. Routledge.

Lanne, Markku and Helmut Lütkepohl (2008). Identifying Monetary Policy Shocks via Changes in Volatility. *Journal of Money, Credit and Banking*, 40(6), 1131–1149.

Lavoie, Donald (1985). *Rivalry and Central Planning: The Socialist Debate Reconsidered*. Cambridge University Press.

Levy, David M. (2002). Robust Institutions. *The Review of Austrian Economics*, 15(2/3), 131–142.

Lohmann, Susanne (1992). Optimal Commitment in Monetary Policy: Credibility versus Flexibility. *The American Economic Review*, 82(1), 273–286.

Lossani, Marco, Piergiovanna Natale, and Patrizio Tirelli (1998). Incomplete Information in Monetary Policy Games: Rules Rather Than a Conservative Central Banker. *Scottish Journal of Political Economy*, 45(1), 33–47.

Lothian, James (2009). Milton Friedman's Monetary Economics and the Quantity-Theory Tradition. *Journal of International Money and Finance*, 28(7), 1086–1096.

Meiselman, David I. (1986). Is There a Political Monetary Cycle? *Cato Journal*, 6(2), 563–586.

Meltzer, Allan (2014). Federal Reserve Independence. *Journal of Economic Dynamics and Control*, 49(December), 160–163.

Mishkin, Frederic (2009). Globalization, Macroeconomic Performance, and Monetary Policy. *Journal of Money, Credit and Banking*, 41(1), 187–196.

Morris, Irwin (2002). *Congress, the President, and the Federal Reserve*. University of Michigan Press.

Munger, Michael and Kevin Munger (2015). *Choosing in Groups: Analytical Politics Revisited*. Cambridge University Press.

Nelson, Edward (2007). Milton Friedman and U.S. Monetary History: 1961–2006. *Review of the Federal Reserve Bank of St. Louis*, 89(3), 153–182.

Nelson, Edward and Anna Schwartz (2008). The Impact of Milton Friedman on Modern Monetary Economics: Setting the Record Straight on Paul Krugman's "Who Was Milton Friedman?" *Journal of Monetary Economics*, 55(4), 835–856.

Otahal, Tomas (2011). Rent-Seeking Origins of Central Banks: The Case of the Federal Reserve System. MENDELU Working Papers in Business and Economics 2011-08.

Paciello, Luigi (2012). Monetary Policy and Price Responsiveness to Aggregate Shocks under Rational Inattention. *Journal of Money, Credit and Banking*, 44(7), 1375–1399.

Pennington, Mark (2011). *Robust Political Economy*. Edward Elgar.

Rainie, Harrison and James White (1981). Friedman: Kill the Fed. *Daily News*, p. 38, May 21.

Reis, Ricardo (2013). Central Bank Design. *Journal of Economic Perspectives*, 27(4), 17–44.

Rogers, John, Chiara Scotti, and Jonathan Wright (2018). Unconventional Monetary Policy and International Risk Premia. *Journal of Money, Credit and Banking*, 50 (8), 1827–1850.

Rogoff, Kenneth (1985). The Optimal Degree of Commitment to an Intermediate Monetary Target. *Quarterly Journal of Economics*, 100(4), 1169–1189.

Romer, Christina D. and David H. Romer (1994). Monetary Policy Matters. *Journal of Monetary Economics*, 34(1), 75–88.

(1997). Institutions for Monetary Stability. In Christina D. Romer and David Romer (Eds.), *Reducing Inflation: Motivation and Strategy*. Chicago University Press, pp. 307–334.

Salter, Alexander William (2014). Is There a Self-Enforcing Monetary Constitution? *Constitutional Political Economy*, 25(3), 280–300.

Salter, Alexander William and Daniel Smith (2019). Political *Economists* or *Political Economists*? The Role of Political Environments in the Formation of Fed Policy under Burns, Greenspan, and Bernanke. *Quarterly Review of Economics and Finance*, 71(1), 1–13.

San Francisco Chronicle (1987). Milton Friedman Says He'd Dump the Fed. June 8, p. 23.

Selgin, George (2008). Milton Friedman and the Case against Currency Monopoly. *Cato Journal*, 28(2), 287–301.

(2015). Hayek and Free Banking. *Alt-M*. Available online (accessed May 27, 2020), www.alt-m.org/2015/07/18/hayek-and-free-banking/#3

(2016). Real and Pseudo Monetary Rules. *Cato Journal*, 36(2), 279–296.

Sen, Amartya (1977). On Weights and Measures: Informational Constraints in Social Welfare Analysis. *Econometrica*, 45(7), 1539–1572.

Silber, William L. (2012). *Volcker*. New York: Bloomsbury Press.

Sowell, Thomas (1980). *Knowledge and Decisions*. Basic Books.

Summers, Lawrence H. (1991). The Scientific Illusion in Empirical Macroeconomics. *The Scandinavian Journal of Economics*, 93(2), 129–148.

Taylor, John (2007). Housing and Monetary Policy, *NBER Working Paper* 13682.

(2009). *Getting Off Track: How Government Actions and Interventions Caused, Prolonged, and Worsened the Financial Crisis*. Hoover Institution Press.

Tillmann, Peter (forthcoming). Monetary Policy Uncertainty and the Response of the Yield Curve to Policy Shocks. *Journal of Money, Credit and Banking*.

Wagner, Richard (1986). Central Banking and the Fed: A Public Choice Perspective. *Cato Journal*, 6(2), 519–543.

West, Edwin (1997). Adam Smith's Support for Money and Banking Regulation: A Case of Inconsistency. *Journal of Money, Credit and Banking*, 29(1), 127–134.

White, Lawrence H. (1999). Why Didn't Hayek Favor Laissez Faire in Banking? *History of Political Economy*, 31(4), 753–769.

(2007). What Type of Inflation Target? *Cato Journal*, 27(2), 283–288.

Money and the Rule of Law

6.1 Instead of Discretion

F. A. Hayek, Milton Friedman, and James M. Buchanan were the three great classically liberal economists of the twentieth century who applied their minds to the challenges of monetary institutional design. As we saw in the previous chapter, their ideas and proposals differed, often significantly. However, there is a single unifying theme throughout their writings on monetary theory and policy. Hayek, Friedman, and Buchanan were each trying to bring monetary institutions under the control of the *rule of law*. Their concern was finding monetary arrangements that could work well (stabilize aggregate demand, prevent financial crises, etc.) while satisfying the normative constraints that citizens of self-governing republics rightly place on their public institutions.

In this chapter, we explain what we mean by rule of law, and why monetary institutions ought to be subject to it. In doing so we draw upon a rich tradition of social philosophy and political economy in the classically liberal tradition. This tradition affirms the importance of the rule of law for reasons that are still widely accepted today. Constraining public institutions such that they respect individual rights, adhere to their publicly given mandates, and operate according to the common good (as opposed to the particular good of interest groups) is important to all the political philosophies represented in the public square today. Conservatives, classical liberals, and progressives often disagree on the *consequences* of a policy, that is, whether it does in fact contribute to the common good. But they agree on the ultimate institutional standards by which policy is to be evaluated. This agreement on principles at the "meta-constitutional level" suggests an important and neglected critique of discretionary central banking: it fails to adhere to the rule of law in any meaningful sense.

Readers may find this claim bizarre, especially as applied to the Federal Reserve. After all, the Fed was created by an act of Congress. Throughout the twentieth century, Congress provided the ultimate guidance for monetary policy by specifying objectives (full employment and price stability post-1977)[1] while prudently leaving decisions over the appropriate means to monetary policymakers. The conventional wisdom holds that this is a triumph that reconciled democratic government with expert management, one that has been broadly economically beneficial (Bean et al. 2010). By now readers will not be surprised to learn we strongly dispute the earlier discussion. Beginning with the second consideration, it is far from clear that the Fed has improved US economic performance (Bédard 2014; Boettke and Smith 2013, 2015; Hogan 2015; Hogan et al. 2018; Paniagua 2016; Selgin et al. 2012). For reasons described in the previous chapters on knowledge and incentive problems, the Fed's century-long experiment with discretionary central banking is at best inconclusive, and at worst a failure. Furthermore, the Fed's behavior since its inception does not represent a marriage of democratic self-governance with specialized macroeconomic expertise. It represents the subjugation of the former by the latter. That the Fed was established and guided according to the formal procedures outlined by the US Constitution is necessary for the Fed to be lawful, but it is not sufficient.

Current monetary arrangements represent not the rule of law, but the rule of central bankers (White 2010). Instead of discretion, monetary authorities ought to be constrained by a "higher law" that the monetary authority itself cannot change and is simple enough to admit minimal interpretive latitude (Buchanan 2010a; Hendrickson and Salter 2018; Salter 2014a; White et al. 2015; Yeager 1962). Our argument harkens back to an older understanding of political economy as the body of knowledge informing our conceptions of the "good society," occupying the space "Between predictive science and moral philosophy" (Buchanan 2001). Our work thus can be viewed, along with those of Frankel (1977), Steil and Hinds (2009), and Zelmanovitz (2015), as an analysis of money and monetary policy in the realm of social philosophy more generally.

We make our argument on two separate but complementary lines. First, we build the case for lawful money on the same grounds as lawful institutions more generally. Second, we explore why unlawful monetary institutions yield harmful political, financial, and macroeconomic outcomes. If

---

[1] See Steelman (2011).

we have a rule of law applied to monetary institutions and policy, we can have macroeconomic stability. But if we forsake the rule of law, we inadvertently lose both.

We proceed in this chapter as follows: In Section 6.2 we provide arguments for the rule of law in general, as well as its important role when it comes to money. In Section 6.3 we examine the theory and practice of discretionary central banking. We do this to anticipate and counter the means–ends argument that constrained discretion is so superior to the rule of law that, despite the prima facie importance placed upon the latter, consequentialist considerations impel us to accept the former. In Section 6.4 we consider the implications of our argument more generally, with special focus on the relevance of broader social–philosophic concerns to the analysis of monetary institutions and policy. This last analysis sets the stage for our subsequent and final chapter, on specific institutional alternatives to discretionary central banking that are both lawful and effective.

6.2 The Rule of Law: Generality, Predictability, and Robustness

A crucial component of the rule of law is generality. The rule of law holds when the restraints society places on individual behavior take the form of general rules that can be equally applied to all. General rules serve a crucial *epistemic* function (Epstein 1995; Hayek 1960 [2011]). They provide information in similar ways as the laws of the physical world. Just as nature's laws provide information regarding the consequences of natural phenomena, general rules spell out the consequences of social phenomena (Brennan and Buchanan 1985 [2000b]; Hayek 1973; Ostrom et al. 1994). When rules are general and abstract, they increase coordination and reduce conflict.[2]

Such a rule for monetary policy would serve the important role of anchoring the public's expectations with respect to equal treatment. Viewed this way, information considerations naturally flow into incentive considerations. For example, if the monetary authority were strictly bound by a rule which prevented them from granting liquidity or credit to politically favored firms, these firms would have no incentive to expend resources on maintaining a privileged position. Firms would also be more likely to internalize the risk they take in conducting financial intermediation. If the Fed cannot underwrite the irresponsible behavior of private

---

[2] For instance, see Easterly (2001), Knack and Keefer (1995), and Mauro (1995).

firms during turbulent times, there will be less irresponsible behavior during normal times. A truly general rule for monetary policy would do much to eliminate moral hazard from our financial system.

An essential condition for a free society is that the government ought to "have the monopoly *only* of coercion and that in all other respects it operates on the same terms as everybody else" (Hayek 1960 [2011], p. 332, emphasis added). Note that operating "on the same terms as everybody else" is not an argument against public authority having some role in monetary institutions, but rather against agents empowered by that authority operating outside a framework of rules. If monetary policy-makers are not bound by a rule, they are in a privileged position to dictate to market actors the terms of the commercial game by meddling with the medium of exchange. And as we have seen since the 2007–2008 financial crisis, they are also in a privileged position to allocate credit to politically connected firms at the expense of systemic liquidity.

Predictability is the second necessary constituent of the rule of law. Both generality and predictability require a degree of abstractness, and both are embodiments of our moral intuitions regarding "fair play" and the import-ance of process in matters of governance. Whereas generality is concerned primarily with equal treatment, predictability is concerned primarily with effective behavior. Rules should be predictable because predictability enables those subject to the rules to form reliable expectations about the future. Predictability also requires that rules be created and enforced in a nonarbitrary fashion. If a law is general in its applicability but is not predictable in its content, or how it will be applied, then that law will not do much to promote social cooperation under the division of labor. In fact, the law may even impede it.

In the previous chapter, we encountered predictability in the form of a stable purchasing power of money (cf. Buchanan 1962). While this is a valid means of institutionalizing predictability, we do not necessarily endorse it. What we do endorse is achieving predictability through general agreement on the rules that underpin monetary policy. Securing this agreement requires that we bring a "constitutional attitude" (Buchanan 1999) to the study of monetary institutions and policy (Boettke et al. 2018). We must avoid both majoritarian passions and elitist tinkering in order to achieve predictability. The former subjects monetary policy to the unstable and arbitrary vagaries of day-to-day electoral politics; the latter represents the capture of monetary policy by a technocratic class that regularly fails to appreciate "how little they really know about what they imagine they can design" (Hayek 1988, p. 76).

The last feature is robustness. Robust rules will be general and predictable, but not all general and predictable rules are robust. Robustness often goes hand-in-hand with generality and predictability, but nonetheless is conceptually distinct. For a rule to be robust, it must work well even when those subject to the rule have limited knowledge and confront opportunistic incentives (Boettke and Leeson 2004; Leeson and Subrik 2006; Levy 2002; Pennington 2011). Taking robustness seriously requires that we get beyond what Coase (1990) dismissively refers to as blackboard economics: assuming that agents have all the relevant information and confront all the right incentives to behave in the manner prescribed by economists' models. In monetary theory and policy, this often takes the form of devising an optimal monetary policy, calibrated to the foibles and follies of the market, while assuming that the implementers of this policy can access the pertinent information and themselves do not confront any perverse incentives. This is an unacceptable asymmetry because it is assumed rather than demonstrated.

In the context of monetary rules, Selgin (2016, p. 282) argues that "that the rule must be capable of perpetuating itself, by not giving either politicians or the public reason to regret its strict enforcement and to call either for its revision or its abandonment in favor of discretion." Thus, robustness embodies both generality and predictability, but it also entails additional requirements. Orthodox monetary theory and policy are most likely to deliver promising results in terms of these additional requirements. The tools and techniques most economists use when studying these issues are well-adapted to answer questions of comparative efficacy. But they cannot be the whole story. Monetary policy will never be truly robust until it incorporates generality and predictability concerns as well.

Generality, predictability, and robustness are all required by monetary institutions because of the essentially public role these institutions perform. Whatever their origin, form, or function, monetary institutions are a crucial component of the social order. They do not only affect markets, but politics and civil society as well. The social role of money makes securing regular and predictable conduct within monetary institutions crucially important (Zelizer 1994; Zelmanovitz 2015). Thus, in spite of comparative scholarly neglect, the rule of law is of primary importance for monetary institutions and policy.

Money is one of civilization's greatest labor-saving technologies. Because money is, in essence, a society's most saleable good (Menger 1892), it economizes on the transaction costs associated with exchange. These saved resources, especially time, can then be directed elsewhere, constituting real wealth gains. Furthermore, money permits the coordination of production and consumption plans by providing a common denominator for adjudicating between these plans (Frankel 1977; Simmel 2011). Without monetary calculation, there would be no way of making comparisons of the value of various consumption and productive plans (Kirzner 1997). This process of "intersubjective" communication shows that money is the structure of the language market actors "speak" to each other when trading (Hayek 1945; Wagner 2010). Money is thus a basic institution of proper concern not just to monetary economists and macroeconomists, but political economists and social philosophers. That money has been neglected by the latter is no reason to concede its de facto monopolization by the former.

When the rules governing money are not general, predictable, and robust, it impedes the efficacy of the market process by obstructing the ability of traders to coordinate their desires and plans through the medium of money. When monetary governance takes the form of discretionary central banking, it transforms money from an enabler of mutual cooperation into an instrument of control, subordinating the goals of market actors to the goals of monetary policymakers. Ordinarily the market, provided it operates under the rule of law, enables individuals to achieve their plans and pursue their projects while allowing others the same freedom (Lomasky 1990). Unlawful money, while it does not necessarily destroy this freedom, does *impede* it. It thus requires justification.

We used the earlier discussed example of markets and property rights for a reason: Monetary relationships *are* property relationships. Because money is a good, property rights to goods in general are also applicable to money in particular. If money is subject to arbitrary manipulation by public authorities, this amounts to a de facto infringement on property rights. To prevent this, we need the rule of law in monetary institutions. General, predictable, and robust rules, applied to monetary institutions, add protections against discretionary and ad hoc interferences in the purchasing power of money. They also prevent the monetary authority from abusing its power to engage in de facto fiscal policy, such as preferential credit allocation, as many central banks around the world have done for the past decade (Meltzer 2011; Selgin 2012). A society that does not conform its monetary institutions to the rule of law thus leaves its members vulnerable on several dimensions regarding the security of their property.

6.3 "Higher Law" and the Constitutional Turn

What the thinkers surveyed in the previous chapter have in common is their emphasis on getting the "rules of the game" right. Whatever their differences, Hayek, Friedman, and Buchanan each recognized that monetary policy does not occur within a vacuum. The way to get better monetary policy is not to develop more "accurate" models, nor to employ more public-spirited central bankers. Instead, the solution had to take the form of *binding constraints* on the range of options available to monetary policymakers, or whatever institutions are chosen to implement monetary policy.

If the Fed's ordinary operating procedure is a matter of law, then the solution to the problems of monetary policy – which are really problems with discretionary central banking – is to bind the monetary authority's hands by invoking a "higher law." This higher law should not be thought of in a normative sense, as is typical in the literature on the natural law, for example. Instead, higher law refers to a set of constraints, rationally chosen, that stave off the anticipable pernicious consequences of monetary discretion, in favor of true monetary rules. These rules must be clear and specified in advance; they must actually constrain the operation of monetary policy; and there must be negative consequences for those who break them.

Of the classical liberal thinkers who have turned their attention to the promise of a higher law for monetary policy, James Buchanan is the most explicit in his treatment of the rules of the game, as opposed to the expected outcome of the game played within given rules. This dichotomy is central to his entire research program. During his time as president of the Southern Economics Association, Buchanan gave an address with the intriguing title, "What Should Economists Do?" (Buchanan 1964). In this speech, he cautioned economists away from the strict Robbinsean conception of their science, as that which studies the allocation of scarce means among alternative competing ends. This reduces economics to nothing more than a mechanical decision science, which Buchanan believed limited the power of economics. Instead, Buchanan proposed economics be conceived as the study of exchange behavior, with analytical focus on the institutions within which exchange takes place. Economics is still a science of rational choice, only rational choice is relegated to the analytical background. In the foreground are the rules that govern the various spheres of exchange in which we find ourselves: markets, politics, and civil society. It is the rules of the game that determine whether we confront competitive or cooperative scenarios.

The link between this conception of economics and the rule of law is obvious: The rule of law is that feature of governance institutions that promote generality, predictability, and robustness, and hence facilitate the widest possible social cooperation under the division of labor. Given the stakes, the practicing economist naturally turns his attention to these institutions: what they are, where they come from, and whether they can be rationally reflected upon and improved. Buchanan's application of the tools of economics to the study of rulemaking can be thought of as the *constitutional turn* in economics, and hence the rebirth of contractarian political economy in the mid-twentieth century. "Constitutional political economy" is the name of the subfield Buchanan pioneered, for which he was awarded the Nobel Prize in 1986 (cf. Buchanan 1987). It is important to note that for students of constitutional political economy (also called constitutional economics), a constitution is the set of rules for making rules. These "meta-rules" are the object of analysis, both positively and normatively, within constitutional political economy. The concept of a constitution should not be confused with the Constitution of the United States, or any particular formal constitution. Indeed, the US Constitution was the lodestar for the rebirth of contractarian political economy (cf. Buchanan and Tullock 1962; Meadowcroft forthcoming), but any social system that operates according to a set of rules within which "ordinary" or "regular" behavior takes place operates according to a constitution, either de facto or de jure. It is this conception of a constitution that Buchanan brought to the study of monetary policy, which includes his arguments for the constitutionalization of money (Buchanan 2010a, 2010b).

As a normative individualist and a positive contractarian, Buchanan has reasons to prefer formal constitutions, both for the basic governance of society (US Constitution) and for particular institutions of public import (a constitution for monetary policy). The task of political economists is to use economic reasoning to ascertain the predictable consequences of alternative sets of rules, as an input into democratic deliberation over what rules we will voluntarily adopt, so as to turn social dilemmas into opportunities for mutually beneficial cooperation (Buchanan 1987; Brennan and Buchanan 1985). Constitutional rules exist in order to constrain, and constitutional economics informs our choice among constraints (Buchanan 1990, p. 3). Ideally, these constraints are adopted to prevent factions from operating the machinery of governance to the benefit of some groups at the expense of others, promoting instead governance that is in the interest of all. This quest for a "generality norm" (Buchanan and Congleton 1998 [2003]) seeks to "eliminate the off diagonals" in the various social interactions that can be modeled as Prisoners' Dilemmas, thus incentivizing the agents subject to the constraints to pick strategies that result in maximal social payoffs.

Applied to monetary policy, the purpose of subjecting the monetary authority to a higher law via constitutional constraints is preventing discretion from perverting the goals associated with macroeconomic stabilization. As one well-known example, Fed officials historically had strong incentives to err on the side of being too "loose" in their creation of liquidity and credit. After all, no Fed official wants to be remembered as being at the helm while a second Great Depression brewed. But these officials' predilection for creating "soft landings" is precisely what incentivizes market actors to engage in the sorts of behaviors that place their firms, and sometimes the entire financial system, at risk in the first place. A monetary constitution restricting the Fed's ability to create liquidity and credit except in specific ways that are general, predictable, and robust can thus improve the efficacy of the Fed while forestalling moral hazard.

6.4 Unconstitutional Money

Whatever else might be said in its favor, contemporary scholarship on macroeconomics and monetary economics almost entirely ignores the importance of the rule of law for monetary institutions. Much of monetary theory today is implicitly romantic (Hogan et al. 2018). It does not make realistic appraisals of the incentives and information confronted by both private and public actors. Instead, monetary policymakers are assumed to confront no serious incentive problems, and confront no serious information problems, when implementing policy. Given these assumptions, of course, monetary discretion seems appropriate. But once we take seriously that public actors just as much as private actors confront less-than-ideal incentives and possess less-than-perfect information, the institutional space for alternative monetary arrangements significantly expands. It is because we live in an imperfect world that we must take robustness seriously. This is why the rule of law matters for all institutions of public importance, which, without question, includes monetary policy.

6.4.1 Discretionary Central Banking: Enabling the Juggler

Long ago, Adam Smith (1776 [1981], p. 930) warned of the "juggling trick" in which all governments are tempted to engage. This juggling trick consists of a trifecta of deficits, debt, and debasement of the currency.

The incentives of public actors to finance government spending with debt rather than taxation is obvious: citizens enjoy receiving public benefits but do not enjoy paying for them. Unlike current citizens, future citizens do not (yet) get a vote. Therefore, public actors, especially elected officials, face strong pressure toward deficit spending, and hence accumulating deficits. This, in turn, creates a tense situation for the monetary authority. Passive accommodation by the monetary authority creates an environment favorable to political actors; central banking, as a political job, cannot ignore the political incentives incumbent in its activities. The pressure for easy money to accommodate profligate politicians was a danger recognized even by John Maynard Keynes (1920, p. 236), who well understood the destructive consequences:

There is no subtler, no surer means of overturning the existing basis of society than to debauch the currency. The process engages all the hidden forces of economic law on the side of destruction, and does it in a manner which not one man in a million is able to diagnose.

The juggling trick of debt, deficits, and debasement is a political "loose joint" that is the result of a number of imperfections in public institutions. One such defect is a failure to enshrine the rule of law in monetary affairs. We do not argue that adopting a true monetary rule under a monetary constitution will be sufficient to prevent the juggling trick from continuing. But we do argue that it is necessary. The political–institutional environment created by unlawful money is one that is inherently favorable to technocratic tinkering in the short run, and passive debt accommodation in the long run. This is not in any way a consequence of malice or irresponsibility on the part of central bankers. Rather it is the outcome selected for by the environment. Without the rule of law binding to the mast the hands of monetary policymakers, they cannot help but dash the macroeconomy on the rocks in response to the urge for technocratic tinkering in ordinary times, moral hazard-inducing bailouts during extraordinary times, and passive accommodation to perpetual deficits in both (Ball 2016; Boettke and Smith 2013; Hogan et al. 2015; Salter and Luther 2019; Salter and Smith 2018).

The deficits problem has largely been dismissed by monetary economists, who argue that the public's incorporation of inflation expectations in response to excessively easy monetary policy implies that the monetary authority cannot consistently ease the real debt burden. This point is correct, but as is the norm in modern monetary scholarship, neglects foundational institutional considerations that complicate the story. The ultimate reason for concern is the informal feedback loop between fiscal and monetary agents. Deficits undermine the ability of monetary authorities to pursue independent monetary policy. When the federal government spends more than it takes in as revenue, the Treasury must finance the deficit by borrowing from the private sector in the form of government bonds. As government issues more bonds, increased demand for loanable funds pushes interest rates up (Hein 1991). Monetary authorities often are under pressure to create conditions that favor new debt issuance by offsetting interest rate increases (Cochrane 2011a, 2011b). Historically, such cases are not uncommon, occurring even in the United States following World War II.

There are several channels through which debt accommodation by discretionary monetary policymakers may work (Boettke and Smith 2013). As one example, legislative, executive, and Treasury officials typically push for maintaining lower interest rates to both keep the interest rate cost of issuing debt low and stimulate the economy. As Alan Blinder (2000, p. 1429) explains:

A large fiscal deficit (or debt) can undermine central-bank credibility in a number of ways. Most obviously, if the country has a limited (or zero) capacity to float interest-bearing debt, the central bank may be forced to monetize any budget deficits–with inflationary, or even hyperinflationary, consequences. This danger is greater if the central bank lacks independence . . ... But even if massive inflationary finance is unlikely, outsized fiscal deficits and/or large accumulations of public debt (relative to GDP) put upward pressure on interest rates, which may induce a more accommodative policy from the central bank.

Ultimately, because of the political logic linking fiscal and monetary strategies, monetary policy and perpetual deficits are inseparable (Bach 1949, p. 1175; Brennan and Buchanan 1981; Buchanan and Wagner 1977 [2000]; Weintraub 1978, pp. 359–360). It may even make more sense to model them as a single institution, at least under contemporary fiscal and monetary institutions. Again, contemporary scholarship largely ignores these institutional considerations. Technical refinement of models, rather than comparative institutional analysis, is viewed by the profession as the ordinary and proper content of published work. Because contemporary monetary theory rarely takes such concerns into account, channels for the mutual impingent of fiscal and monetary affairs rarely make it into the model.

Our argument is backed by empirical evidence suggesting a link between fiscal deficits and monetary accommodation (Allen and Smith 1983; Blinder 1982; Bradley 1985; Canzoneri et al. 2001; Fair 1978; Freedman et al. 2010; Friedman 1994; Grier and Neiman 1987; Hamburger and Zwick 1981; Levy 1981; Smith and Boettke 2015; Weintraub 1978). Monetary accommodation, in turn, undermines economic coordination and causes misallocations of capital (Salter 2014b). It is admittedly not the case that fiscal policymakers consciously create excessive debt, and monetary policymakers consciously accommodate them. Rather, contemporary fiscal institutions *select for* perpetual debt, and contemporary monetary institutions *select for* accommodation (cf. Alchian 1950). A constitutional perspective on monetary institutions brings this into focus, whereas in much modern monetary scholarship they remain obscure if analyzed at all.

6.4.2 The Failure of Nonconstitutional Constraints

Many of the proposed solutions to political economy concerns in the contemporary monetary literature amount to pseudo-rules. As Selgin (2016, p. 282) recognizes, the problem with pseudo-monetary rules is that they are "either not well enforced or not expected to last." When they are adopted, they tend to be ineffective precisely because they are pseudo-rules. They are gestures toward the rule of law, rather than the rule of law itself. For example, debt limits and balanced budget requirements have not restrained excessive public spending and hence have not relieved monetary authorities from the pressures of accommodative policy (Boettke and Luther 2010). In addition, spending constraints in both the United States and the European Union have not stopped the juggling trick (Wagner 2012, chs. 1 and 2). While some expenditure rules are more effective than others, even the more effective pseudo-rules have been worked around, modified, or ignored (Cordes et al. 2015; Primo 2007). On the monetary side explicitly, voluntarily followed monetary rules were abandoned prior to the financial crisis (Taylor 2009a, 2009b). Although the "effective degree of independence has gradually increased over time" (Bernanke 2010), the Fed's independence repeatedly has been compromised by political pressures and pressures for debt accommodation (Boettke and Smith 2013; Smith and Boettke 2015).

Inflation targeting in some form is frequently treated as a monetary rule that has been agreed upon by scholars and practiced by policymakers. For instance, New Zealand, Canada, the United Kingdom, and Australia, among others, have adopted the practice of inflation-targeting (Meyer 2001). But again, this is not a true rule, at least not by itself. Bernanke et al. (1999, p. 4, italics in original) carefully stress that inflation targeting "serves as a *framework* for monetary policy rather than a *rule* for monetary policy." Inflation targeting comes in a variety of forms, with varying degrees of flexibility in the lengths of the adjustment period and even with built-in escape clauses (Meyer 2001). For instance, the European Central Bank (ECB) maintains a stated medium-term inflation target in order to pursue its formal objective of price stability (Meyer 2001; White 2011, p. 3).

However, it is far from clear that inflation targeting constrains central banks (Taylor 2007; White 2007; see also Arestis and Sawyer 2003). The problem is the broad flexibility inflation targeting offers when it comes to setting and defining targets. Such flexibility emerges, in part, because of the genuine uncertainty of what the target inflation rate should be (Epstein and Yeldan 2009, p. 9; Pollin and Zhu 2009, p. 130). For instance, New Zealand, the first country officially to implement inflation targeting, started in 1989 with an inflation target of 0–2 percent, but gradually widened it to 0–3 percent, and then to 1–3 percent.

Importantly, not all de jure restrictions count as true constitutional constraints. The ECB has an inflation-targeting mandate that looks very much like a constitutional constraint. But looks can be deceiving. The rule is not self-enforcing, in part because there are no costs to ECB decision-makers for deviation. The ECB's inflation-targeting mandate was ignored when the ECB effectively monetized the debt of Greece, Ireland, and Portugal in response to fears over a sovereign debt crisis (White 2011, p. 3). With no penalty for noncompliance with its stated inflation target, the ECB persistently has maintained inflation rates above its constitution-alized target (Salter 2014a, p. 4).

Some form of inflation targeting is popular especially with advocates of constrained discretion (Bernanke and Mishkin 1997; see also Woodford 2012). The fatal flaw in this view is that it conceives discretionary central bankers as disinterested technicians trying to advance social welfare. "If this is the case, some discretion may achieve an outcome that is closer to fulfilling the overall mandate, even if there is a thin line separating the principles handed to the central bank and the operational targets it sets for itself" (Reis 2013, p. 19). But that reasoning misses the point completely. Remember one of the first and most crucial points about true rules: If central bankers can choose whether to follow a rule or not, then it is not a rule in any meaningful sense (Dellas and Tavlas 2016, p. 313). The direction that the rules-versus-discretion literature has taken since Bernanke and Mishkin (1997) does not represent the gradual adoption of "best practices" in central banking. In contrast to this "Whig history" of monetary economics (cf. Mishkin 2009), it is more nearly the case that the literature has ignored what really matters. If true rules do not exist, then de facto what we have is monetary discretion, which is a failure of the rule of law (Brennan and Buchanan 1980 [2000a], ch. 6, 1981).

6.5 What Ought to Be Done?

Our argument boils down to the following: Rule-like behavior is no substitute for true rules. Without true rules as informed by the constitutional perspective on political economy, the rule of law does not prevail. At best, we have somewhat-regular behavior by discretionary central bankers, until we do not. Brennan and Buchanan cogently express this position:

> We cannot, and should not, expect the decision-makers in the Bank of England or the United States Federal Reserve Board to behave "as if" they are bound by a non-existent constitutional rule for monetary issue. They will behave in accordance with such a rule only if it exists. (Brennan and Buchanan 1981, p. 65)

More than a decade since the financial crisis, "monetary economics" in practice still mostly means "an interest rate policy rule." We do not contend that the standard toolkit is inappropriate, but we do contend that it is insufficient. As Buchanan (1962, p. 157, emphasis in original) wrote, "[technical] issues such as these, regardless of individual views, *need not be raised* in the basic consideration of alternative monetary constitutions. And I think that the air would be cleared substantially if we should agree to leave aside these essentially subsidiary issues until the more basic ones are settled." By "these" Buchanan had in mind the technical aspects of monetary economics and policy models that specified how the relevant macroeconomic variables behave. We reiterate that we do not believe these analyses to be unimportant. But nonetheless, they are properly of secondary importance. As Friedman (1947, p. 415) argues, one cannot decide on the suitability of an institutional arrangement based on formal equilibrium conditions. Rather, one must consider the range of alternative institutions, considering issues such as administrative costs, induced unintended consequences, and ethical values. The reason is simple: Formal equilibria are frequently institutionally dependent and require taking seriously the possibility that governors face incentive and information problems just as severe as the governed. Comparative institutional analysis belongs in the analytical foreground; technical models belong in the analytical background.[3]

The mainstream literature on monetary policy overlooks political economy concerns because scholars fail to challenge the premise that central

---

[3] Friedman (1947, p. 405) writes, "the formal analysis is almost entirely irrelevant to the institutional problem."

bankers should be judges in their own cause. The policies of central banks in recent crises, as well as the modern record of inflation targeting more generally, demonstrate that central bank discretion is far more problematic than currently appreciated. That is why we need the rule of law. Embracing the constitutional turn in monetary economics can be an important first step in incorporating the necessary breath it has lacked thus far. The most important novel avenue would be reforms to the basic institutional framework of central banking.

As we have seen, money is a "meta-rule." The processes governing how money is produced and supplied to the market – the constitution of monetary policy – set the background conditions against which economic activity takes place. While tinkering for the purposes of achieving specific post-constitutional outcomes is impractical, "getting the constitution right" is a valid concern that, taken seriously, can yield systematically better macroeconomic outcomes. Monetary constitutions thus are an important and potentially fruitful research avenue in post-financial-crisis macroeconomics. Scholarship focused on the comparative properties of various monetary constitutions can move us toward an economic environment conducive to growth and efficiency, while also avoiding the vagaries of day-to-day politics, such as capture by special interest groups.

Grounding money in the rule of law offers a way forward for research areas that, without an appreciation of the pre- and post-constitutional aspects of monetary policy, confront a dead end. This is particularly concerning for the post-crisis conversation on macroeconomic and financial stability. Much of this literature highlights various market failures that explain why private sector financiers, owing to a divergence between private and social costs associated with financial intermediation, precipitated the crisis. They also purport to show that well-crafted policy, such as "macroprudential" policy, can prevent such crises in the future (Galati and Moessner 2013; Hanson et al. 2011; Kahou and Lehar 2017). What those studies fail to realize is the reciprocal relationship between financial intermediation and monetary institutions (Hendrickson and Salter 2018; Salter 2017). Especially worrisome is that a central bank's monopoly on high-powered money creation presents nonnegligible temptations to allocate credit under the cover of stabilization policy (Salter 2014b). As De Paoli and Paustian (2017, p. 319) write, "when trade-offs [between monetary authorities and macroprudential regulators] are present and policy is discretionary, the institutional arrangements become crucial." The link between money and finance does not weaken the argument for true rules. If anything, it makes it much stronger.

Embracing the constitutional paradigm shows that supposed market failures are the predictable results of flawed monetary institutions, because these institutions do not create a structure of incentives and information conducive to macroeconomic and financial stability. Furthermore, we cannot simply assume that policymakers can correct those failures when they are subject to the same imperfections as market agents. A robust monetary constitution, the object of which is to bring money under the rule of law, must provide the mechanisms for channeling self-interested behavior by private *and public* actors into socially beneficial outcomes. Constitutional political economy applied to monetary institutions and policy provides the analytical framework for discovering those kinds of constitutions.

References

Alchian, Armen (1950). Uncertainty, Evolution, and Economic Theory. *Journal of Political Economy*, 58(3), 211–221.

Allen, Stuart and Michael Smith (1983). Government Borrowing and Monetary Accommodation. *Journal of Monetary Economics*, 12(4), 605–616.

Arestis, Philip and Malcolm Sawyer (2003). Inflation Targeting: A Critical Appraisal. The Levy Economics Institute of Bard College, Working Paper No. 338.

Bach, George (1949). The Federal Reserve and Monetary Policy Formation. *The American Economic Review*, 39(6), 1173–1191.

Ball, Laurence (2016). Ben Bernanke and the Zero Bound. *Contemporary Economic Policy*, 34(1), 7–20.

Bean, Charles, Matthias Paustian, Adrian Penalver, and Tim Taylor (2010). Monetary Policy after the Fall, Macroeconomic Challenges: The Decade Ahead Available online (accessed May 28, 2020), www.kansascityfed.org/publicat/sympos/2010/Bean_final.pdf

Bédard, Mathieu (2014). Robust Political Economy and the Insolvency Resolution of Large Financial Institutions. SSRN Working Paper. Available online (accessed May 27, 2020), www.ssrn.com/abstract=2494684

Bernanke, Ben (2010). Central Bank Independence, Transparency, and Accountability. Speech at the Institute for Monetary and Economic Studies International Conference. Tokyo, Japan. May 26. Available online (accessed May 28, 2020), https://fraser.stlouisfed.org/title/statements-speeches-ben-s-bernanke-453/central-bank-independence-transparency-accountability-9072

Bernanke, Ben, Thomas Laubach, Frederic Mishkin, and Adam Posen (1999). *Inflation Targeting: Lessons from the International Experience*. Princeton University Press.

Bernanke, Ben and Frederic Mishkin (1997). Inflation Targeting: A New Framework for Monetary Policy? *Journal of Economic Perspectives*, 11(2), 97–116.

Boettke, Peter and Peter Leeson (2004). Liberalism, Socialism, and Robust Political Economy. *Journal of Markets and Morality*, 7(1), 99–111.

Boettke, Peter and William Luther (2010). The Ordinary Economics of an Extraordinary Crisis. In Stephen Kates (Ed.), *Macroeconomic Theory and Its*

Failings: Alternative Perspectives on the Global Financial Crisis. Edward Elgar, pp. 14–25.

Boettke, Peter and Daniel Smith (2013). Federal Reserve Independence: A Centennial Review. *Journal of Prices and Markets*, 1(1), 31–48.

Boettke, Peter, Alex William Salter, and Daniel Smith (2018). Money as Meta-Rule: Buchanan's Monetary Economics as a Foundation for Monetary Stability. *Public Choice*, 176(3), 529–555.

Blinder, Allan (1982). Issues in the Coordination of Monetary and Fiscal Policy. In Monetary Policy Issues in the 1980s [Symposium Sponsored by the Fed Bank of Kansas City].

(2000). Central-Bank Credibility: Why Do We Care? How Do We Build It? *American Economic Review*, 90(5), 1421–1431.

Bradley, Michael (1985). Federal Deficits and the Conduct of Monetary Policy. *Journal of Macroeconomics*, 6(4), 411–431.

Brennan, Geoffrey and James Buchanan (1980 [2000a]). *The Power to Tax: Analytical Foundations of a Fiscal Constitution*. In Collected Works of James Buchanan, volume 9. Liberty Fund, Inc.

(1981). Monopoly in Money and Inflation: The Case for a Constitution to Discipline Government. Institute of Economic Affairs Hobart Paper No. 88.

(1985 [2000b]). *The Reason of Rules: Constitutional Political Economy*. In Collected Works of James Buchanan, volume 10. Liberty Fund, Inc.

Buchanan, James (1962). Predictability: The Criterion of Monetary Constitutions. In Leland Yeager (Ed.), *In Search of a Monetary Constitution*. Harvard University Press, pp. 155–183.

(1964). What Should Economists Do? *Southern Economic Journal*, 30(3), 213–222.

(1987). The Constitution of Economic Policy. *The American Economic Review*, 77(3), 243–250.

(1990) The Domain of Constitutional Economics. *Constitutional Political Economy*, 1(1), 1–18.

(1999). The Ethics of Constitutional Order. In *The Collected Works of James M. Buchanan*, volume 1: The Logical Foundations of Constitutional Liberty. Liberty Fund, Inc., pp. 368–373.

(2001). The Domain of Subjective Economics: Between Predictive Science and Moral Philosophy. In *Collected Works of James M. Buchanan*, volume 17. Liberty Fund, Inc., pp. 24–39.

(2010a). The Constitutionalization of Money. *Cato Journal*, 30(2), 251–258.

(2010b). Chicago School Thinking: Old and New. Draft of Remarks Given at the Summer Institute, University of Virginia.

Buchanan, James and Roger Congleton (1998 [2003]). *Politics by Principle, Not Interest: Towards Nondiscriminatory Democracy*. Liberty Fund, Inc.

Buchanan, James and Gordon Tullock (1962). *The Calculus of Consent*. University of Michigan Press.

Buchanan, James and Richard Wagner (1977 [2000]). *Democracy in Deficit: The Political Legacy of Lord Keynes*. Liberty Fund, Inc.

Canzoneri, Matthew, Robert Cumby, and Behzad Diba (2001). Is the Price Level Determined by the Needs of Fiscal Solvency? *The American Economic Review*, 91(5), 1221–1238.

Coase, Ronald (1990). *The Firm, the Market, and the Law.* University of Chicago Press.

Cochrane, John (2011a). Determinacy and Identification with Taylor Rules. *Journal of Political Economy,* 119(3), 565–615.

(2011b). Inflation and Debt. *National Affairs,* 45(Fall), 56–78. Available online (accessed December 8, 2020), www.nationalaffairs.com/publications/detail/infla tion-and-debt

Cordes, Till, Tidiane Kinda, Priscilla Muthoora, and Anke Weber (2015). Expenditure Rules: Effective Tools for Sound Fiscal Policy? (No. 15–29). International Monetary Fund.

Dellas, Harris and George S. Tavlas (2016). Friedman and the Bernanke-Taylor Debate on Rules versus Constrained Discretion. *Cato Journal,* 36(2), 297–313.

De Paoli, Bianca and Matthias Paustian (2017). Coordinating Monetary and Macroprudential Policies. *Journal of Money, Credit and Banking,* 49(2–3), 319–349.

Easterly, William (2001). Can Institutions Resolve Ethnic Conflict? *Economic Development and Cultural Change,* 49(4), 687–706.

Epstein, Richard (1995). *Simple Rules for a Complex World.* Harvard University Press.

Epstein, Richard and Erinç Yeldan (Eds.) (2009). Beyond Inflation Targeting: Assessing the Impacts and Policy Alternatives. In Gerald Epstein and Erinc Yeldan (Eds.), *Beyond Inflation Targeting: Assessing the Impacts and Policy Alternatives.* Edward Elgar, pp. 3–27.

Fair, Ray (1978). The Sensitivity of Fiscal Policy Effects to Assumptions about the Behavior of the Fed. *Econometrica,* 46(5), 1165–1179.

Frankel, Stephen (1977). *Two Philosophies of Money.* Palgrave Macmillan.

Freedman, Charles, Michael Kumhof, Douglas Laxton, Dirk Muir, and Susanna Mursula (2010). Global Effects of Fiscal Stimulus during the Crisis. *Journal of Monetary Economics,* 57(5), 506–526.

Friedman, Milton (1947). Lerner on the Economics of Control. *Journal of Political Economy,* 55(5), 405–416.

(1994). *Money Mischief: Episodes in Monetary History.* Harcourt Brace & Company.

Galati, Gabriele and Richhild Moessner (2013). Macroprudential Policy: A Literature Review. *Journal of Economic Surveys,* 27(5), 846–878.

Grier, Kevin and Howard Neiman (1987). Deficits, Politics and Money Growth. *Economic Inquiry,* 25(2), 201–214.

Hamburger, Michael and Burton Zwick (1981). Deficits, Money and Inflation. *Journal of Monetary Economics,* 7(1), 141–150.

Hanson, Samuel, Anil Kashyap, and Jeremy Stein (2011). A Macroprudential Approach to Financial Regulation. *Journal of Economic Perspectives,* 25(1), 3–28.

Hayek, Friedrich August (1945). The Use of Knowledge in Society. *The American Economic Review,* 35(4), 519–530.

(1960 [2011]). *The Constitution of Liberty.* University of Chicago Press.

(1973). *Law Legislation and Liberty,* volume 1: *Rules and Order.* University of Chicago Press.

(1988). *The Fatal Conceit.* University of Chicago Press.

Hein, Scott (1991). Deficits and Inflation. *Federal Reserve Bank of St. Louis Review,* 63 (3), 3–11.

Hendrickson, Joshua and Alexander William Salter. (2018). Going Beyond Monetary Constitutions: The Congruence of Money and Finance. *The Quarterly Review of Economics and Finance*, 69(C), 22–28.

Hogan, Thomas (2015). Has the Fed Improved U.S. Economic Performance? *Journal of Macroeconomics*, 43, 257–266.

Hogan, Thomas, Linh Le, and Alex William Salter (2015). Ben Bernanke and Bagehot's Rules. *Journal of Money, Credit, and Banking*, 47(2–3), 333–348.

Hogan, Thomas, Daniel Smith, and Robin Aguiar-Hicks (2018). Central Banking without Romance. *European Journal of Comparative Economics*, 15(2), 293–314.

Kahou, Mahdi Ebrahimi and Alfred Lehar (2017). Macroprudential Policy: A Review. *Journal of Financial Stability*, 29, 92–105.

Keynes, John Maynard (1920). *The Economic Consequences of the Peace*. Harcourt, Brace & Company.

Kirzner, Israel M. (1997). Entrepreneurial Discovery and the Competitive Market Process. *Journal of Economic Literature*, XXXV(March), 60–85.

Knack, Stephen and Philip Keefer (1995). Institutions and Economic Performance: Cross-Country Tests Using Alternative Institutional Measures. *Economics & Politics*, 7(3), 207–227.

Lomasky, Loren (1990). *Rights, Persons, and the Moral Community*. Oxford University Press.

Leeson, Peter and J. Robert Subrik (2006). Robust Political Economy. *The Review of Austrian Economics*, 19(2–3), 107–111.

Levy, David M. (2002). Robust Institutions. *The Review of Austrian Economics*, 15(2/3): 131–142.

Levy, Mickey D. (1981). Factors Affecting Monetary Policy in an Era of Inflation. *Journal of Monetary Economics*, 8(3), 351–373.

Mauro, Paolo (1995). Corruption and Growth. *The Quarterly Journal of Economics*, 110 (3), 681–712.

Meadowcroft, John (forthcoming). Buchanan at the American Founding: The Constitutional Political Economy of a Republic of Equals. *Public Choice*.

Meltzer, Allan (2011). Politics and the Fed. *Journal of Monetary Economics*, 58(1), 39–48.

Menger, Carl (1892). On the Origins of Money. *Economic Journal*, 2(6), 239–255.

Meyer, Laurence (2001). Inflation Targets and Inflation Targeting. Remarks by Governor Laurence Meyer. University of California at San Diego Economics Roundtable. July 17. Available online (accessed May 28, 2020), https://research.stlouisfed.org/publications/review/2001/11/01/inflation-targets-and-inflation-targeting/

Mishkin, Frederic (2009). Will Monetary Policy Become More of a Science? In Heinz Hermann (Ed.), *Monetary Policy over Fifty Years: Experiences and Lessons*. Routledge, pp. 81–103.

Ostrom, Elinor, Roy Gardner, and James Walker (1994). *Rules, Games, & Common-Pool Resources*. University of Michigan Press.

Paniagua, Pablo (2016). The Robust Political Economy of Central Banking and Free Banking. *The Review of Austrian Economics*, 29(1), 15–32.

Pennington, Mark (2011). *Robust Political Economy: Classical Liberalism and the Future of Public Policy*. Edward Elgar Publishing Limited.

Pollin, Robert and Andong Zhu (2009). Inflation and Economic Growth: A Cross-Country and Non-Linear Analysis. In Gerald Epstein and Erinc Yeldan (Eds.), *Beyond Inflation Targeting: Assessing the Impacts and Policy Alternatives*. Edward Elgar, pp. 116–136.

Primo, David (2007). *Rules and Restraint: Government Spending and the Design of Institutions*. Chicago University Press.

Reis, Ricardo (2013). Central Bank Design. *Journal of Economic Perspectives*, 27(4), 17–44.

Salter, Alex William (2014a). Is There a Self-enforcing Monetary Constitution? *Constitutional Political Economy*, 25(3), 280–300.

(2014b). Debt Erosion and the Market Process. *Economic Affairs*, 34(3), 370–378.

(2017). The Imprudence of Macroprudential Policy. *Independent Review*, 19(1), 5–17.

Salter, Alex William and Daniel J. Smith (2018). Political *Economists* or *Political Economists?* The Role of Political Environments in the Formation of Fed Policy under Burns, Greenspan, and Bernanke. *Quarterly Review of Economics and Finance*, 71(1), 1–13.

Salter, Alex William and W. J. Luther (2019). Adaptation and Central Banking. *Public Choice*, 180(3–4), 243–256.

Selgin, George (2012). L Street: Bagehotian Prescriptions for a 21st Century Money Market. *Cato Journal*, 32(2), 303–332.

(2016). Real and Pseudo Monetary Rules. *Cato Journal*, 36(2), 279–298.

Selgin, George, William Lastrapes, and Lawrence H. White (2012). Has the Fed Been a Failure? *Journal of Macroeconomics*, 34(3), 569–596.

Simmel, George (2011). *The Philosophy of Money*. D. Frisby (Ed.), Routledge.

Smith, Adam (1776 [1981]). *An Inquiry into the Nature and Causes of the Wealth of Nations*. Liberty Fund Inc.

Smith, Daniel and Boettke, Peter (2015). An Episodic History of Federal Reserve Independence. *The Independent Review*, 20(1), 99–120.

Steelman, Aaron (2011). The Federal Reserve's "Dual Mandate": The Evolution of an Idea. The Federal Reserve Bank of Richmond *Economic Brief* (December), 1–6.

Steil, Benn and Manuel Hinds (2009). *Money, Markets, and Sovereignty*. Yale University Press.

Taylor, John (2007). Housing and Monetary Policy. NBER Working Paper No. 13682.

(2009a). The Financial Crisis and the Policy Responses: An Empirical Analysis of What Went Wrong. *Critical Review*, 21(2–3), 341–364.

(2009b). *Getting off Track: How Government Actions and Interventions Caused, Prolonged, and Worsened the Financial Crisis*. Hoover Institution Press.

Wagner, Richard (2010). *Mind, Society, and Human Action: Time and Knowledge in a Theory of Social Economy*. Routledge.

(2012). *Deficits, Debt, and Democracy: Wrestling with Tragedy of the Fiscal Commons*. Edward Elgar.

Weintraub, Robert (1978). Congressional Supervision of Monetary Policy. *Journal of Monetary Economics*, 4(2), 341–362.

White, Lawrence (2007). What Type of Inflation Target? *Cato Journal*, 27(2), 283–288.

(2010). The Rule of Law or the Rule of Central Bankers? *Cato Journal*, 30(3), 451–463.

White, Lawrence H. (2011). The Euro's Problems are Fundamental. *AIER Economic Bulletin*, LI.

White, Lawrence H., Victor Vanberg, and Köhler Ekkehard (2015). *Renewing the Search for a Monetary Constitution*. Cato Institute.

Woodford, Michael (2012). Inflation Targeting and Financial Stability. *Sveriges Riksbank Economic Review*, 1, 7–32.

Yeager, Leland (1962). *In Search for a Monetary Constitution*. Harvard University Press.

Zelizer, Viviana (1994). *The Social Meaning of Money*. Basic Books.

Zelmanovitz, Leonidas (2015). *The Ontology and Function of Money: The Philosophical Fundamentals of Monetary Institutions*. Lexington Books.

7

Conclusion

Money and Liberalism in the Twenty-First Century

7.1 Monetary Policy: "Seeing Like a State" vs. "Seeing Like a Citizen"

In *Seeing Like a State*, James C. Scott (1998) argues that states purposefully try to "rationalize" the societies they oversee. The modern state, because it is hierarchical and centralized, has a difficult time exercising its power over the organic developments of civil society. From grid-like urban plans, to uniform weight, measure, and language requirements, to replacing place-names with an organized numbering scheme, politicians and bureaucrats have an incentive to deal with the "crooked timber of humanity" by imposing a kind of rationalist legibility. The goal is the ability to "read" society, for the purposes of social control. This is a necessarily technocratic project, one that does violence to the spontaneous, bottom-up living patterns of the state's subjects.

Contemporary scholarship on monetary theory and policy is a perfect example of the "seeing like a state" mentality. It is openly technocratic and rationalistic and treats these features not only as virtues, but as the only legitimate way of doing *scientific* monetary economics. The structure and operation of central banks, such as the Federal Reserve, reflect this mentality.

One way to interpret our project is as a challenge to this paradigm. We rejected the scientific monopoly of the "seeing like a state" program for the study of monetary policy and its associated institutions. We argued that this paradigm was means–ends inconsistent on its own terms: neither its theory nor its practice can help us secure macroeconomic stability or financial robustness. We also argued that this paradigm was normatively incompatible with liberal democracy and self-governance.

As an alternative for monetary economics, we proposed what might be called the "seeing like a citizen" paradigm (cf. Aligica 2018; Aligica et al. 2019), one rooted in the rule of law. We treated money as a cooperative project among citizens, not a prerogative of central bankers. We drew upon several notable thinkers who wrote on monetary economics and gave serious attention to the pertinent questions of generality, predictability, and robustness. Finally, we argued in favor of a "constitutional turn" by which society's monetary institutions are subject to the reasoned deliberation of coequal citizens. We embraced neither elitist technocracy nor majoritarian passions, but self-governance under the liberal principles of constitutional justice.

One of the thinkers we surveyed, F. A. Hayek, thought long and hard about these questions. "If the old truths are to retain their hold on men's minds," Hayek writes at the beginning of *The Constitution of Liberty*,

they must be restated in the language and concepts of successive generations. What at one time are their most effective expressions gradually become so worn with use that they cease to carry a definite meaning. The underlying ideas may be as valid as ever, but the words, even when they refer to problems that are still with us, no longer convey the same conviction; the arguments do not move in a context familiar with us; and they rarely give us direct answers to the questions we are asking. (1960, p. 1)

We took up Hayek's challenge to restate the basic principles of monetary policy in a free society. This is why the rule of law has been so vital to our endeavor: The consistent application of freedom under the law in the realm of monetary policy is the core of our argument.

Law, in this Hayekian sense, guarantees our individual liberty while enabling us to enjoy the great gains from social cooperation under the division of labor. We can, and indeed do, live better together than we ever could in isolation. This is possible because we follow abstract rules that are independent of particular interests. Centuries ago, Rousseau (1762) famously asked, how can a man be free while subject to wills other than his own? The liberal answer was to live under the rule of law, subject to arbitrary coercion by neither oligarchs on the one hand or the mob on the other. General and abstract rules of just conduct govern our social interactions. Adopting this principle enables society to move from being defined by *status* to those defined by *contract*. As Hayek puts it: "The true contrast to a reign of status is the reign of general and equal laws, of the rules which are the same for all" (1960, p. 154). Law in this sense is opposed to state-sanctioned privilege. Hence, a society ruled by law is one that eschews legal privilege, and thus institutionalized discrimination. The chief safeguard of this is the requirement that rules must apply to all, including those in positions of power. The rule-of-law approach to public policy is intricately connected to the liberal constitutional project of devising a system of governance that exhibits neither discrimination nor dominion.

Monetary theory is a technical branch of positive economics but monetary policy is an application of that science within the broader context of political and social arrangements. We need a creative act of political economy to render monetary policy consistent with the aims of a free society. Since money, as the hub of the wheel of commerce, is the unifying link among all exchange relations, disturbances caused by monetary mischief damage the operation of the entire system (Yeager 1997).

Governments are constantly tempted to assume greater control over money by increasing their discretionary authority. Hayek's argument, and ours, is easy to state: a "rule which aims at what is desirable in the long run and ties the hands of the authority in its short-term decisions is likely to produce a better monetary policy than principles which give to the authorities more power and discretion and thereby make them most subject to both political pressure and their own inclination to overestimate the urgency of the circumstances of the moment" (1960, p. 333). This principle must become the bedrock of our thinking about monetary institutions.

There is an old saying in political science: where you sit depends on where you stand (Miles 1978). Applied to economics and economic policy, this means context matters greatly. One way it matters is for the question of *theory choice* among economic policy decision-makers. What determines which theoretical window we look through? This choice is often made based on political, rather than scientific, criteria. The window we choose is one with a view to the fundamental jurisprudential tenets of liberalism. Similarly, Hayek (1948) argued that what David Hume and Adam Smith sought to develop in their approach to classical liberal political economy was a social system that would be so governed that bad men could do the least harm, and in so doing could grant freedom to all (cf. Boettke and Leeson 2004). The checks and balances against the arbitrary abuse of power were sought, however imperfectly, to forestall discrimination and domination. Opposed to this was the romantic tradition of the French Enlightenment, which sought through reason to ensure that the best and the brightest would be granted freedom to rule.

The distinction between a system that seeks to govern *with* versus a system that seeks to govern *over* was a major sticking point in the economic debates in the first half of the twentieth century. Frank Knight and Henry Simons, for example, both were upset with the arguments developed in Keynes' *General Theory* not only because of technical disagreements in economic science, but also the broader social–philosophical implications of Keynesian policy. These scholars, especially Simons, saw their projects as the neoclassical economics counterpart to the classical liberal argument for rules in matters of public policy. Milton Friedman, who was a student of both Knight and Simons, would become the most notable advocate for rules during the era of Keynesian hegemony in the academy and in Washington. It is important, given how we are framing this summary, to remember Friedman's warning that any institution in which errors by a few can threaten the entire system is perhaps an institution we should do without. This was Friedman's position in *Capitalism and Freedom* (1962) with respect to discretionary central banking. James Buchanan, also a student of Frank Knight, argues in his own Nobel lecture (1986) that economists must cease offering policy advice as if to a benevolent despot.[1] The potential for abuse must be built into economists' models and, more fundamentally, the design of our political institutions. Our business is not to be elite-trained social engineers for powerful benevolent social planners. That model, even conceptually, must be rejected if our goal is to discuss economic policy in a free society.

7.2 Monetary Policy Amid the Pandemic

We wrote this book more than a decade after a severe challenge to the idea of rule-based monetary policy. The profession has learned much since the global financial crisis of 2007–2008 and the ensuing slow recovery. We drew upon those lessons and restated the case philosophically, analytically, and empirically for the rule-of-law approach to monetary policy, contingent on the existence of a central bank. But as we were wrapping up this project, a new stress to the liberal order arose, that of a global pandemic. In the United States, to combat the spread of COVID-19, nine states issued stay-at-home orders as of March 23; this expanded to twenty-one states three days later, and thirty states a week later. The orders, along with accompanying restrictions on nonessential business activity, had devastating economic consequences. As of this writing, US unemployment claims

---

[1] Buchanan was formally a dissertation student of Roy Blough. Knight served on Buchanan's dissertation committee and was a major influence on his thinking throughout his career (Johnson 2014).

have exceeded 30 million, or roughly 20 percent of the labor force, the highest since the Great Depression. Analysts project a 16 percent decline in GDP for 2020, a number that took three years into the Great Depression to reach.

The response by the Fed has been extraordinary.[2] In terms of conventional tools, the Fed lowered its target for the federal funds rate to between 0 and 0.25 percent. Its statements concerning the future path of the federal funds rate makes it clear that they will keep rates near-zero for the foreseeable future. The discount rate, for direct lending to banks, has been cut to 0.25 percent. It has eliminated reserve requirements and eased post-financial crisis capital requirements. In addition, in support of its new federal funds rate target, it has *significantly* increased its presence in the repurchase agreement (repo) market. Before the pandemic, the Fed offered $100 billion in overnight repo and $20 billion in two-week repo. In response to the pandemic they expanded it to $1 trillion in overnight repo and $500 billion each in one-month and three-month repos.

The Fed has also revived a number of programs from the 2007–2008 crisis. It started another round of quantitative easing (QE), beginning with purchasing $500 billion in Treasuries and $200 billion in government-supported mortgage-backed securities. On March 23, the Fed announced this bout of QE would continue indefinitely. It resumed loans to the primary dealers through the Primary Dealer Credit Facility, at a rate of 0.25 percent. The Money Market Mutual Fund Liquidity Facility (MMLF), another financial crisis innovation, is also back in operation. Similarly, through Commercial Paper Funding Facility (CPFF), the Fed is buying unsecured short-term corporate debt directly. Finally, the Fed has stepped up loans through the Term Asset-Backed Securities Loan Facility (TALF), but with expanded eligible collateral for loans to households, consumers, and firms. The Treasury has provided $10 billion to protect against losses incurred by the Fed through MMLF, CPFF, and TALF, which means these operations are being underwritten by taxpayers.

The Fed is engaged in a host of truly novel activities, as well. The Fed is now lending directly to US corporations through two new programs: the Primary Market Corporate Credit Facility (PMCCF) and the Secondary Market Corporate Credit Facility (SMCCF). The former includes purchasing newly issued corporate debt, as well as providing loans. The latter includes purchasing existing corporate debt, as well as exchange-traded

---

[2] The Brookings Institution provides a useful summary of the Fed's response to the COVID-19 pandemic, which is periodically updated (Cheng et al. 2020).

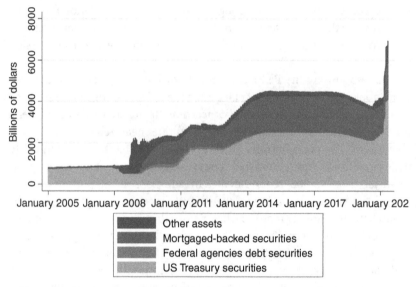

Figure 7.1. Federal Reserve balance sheet.
Source: FRED, Federal Reserve Bank of St. Louis

funds that invest in high-grade corporate debt. Total support through these programs tops out at $750 billion, with taxpayers covering up to $75 billion in losses. Through its Main Street Lending Program, the Fed is supporting up to $600 billion in small- and medium-sized business loans. Again, taxpayers are responsible for covering up to $75 billion in losses. Most concerningly, the Fed is also making loans directly to state and local governments. Through its Municipal Liquidity Facility, the Fed will purchase up to $500 billion in state and local government debts, with taxpayers responsible for up to $35 billion in losses.

In total, the Fed's interventions amount to $2.3 trillion. The predictable result was a significant expansion in the Fed's balance sheet, as shown in Figure 7.1. Chairman Jerome Powell frankly acknowledged the magnitude of the Fed's response: "We are deploying these lending powers to an unprecedented extent ... We will continue to use these powers forcefully, proactively, and aggressively until we are confident that we are solidly on the road to recovery" (Powell 2020). In other words, the Fed is continuing down the trail it blazed during the financial crisis. Whether or not the Fed's activities are effective at stabilizing markets, this is a profound and troubling expansion of its mandate, with worrying implications for the rule of law. That many of the Fed's activities were Congressionally authorized is of little comfort.[3] After the 2007–2008 crisis, Meltzer (2011) worried that the distinction between monetary and fiscal policy was becoming blurred. With their pandemic response, the Fed has not so much blurred as it has destroyed this distinction. "But is this really the function of the Federal Reserve?" John Cochrane (2020) asks. "Where is the outrage? Where are the financial economists? Where is the reform plan so we don't do this again?" Indeed, the lack of concern among monetary and financial economists is just as alarming as is the Fed's brazenness. Now more than ever, economists must attend to the realities of mandate creep within, and moral hazard without, the world's most important central bank.

The scope for political interference in monetary policy decision-making has also been greatly expanded. Because the Fed is engaging in de facto fiscal policy, we must worry that Congress will try to use the Fed's balance sheet to accomplish political goals that cannot be achieved through the budgeting process. Congresswomen Maxine Waters (2020), the Chairwomen of the House Financial Services Committee, wrote a letter to Chairman Powell, urging the Fed to "use its authority to impose conditions that protect existing collective bargaining agreements and require eligible businesses to guarantee workers full paid leave, worker representation on corporate boards, and a $15 minimum wage." In the letter, Waters also urged the Fed to allow nonprofits and community development financial organizations to be eligible for the program and to favor certain kinds of enterprises, such as community banks and credit unions. There is also the risk the Fed will be further exposed to other kinds of political influence. Recent expansions in the Fed's Municipal Liquidity Facility were also the result of political pressure. Initially, the program was restricted to cities of more than 1 million residents and counties of more than 2 million residents, but those restrictions were dropped to cities of 250,000 and counties of 500,000 residents (Politi and Smith 2020).

Additionally, the Fed's backstopping of municipal and state debt may undermine federalism. The American system of governance is predicated on multiple authorities, such as local and state governments, meeting citizens' demands for public output, as well as resisting overreach by Washington. But if the Fed makes

---

[3] For example, the Fed's loans to small- and medium-sized businesses, as well as to state and municipal governments, were authorized by the CARES Act. But this does not make such activities compatible with the rule of law. Compliance with official de jure procedures may be a necessary condition for the rule of law to hold, but it is never a sufficient condition. As we have argued, public policy must be general and predictable to qualify as lawful. Fed activity – indeed, most government policy – in the wake of COVID-19 has failed to satisfy these criteria. Menand (2020), however, argues that many of the facilities invoked by the Fed in response to COVID-19 did not even meet the legality standard of de jure law.

financing artificially cheap for local governance entities, then these entities risk becoming dependent on those funds. Public finance at the local and state level will increasingly be a function, not of genuine budgeting decisions according to the democratic process, but the whims of central bankers. Those who value liberal democracy and self-governance should be worried about the danger the Fed's actions pose to these foundational public commitments.

We believe that the argument for rules is even more critical during emergencies. Both the Fed and the Treasury have engaged in extraordinary measures to address the economic crisis born of the public health crisis. Understanding and responding to this turmoil requires thinking in terms of the unavoidable trade-offs involved. We can, and future scholars will, debate the epidemiological evidence, public health officials' policy stances, and government interventions at the federal, state, and local levels. But if we are to learn anything from this episode, the depiction of the relevant trade-offs must occupy a prominent position.

What exactly the appropriate macroeconomic measures are will continue to be a subject of intense debate. Our contribution to this debate is to suggest that a rule-bound approach to monetary policy may have been more effective in addressing the pressing issues without causing the distortions and dysfunctions in the operation of labor markets, capital markets, and the economy as a whole. That the COVID-19 pandemic required an immediate and vigorous response does not mean it was wise to engage in policies that emphasize short-run relief at the expense of the long-run economic health. Stable and predictable rules reflect a "first, do no harm" norm for monetary authorities by ensuring that they do not jumble together an ad hoc response, contributing to economic uncertainty during already uncertain times. This was our critical argument against "triage economics" in the book, and it is our argument for the situation today.

We are not adopting a "do nothing" stance, nor are we cynically denying the reality of the crisis. We take precisely the same position as the one we articulated in the wake of the global financial crisis. We advocate not a head-in-the-sand policy, but an eyes-wide-open policy, one that respects the basic philosophical and jurisprudential tenets of liberalism. As Hayek stressed, the short-run *and* the long-run consequences must be accounted for in any serious economic analysis.

7.3 Liberalism, Even When It's Hard

Since the days of Smith and Hume, liberal political economists have recognized that the specter of social conflict · looms large among individuals. The conflicts arising over lockdowns in response to COVID-19 offer a striking example. The threat of conflict impels the need for institutions of public governance to ward off predation while promoting peaceful social cooperation.[4] J. S. Mill argues in *On Liberty* that:

> The principles asserted in these pages must be more generally admitted as the basis for discussion of details, before a consistent application of them to all the various departments of government and morals can be attempted with any prospect of advantage. The few observations I propose to make on questions of detail, are designed to illustrate the principles, rather than to follow them out to their consequences. I offer, not so much applications, as specimens of application; which may serve to bring into greater clearness the meaning and limits of the two maxims which together form the entire doctrine of this Essay, and to assist the judgment in holding the balance between them, in the cases where it appears doubtful which of them is applicable to the case.
>
> The maxims are, first, that the individual is not accountable to society for his actions, in so far as these concern the interests of no person but himself. Advice, instruction, persuasion, and avoidance by other people, if thought necessary by them for their own good, are the only measures by which society can justifiably express its dislike or disapprobation of his conduct. Secondly, that *for such actions as are prejudicial to the interests of others, the individual is accountable, and may be subjected either to social or to legal punishments, if society is of opinion that the one or the other is requisite for its protection.* (1859, pp. 177–178, emphasis added)

Liberal political economists, in their classic or contemporary form, understand that our social interactions can give rise to unfortunate consequences. Some are mere annoyances, while others are real harms. The basic Coasean analysis of bargaining away conflicts between parties is grounded in a recognition of the reciprocal nature of harms (Coase 1960). In our bargaining, however, as Buchanan and Tullock (1962) stressed, we have to realize that there are different interests colliding that demand reconciliation. Buchanan and Tullock used the example of a swamp and a mosquito abatement program, and the *political* bargain that must be struck between those who live near the swamp and those who live farther from the swamp in order to address the social problem.

In the context of political exchange, the argument for fiscal federalism and political decentralization is grounded in the principle of subsidiarity:

---

[4] See Boettke and Leeson, ed., *The Economic Role of the State* (2015) for a documentary history of this debate among economists and political economists; also see Boettke (2018) "Economics and Public Administration" and Aligica et al. (2019) *Public Administration and the Classical Liberal Perspective* for a presentation of the positive agenda for laissez-faire by modern representatives of liberalism.

When we choose in groups, we should strive to match the size of the potential harms from social conflicts with the most local governmental decision unit capable of addressing those harms. We live better together, but our living together necessarily entails confronting each other as potential sources of harm. The point of liberal institutions of governance, which include the formal rules of public governance as well as informal rules of civil society, is to turn our bumping and bargaining into a situation where the rough-and-tumble of social life may leave us bruised but never mortally wounded. Only by doing so can we realize the great material bounty provided by sustained economic growth, which is an important component of human flourishing (Deaton 2013; Fogel 2004).

In making our case for general and abstract rules, it is always important to remember that argument made by J. S. Mill in *Principles of Political Economy* (1848 [2006], pp. 944–945) in deciding how to address harms, and who is responsible for addressing harms. "The preceding," Mill writes, "are the principal reasons, of a general character, in favor of restricting to the narrowest compass the intervention of a public authority in the business of the community: and few will dispute the more than sufficiency of these reasons, to throw, in every instance, the burden of making out a strong case not on those who resist, but on those who recommend, government interference. *Laissez-faire, in short, should be the general practice: every departure from it, unless required by some great good, is a certain evil*" (emphasis added).

Following Mill, we have a laissez-faire principle, but we confront actions that are *prejudicial to the interests of* others. Thus, there is a tension that must be wrestled with. Our current political arrangements, let alone the prevailing public ideology, are a long way from J. S. Mill's formulations in the nineteenth century, and even from the formulations suggested by Hayek's *The Constitution of Liberty* (1960). It is our sincere hope that the severity of both the pandemic and the lockdown will impress on the public imagination the need for a liberal reawakening. An open society, grounded on a liberal order, can both withstand shocks and provide an environment suitable for a society of free and responsible individuals who treat one another as dignified equals.

All this may seem far afield of monetary theory and policy. On the contrary, these remarks are essential for understanding monetary theory and policy *in a democratic and self-governing society*. If we care about these things, monetary policy cannot be something done *to* the public at large *by* a privileged subset of the public. Nor can monetary institutions operate under the exclusive purview of a cadre of unaccountable experts (cf. Koppl

2019). This is why the Fed's behavior in the wake of the COVID-19 pandemic is so concerning. It inevitably moves us further down the path toward technocratic fiat, away from the rule of law. Whatever the public stances or political predilections of central bankers, in no way can their actions over the past decade qualify as liberal. The larger the role the Fed plays in allocating resources, and the greater markets come to rely on direction via bureaucratic control, the more likely it is that the US central bank will become an agency promoting conflict, rather than ameliorating it. Furthermore, due to the institutionalization of moral hazard, extraordinary Fed policies in one crisis inadvertently sow the seeds of another.

Money, banking, and finance are indisputably one of the economy's "commanding heights." But this makes increasing nonmarket control more concerning, not less. Instead of policy that is general, predictable, and robust, the Fed has doubled down on its failures since the 2007–2008 crisis and operated in a manner that is privileged, opaque, and susceptible to capture by special interests. Whatever else they have been, the actions of the Fed certainly were not predictable, general, or robust, as demonstrated by its response to COVID-19, which contained a host of unprecedented tools, directed at specific sectors of the economy (and state and local governments!), that are not designed robustly against knowledge and incentive problems. In brief, the Fed's response to the pandemic is the antithesis of the liberal–democratic approach to monetary policy.

Liberal political economy has never denied that human conflict is omnipresent and that such conflict can undermine society's ability to engender social cooperation through peaceful exchange. Conflict and strife are real. Actions prejudicial to the interest of others take place and must be ameliorated. The question is always, who best can deal with them? And what does dealing with them entail? For the liberal, commerce and civil society tend to be more effective arenas for resolving conflicts than the state. The burden of proof falls on those who advocate governmental privilege and state coercion to achieve the common good. The liberal, in contrast, is predisposed to solutions that fruitfully employ human sociability and the voluntary adoption of norms to ameliorate potential harms. In the context of our work, we want the burden of proof to rest squarely on the shoulders of those who argue that the urgency of the moment demands discretion rather than rules. The repudiation of lawful conduct, and the apparent lack of humility and perspective, by the Fed seriously calls into question whether discretionary central banking is compatible with liberal democracy.

7.4 Mises, Money, and Maladies

Challenges to liberalism and self-governance from crisis events – pandemics, wars, economic collapse, and the like – are nothing new. Throughout the twentieth century, liberal political economists confronted such challenges, as well as contended with those who argued the liberal doctrines of private property, freedom of contract, and the rule of law were obsolete. From World War I, the pandemic of 1918, the Great Depression, World War II, the pandemic of 1957, and the long Cold War, they had to grapple with issues that struck at the heart of civilization.

One of the staunchest liberals of the era was Ludwig von Mises. He was simultaneously capable of technical precision and comprehensive vision. His critique of socialism was decisive, and his price-theoretic rending of the manipulation of money and credit remains, as we have argued, a top contender for an *economic* theory of macroeconomic volatility. In developing both his systematic critique of socialism and his analysis of the monetary system (including the problems associated with the manipulation of money and credit), Mises articulated a theory of the entrepreneurial market process that demands our theoretical attention. Critical to his theory of how the price system and market economy work is monetary calculation. Money is central to the Misesian approach to economic theory and not an appendage attached to an analysis of a "natural" economy. To Mises, in the study of an advanced civilization with modern economic conditions, there is no "real" economy that operates apart from monetary mediation. This belies the criticisms of those who argued the introduction of money undermined the self-regulating properties of markets, and it distances Mises from the "new classical" economists who insist on modeling conventions that render money sterile.[5] It is our contention that Mises, as an economist and monetary theorist, remains just as relevant today as he was during his lifetime. We must continue his research program to advance our understanding of money and monetary institutions in the context of a general theory of social cooperation.

The high esteem with which we hold Mises' contributions to economic science, and monetary economics in particular, is relevant to the current situation. Mises was not only a pure academic economist, but also a broadly engaged intellectual. It is his role as an economic policy advisor and analyst that we want to explore briefly. In the context of World War I,

---

[5] As Roger Garrison (1984, 2001) notes, the two universals of macroeconomic reality are time and money.

Mises wrote the following: "When there is a fire, it is paramount to utilize fireman, hoses, and water; how to pay the fire brigade is a secondary consideration at that point" (Mises 1918 [2000], p. 218). And, he argues that when it is an exogenous threat, "The favorable outcome of a war is not solely dependent on the number of soldiers, or the valor and brilliance of their military commanders. An equally important factor is the capacity to provide the army with supporting material, arms, and military equipment of every kind" (Mises 1918 [2000], p. 216). Since the COVID-19 pandemic has often been likened to a war, we think this attitude is appropriate in situating our thinking.

As we have already said, we can debate many things about the COVID-19 situation, and historians will certainly do so. But there are two critical facts that must be clearly stressed. First, the current economic malaise was not generated by manipulation of money and credit. We do not indict the Fed for the economic shock caused by the pandemic. In addition, because of voluntary social distancing, combined with the various stay-at-home orders and other shutdown policies, capital and labor are not being reallocated as they normally would in a time of structural adjustment. The self-corrective mechanism has been partly impeded by diktat. In short, our precarious economic condition is a consequence of a work stoppage, with both private and public sources, following a public health crisis. Perhaps the magnitude of the externality represented by the virus makes the various shutdown policies justifiable. But it poses serious difficulties for tens of millions of Americans nonetheless.

Second, the public health crisis is a textbook exogenous shock, the effects of which were amplified by a host of government failures, such as the CDC's unnecessary regulatory roadblocks and its bungling of testing. But those issues are not relevant for discussing the proper future course of policy; they are the constraints against which the next steps must be made. We can adjudicate guilt and innocence down the road. The same holds true about the debate over epidemiological findings and public health officials' use of statistics. As economists, we are trained to think in terms of trade-offs. Our attention is drawn to the necessity of thinking through the alternative paths forward that are effective at ending the public health crisis without threatening our economic future.

Massive expansion in the powers of the Fed, and ramped-up deficit spending by Congress, are not recipes for a speedy recovery any more than other proposed policies that are emerging from the political negotiations caused by the crisis, such as restrictions on trade and immigration. The situation is continually evolving as we write, so we are necessarily short of details in our analysis compared to what we know about 2007–2008. To start, any and all fiscal matters – cases where resources are being allocated directly – should be the purview of the people's representatives, in Congress assembled. The Fed should have restricted itself to providing ample liquidity to the market, and perhaps also acting as a Bagehotian lender of last resort.[6] The combination of the Fed's monopoly on the creation of high-powered money with programs that directly allocate credit, as well as prop up specific asset prices, transgress the proper bounds of a central bank. By its very nature, the Fed is a Big Player (Koppl 2019), because it operates with minimal constraints and yet can significantly affect markets. The Fed can use its balance sheet to redirect economic activity to a degree that other market and nonmarket actors cannot achieve. It is a truism that great power comes with great responsibility. But truisms become so for a reason. Currently, the Fed is wielding significant power in the absence of any clear responsibility mechanism, or even a discussion about the future implementation of responsibility mechanisms. But such a mechanism is a non-negotiable component of the rule of law. As with all rule-of-law approaches to public policy, the critical test is the strict adherence to generality: no picking of winners and losers. This generality norm does not eliminate all public policies that might fit our respective preferences, but it does an admirable job of first-level sorting. In particular, it would rule out using the Fed's balance sheet to give preferential treatment to favored firms. Ultimately, since money is the hub of the wheel of commerce, we must always be mindful of the downside risk of monetary mischief.

This is why we insist Mises is a relevant thinker on monetary matters – indeed, perhaps the perennial thinker on monetary matters. In his classic essay, *Economic Calculation in the Socialist Commonwealth*, Mises develops the argument that rational economic calculation under socialism is impossible. Included in this essay is a discussion of banking and finance. Quoting the socialist economist Otto Bauer, Mises (1920 [2012], p. 39) writes that, "Only by nationalization of the banks does society obtain the power to regulate its labor according to a plan, and to distribute its

---

[6] In addition, the noticeable fall in inflation expectations suggests the Fed is failing in its primary macroeconomic responsibility: maintaining nominal (aggregate demand) stability. See the FRED data on, for example, five-year breakeven inflation rate: https://fred .stlouisfed.org/series/T5YIE. This is even more pronounced when we remember that the pandemic undoubtedly came with a massive negative supply shock, which ceteris paribus should raise expected inflation.

resources rationally among the various branches of production, so as to adapt them to the nation's needs." Mises (1920 [2012], pp. 40–41) criticizes Bauer by noting, rightly, that socialists "do not realize that the bases of economic calculation are removed by the exclusion of exchange and the pricing mechanism, and that something must be substituted in its place, if all economy is not to be abolished and a hopeless chaos is not to result."

Obviously, in the United States, there is no serious proposal to nationalize the financial sector. Yet Mises' critique of socialized finance is still relevant, because the essence of his argument is the *subsumption of the market mechanism to bureaucratic control.* Such control throws a wrench in the gears of the economic system. Here is what this means for us today: By crossing the line from liquidity provider to credit allocator, the Fed is centrally directing a nontrivial portion of the financial sector. Private sector balance sheets may be healthier as a result, but healthy balance sheets do not *mean the same thing* when they are propped up by interminable high-powered money creation, as opposed to reflecting patterns of sustainable specialization and trade (cf. Kling 2016) in the market.

The long-run result of the Fed's actions will be greater fragility, as the entire financial system becomes increasingly dependent on the whims of whoever sits on the Board of Governors. This point – the asymmetry of economic information when generated by market processes as opposed to political processes – is Mises' most important message. It has yet to be heard by the vast majority of monetary policymakers.

7.5 Monetary Institutions as if Liberalism Mattered

In *Lombard Street* (1873, pp. 207–208), Walter Bagehot argued that "unhappily, the rule which is most simple is not always the rule which is most to be relied upon. The practical difficulties of life often cannot be met by very simple rules; those difficulties being complex and many, the rules of countering them cannot be single and simple. A uniform remedy for many diseases often ends by killing the patient." In short, the pragmatic stance has long contended that there are times when rules cannot be broken, and others when the rules must be broken in order to ensure safety. But this pragmatism must be tempered by a sober recognition that the temptation is to err on the side of breaking rules, not following them. As one notable political entrepreneur put it: "Never let a crisis go to waste." Liberalism stands or falls on how we deal with this temptation when it arises.

Our argument is that there are costs to breaking those rules that are often clouded in the fog of emergency, and that they must be taken into account if monetary policy is going to be practiced in a way that does not endanger long-run economic prosperity. Economic growth is a moral imperative not because of the increase in consumption and luxury goods, but because of the accompanying improvements in medicine, living conditions, educational opportunities, leisure, and social equality (McCloskey 2006, 2010, 2016). The free society is an *opportunity-maximizing* society, and with opportunity comes betterment and well-being.

But any time the liberal tenets of generality, predictability, and robustness are overlooked, the promise of the free society is threatened. We have identified major structural issues that must be accounted for not just in the wake of emergencies, but during the normal operations of politics as well. This insight, which is fairly standard in political economy, has yet to be applied to central banking in a systematic way. We wrote this book to correct that oversight.

The peculiar nonmarket situation of central banks, we argued, translates into a knowledge problem that monetary policymakers face in attempting to steward the macroeconomy. Matching money supply with money demand is an intricate and complex process, requiring constant adaptations and adjustments along a multiplicity of margins to keep the system tending toward the right balance. Failing to achieve that balance results in macroeconomic volatility. The knowledge problem presents a challenge to discretionary management that is, in fact, insurmountable.

The other problem is incentive alignment. Without a generality norm, there is nothing preventing groups from using the means of public governance to benefit themselves at the expense of others. This is no less relevant for monetary policy than it is for other, more conventional political arenas. Monetary policy, and hence central banking, *is* political. Failure to recognize this, and address it with careful institutional design, predictably results in monetary policy failures. Monetary mischief – the use of the Fed's balance sheet for reasons other than the maintenance of systemic liquidity – wreaks havoc on the market process by impeding economic calculation, and it generates distributional consequences that cannot but be discriminatory.

We argued throughout *Money and the Rule of Law* that the knowledge problem and the incentive problem cannot be brushed aside for the sake of expediency. These problems become even more severe during a crisis, precisely when the pressure to "do something" reaches its peak. We buttressed the case for rules beyond the technical arguments in monetary economics, and in doing so we showed that constrained discretion is not the "golden mean" between rules and discretion, but discretion with rule-like window dressing. The only alternative that can deliver macroeconomic stability and meet the demands of justice is the rule of law, which means a true monetary rule.

The two economic crises of the twenty-first century bring us to a crossroads for monetary institutions and policy. Getting money right is crucial. At stake are both short-run economic stability and long-run economic growth. Furthermore, given the public's current preoccupation with distributive injustices and the machinations of "elites," it is all the more important that our monetary institutions reflect equality under the law. In a constitutional democracy, governance arrangements are never settled. The choices we make in the next few years regarding the institutional underpinnings of monetary policy will affect us for decades to come. We hope we have contributed to the academic discourse, as well as the public deliberation, that must occur for us to make these choices wisely.

References

Aligica, Paul Dragos (2018). *Public Entrepreneurship, Citizenship, and Self-Governance.* Cambridge University Press.

Aligica, Paul Dragos, Peter J. Boettke, and Vlad Tarko (2019). *Public Administration and the Classical Liberal Perspective.* Oxford University Press.

Bagehot, Walter (1873). *Lombard Street: A Description of the Money Market.* Henry S. King & Co. Available online (accessed May 27, 2020), www.econlib.org/library/Bagehot/bagLomCover.html

Boettke, Peter (2018). Economics and Public Administration. *Southern Economic Journal,* 84(4), 938–959.

Boettke, Peter and Peter Leeson (2004). Liberalism, Socialism, and Robust Political Economy. *Journal of Markets and Morality,* 7(1), 99–111.

(2015). *The Economic Role of the State.* Edward Elgar Publishing.

Buchanan, James (1986). The Constitution of Economic Policy. The Sveriges Riksbank Prize in Economic Sciences in Memory of Alfred Nobel 1986 Prize Lecture. Available online (accessed May 12, 2020), www.nobelprize.org/prizes/economic-sciences/1986/buchanan/lecture/

Buchanan, James and Gordon Tullock (1962). *The Calculus of Consent.* University of Michigan Press.

Cheng, Jeffrey, David Skimore, and David Wessel (2020). What's the Fed Doing in Response of the COVID-19 Crisis? What More Could It Do? Brookings Institute. Available online (accessed May 12, 2020), www.brookings.edu/research/fed-response-to-covid19/

Coase, Ronald (1960). The Problem of Social Cost. *Journal of Law and Economics,* 3 (October), 1–44.

Cochrane, John (2020). Bailout Redux. *The Grumpy Economist.* April 20. Available online (accessed May 12, 2020), https://johnhcochrane.blogspot.com/2020/04/bailout-redux.html

Deaton, Angus (2013). *The Great Escape*. Princeton University Press.

Fogel, Robert William (2004). *The Escape from Hunger and Premature Death, 1700–2100*. Cambridge University Press.

Friedman, Milton (1962). *Capitalism and Freedom*. University of Chicago Press.

Garrison, Roger (1984). Time and Money: The Universals of Macroeconomic Theorizing. *Journal of Macroeconomics*, 6(2), 197–213.

(2001). *Time and Money: The Macroeconomics of Capital Structure*. Routledge.

Hayek, Friedrich August (1948). *Individualism & Economic Order*. University of Chicago Press.

(1960). *Constitution of Liberty*. University of Chicago Press.

Johnson, Marianne (2014). James M. Buchanan, Chicago, and Post-War Public Finance. *Journal of the History of Economic Thought*, 36(4), 479–497.

Kling, Arnold (2016). *Specialization and Trade*. Cato Institute.

Koppl, Roger (2019). *Expert Failure*. Cambridge University Press.

McCloskey, Deidre (2006). *The Bourgeois Virtues*. University of Chicago Press.

(2010). *Bourgeois Dignity*. University of Chicago Press.

(2016). *Bourgeois Equality*. University of Chicago Press.

Meltzer, Alan (2011). Politics and the Fed. *Journal of Monetary Economics*, 58(1), 39–48.

Menand, Lev (2020). Unappropriated Dollars: The Fed's Ad Hoc Lending Facilities and the Rules That Govern Them. European Corporate Governance Institute Working Paper No. 518/2020. Available online (accessed November 24, 2020), https://ecgi .global/sites/default/files/working_papers/documents/menandfinal_0.pdf

Miles, Rufus (1978). The Origin and Meaning of Miles' Law. *Public Administration Review*, 38(5), 399–403.

Mill, John Stuart (1848 [2006]). *Principles of Political Economy*. Liberty Fund, Inc.

(1859). *On Liberty*. The Walter Scott Publishing Co., Ltd.

Mises, Ludwig von. (1918 [2000]). On Paying for the Cost of War and War Loans. In *Selected Writings of Ludwig von Mises*, volume 1. Liberty Fund, Inc., pp. 216–226.

(1920 [2012]). *Economic Calculation in the Socialist Commonwealth*. Mises Institute.

Politi, James and Colby Smith (2020). Fed Extends Municipal Lending to Smaller US Cities and Counties. *Financial Times*. April 27. Available online (accessed May 13, 2020), www.ft.com/content/34a77027-72b9-4a6b-9aa4-7cf9a6fa56e5

Powell, Jerome (2020). COVID-19 and the Economy. Speech at the Hutchins Center on Fiscal and Monetary Policy. The Brookings Institution, Washington, DC. April 9. Available online (accessed May 12, 2020), www.federalreserve.gov/newsevents/ speech/powell20200409a.htm

Rousseau, Jean-Jacques (1762). *Du Contrat Social; Ou Principes du Droit Politique*. Swan Sonnenschein & Co.

Scott, James (1998). *Seeing Like a State*. Yale University.

Waters, Maxine (2020). Waters Urges Fed to Address Concerns Regarding COVID-19 Programs and Facilities Needed to Support Small Businesses and the Economy. U.S. Committee on Financial Services Press Release. Available online (accessed May 12, 2020), https://financialservices.house.gov/news/documentsingle.aspx?DocumentID= 406504

Yeager, Leland (1997). *The Fluttering Veil*. George Selgin (Ed.). Liberty Fund, Inc.

Index

CPSIA information can be obtained
at www.ICGtesting.com
Printed in the USA
BVHW081744250521
608110BV00010B/156